GRACIE HALL-HAMPTON

GRACIE HALL-HAMPTON

The Arkansas Years, 1917-1953

CODIS HAMPTON II

authorHOUSE®

AuthorHouse™ LLC
1663 Liberty Drive
Bloomington, IN 47403
www.authorhouse.com
Phone: 1-800-839-8640

This book is a work of fiction. All the names, events and address are all fictitious.

Published by AuthorHouse   04/01/2014

ISBN: 978-1-4918-3113-7 (sc)
ISBN: 978-1-4918-3112-0 (hc)
ISBN: 978-1-4918-3111-3 (e)

Library of Congress Control Number: 2013919268

TABLE OF CONTENTS

ACKNOWLEDGEMENT I

First and foremost, let me acknowledge Jesus Christ, God almighty, without whom, I would not be here to tell this or any other story.

I dedicate this book to my family, Sandra, my wife of 45 years, Shawn Lynn, my daughter, Richie and Codis B, my sons, and Khayree C Davis, my grandson. To my sisters, Delores A Evans, and Carol R. Cole, my brother, James Edward Hampton, and all my cousins, in-laws and friends, you all know who you are.

To my father, Codis Hampton, and mother, Doretha Cole, along with my Grandmother Gracie Hampton, and Grandfather John Hampton, to all my uncles, especially Calvin, Curtis, Van D (Peach), Clarence D, and Monroe Hampton. To my aunts, like Lacirene, Nookie, Gertharene, cousins, other great grandparents and ancestors that have lived and passed on to an entirety of peace, please know that I will do my best to keep your memories and names alive in our minds. You, with God's help, are the reason I am here. For that, I am forever grateful, and give you all the love and respect I have in my heart.

To my stepmother, Rosalie Hampton (1 of 22 sisters and brothers from her deceased parents, Louis & Mollie Miller, of Fountain Hill, Arkansas), and my mother-in-law, Ruth Gilkey-Moseby, who have passed on to soon, you two are missed. I miss and loved your counseling and showing me how precious a friend can be.

To my cousins Virgie Jenkins, Kathleen Hampton-Lee, Mary K. Belin, my aunt Bea, some and others, who contributed to the events in this book and kept me rooted in who was who and incidents that happened, you also have all my love and thanks for being you and there for me.

It is impossible for me to articulate to anyone how influential the aforementioned people, living, and deceased have meant to me. Although, I will say this, there is no other family, and that would include some famous families that I would want or choose to be a part of than the Hampton family, and our Arkansas family tree. There are so many stories to be told. My wish is that others put those stories out there for public consumption. That is certainly my intention.

And finally, this book's dedicated to another hard working friend, Maureen Kreklow, who performed a herculean effort in helping me edit this book.

ACKNOWLEDGEMENT II

Authors Note: Researching World and American History is a never ending task. In order to write about a certain time line occurrences, one must check and cross check dates and different versions of when an event occurred, how it happened and what was its cause and effect. The following sites and people listed their versions of times gone by were taken into account as I noted certain historical events in this book. Without each and every one of them, the instances of history referenced could not have been specified here.

These are not only the sites I used among other reference points but are also my recommendations when looking for accuracy at reporting history. Having said that, and although every historical event is thought to be factual in this authors mind, there may be errors based on the research found. The bottom line, I was not there and neither was anyone else except the participants in the event. Therefore, the historical dates and events reported in this book are subjective and should be viewed in that manner.

The Origins at Tuskegee Institute

Central Arkansas Library System, Arkansas Black History Online.

The Encyclopedia of Arkansas History & Culture

W.C. Handy's Autobiography

The White House.Gov Web Site.

David Ellery Rison, "Arkansas During the Great Depression" (Ph.D. diss., University of California at Los Angeles, 1974)

The People History at thepeoplehistory.com.

This day in History at History.Com.

The American Experience, 25 years. From PBS.Org.

Television History—The First 75 Years, From TV History.TV

The HistoryOrb site at historyorb.com.

The University of North Carolina Collection, This Month in North Carolina History, unc.edu.

Britannica from Britannica.com

The Free Library.com

The Arkansas Preservation.org

"The Death of President Franklin Roosevelt, 1945 "EyeWitness to History, www.eyewitnesstohistory.com (2008).

The Church of Jesus Christ of Latter-day Saints | Church Websites

Special thanks to Ancestry.com, and the Family Tree Maker software program,

Please direct all letters, comments, or written correspondence regarding this manuscript to the following,

Frosty LTD, Attn: Codis Hampton II, PO Box 668, Pittsburg, CA. 94565

CHAPTER 1

A Tragedy strikes home

Harriett was behind in her chores, thus the reason she rushed to get supper ready on this evening. It was Friday, and as has been the Hall household tradition, fried fish was the main entree along with a side-dish of smothered potatoes, prepared in such a way as one would notice the steaming pearl like surface onions speckled throughout the bowl. She gently placed a serving bowl of hot and creamy vegetable soup on the table alongside the hot buttered biscuits. Already on the table was a bowl of leftover fried chicken that had been reheated for this festive like supper. There was a small can filled with molasses along with a bowl of fresh churned butter to accompany the meal. Bowls of creamed corn and fried okra with freshly cut carrot sticks and sliced tomatoes helped to make up the feast.

She took a step back from the table to view the entire scene so that she could make sure she got everything on the table. The oblong table had three chairs, a two-person bench and a stool, just enough to seat everyone in the Hall family. "Oh, the corn fritters," she said out loud turning to take them off the iron stove top and placing the semi-warm pan on the table. Just in time too, as she could hear the creaky wheels of the family's horse drawn wagon coming down the hill headed for her cabins front door. She knew the sound of the horse team because she heard them returning from old man Jennings' farm six days a week

1

over the last few years. Sometimes seven days a week during the planting and harvesting seasons of the year. She could count on her husband's old hunting dogs, Sadie, the Mama dog, and her three young pups barking at the sight of Frank Hall and the kids coming home.

Harriett, patted her short cropped hair, checked to ensure her full bodied apron was spotless as could be while covering her modest house dress. She smiled as she was once again pleased at the preparation she had put in to make this meal for her loved ones. She opened the front door, shielding her eyes with her right hand and stepped out on the porch into the late evening sun.

It was quite a scene, Sadie and the pups were barking and milling around the walkway to the cabin. You could also tell that Mama Dog was making sure one of the pups didn't run out in the road only to get trampled by a spooked horse or worse, run over by the wagon wheel. "Sadie, stay back there now," commanded Edward Hall, nineteen, the only boy and oldest child of the Halls. He was sitting in his customary place beside his father as the wagon came to a stop in front of the walkway.

"Whoa, whoa team," shouted Frank Hall as he attempted to calm down the skittish horses that were obviously annoyed by the barking and jumping around of the little pups. In defense of the pups, the eight week old dogs had not been around long enough to know if this wagon full of people and especially those two strange and mammoth animals were friend or foe. They were just doing their barking, jumping around, and turning flips routine to alert whoever was there that a possible intrusion of people, wagon, and exceptionally large animals were going on here. Sadie had stopped barking and looked on in amusement at her offspring's act.

"Hi Mama!" Eighteen year old Versia, seventeen year old Lummie, almost thirteen year old Gracie, and eleven year old Lena yelled almost in unison out to their Mama.

"Hey girls, get yourselves in here so you can help me finish setting the table," Harriett instructed half scolding. Gracie and Lena jumped out of the wagon at her command, ran and tried to hug Harriett as shooed them inside the cabin.

The two oldest girls, body style and facial features identical to their mother, moved slow and deliberate like the young ladies they thought they were each waiting for Edward to give them a hand at getting down from the wagon. Afterwards, Edward told his father that he would take the team and wagon down to the half built barn house/stable, unhook them and be back in a flash for supper.

Frank playfully bent his lean five-nine frame down to the dogs' level. By now, he was through stroking and greeting Sadie, nodded his head in approval as all of his attention now turned to his cute and petite five foot, brown skinned wife still standing in front of the cabins doorway looking like a little angel with the slowly disappearing evening sun glistening off her face. There were no words as they both embraced in appreciation of each other. With the pups still barking, arms around the others waist, Frank and Harriett went inside, closing the door behind them.

"How was it?" Harriett asked.

"A day like any other day this time of year, worked our butts off from the time we got there until we left," replied Frank.

At various time throughout the years, the entire Hall family members, excluding Mama Harriett, worked in some capacity for Lee Jennings farm for over eighteen years. This was in spite of the Hall household sitting on land that was given to Harriett by her father, Pete Belin. Old man Belin, like Mr. Jennings' father was an early 1800s settler in the Pleasant Hill community of Banks. By the time, Harriett whom he nicknamed "Haig" and her four brothers became adults they each received forty acres. For Frank and Harriett having the land was one thing, working the land was a slow process. Oftentimes it cost more money than they ever could save. It was even harder to get a local loan on the property. None of the forty acre properties was what one would call prime farming land and all needed a lot of work even with all the brothers helping each other out. Something always came up.

Thus, old man Jennings had come to know Frank Hall as a "nigger he could count on". He might not say it like that to Franks face but Mr. Jennings had grown to respect the hard working Frank and his family. He knew any money he paid Frank or the family members would be used to attend to their own property. Although the children attended school outside of the planting season from March to late June and harvest time in late September through October, Arkansas schools were closed down to allow for all hands on deck at these peak farming periods. There were areas on the Halls' land where they planted the normal food staples such as tomatoes, cabbage, greens, corn, potatoes and beans. Therefore, they had the double duty of attending to their small crops while working for extra money at the Jennings' farm.

The girls washed up and finished setting the table, at least what little was left to do and were already seated while waiting on the rest of the family. Frank and Harriett took their place at the table about the same time as Edward came rushing through the door so as to not miss any food or let it get cold. Edward looked like his father, same body style and disposition.

"Did you wash your hands after messing with those horses?" Harriett asked in her deep southern county motherly way.

"Yeah mama, outside."

"Did you . . . ," Harriett started to ask.

"I know Mama, the water was cold, but I put a lot of the bar soap on my hands to clean them proper," Young Edward added.

"Oh yeah Versia, you gonna have to ask Rollie Mama to get us some more of that homemade bar soap. Besides, somebody else beside you has a special day coming up Sunday, and we want her to be clean and smelling fresh in church, seeing how it's her birthday doings and all," Harriett instructed.

The two youngest girls smiled at the thought of Sunday doings, even though her actual thirteen birthday was today. Nothing was more crucial than the planting season at this time of year. So they looked forward to the festive atmosphere and knowing that she was going to have her favorite chocolate icing cake made and served with some freshly made ice cream. "Yum," Gracie and Lena thought.

Yet that was not what the giggling was about. The girls could not help but imagine what feelings were going through Versia's mind as she thought about becoming the wife of Rollie. Rail Parker was nicknamed Rollie because he was a chubby nineteen year old young man. They were to be married Saturday after

4

next. Girls being girls, just the thought of the wedding night produced an almost uncontrollable giggle. Lummie just looked at the two girls as if they were acting like children.

"Girls, if you are through, can we say grace now?" Papa Frank, as he was sometime called by his kids, interrupted.

As they clasp hands, Frank asked for a blessing of the meal and thanked the Lord in his most personable way for the food provided on the table and for the health and welfare of his family.

"Yeah, let's eat," summarized Edward.

Yes, there was a not-so-minor day coming up this Sunday. Little Gracie would be a year older. The following weekend would be truly memorable as the first of the Hall children would be getting married to a Parker. The family knew a little about the Parker family because they were part of the Gravel Ridge community.

Clement and Cora Parker had three boys, Clement Jr.; Rail (Rollie) and Sammy. Their oldest boy, Clement Jr., had enlisted in the US Army over a year ago. They say his segregated unit was fighting alongside French soldiers in the War. The United States joined its Allies in Britain, France, Russia, Belgium, and Greece to name a few in the "Great War" of World War I by declaring war on Germany the previous month. That was on April sixth, to be exact. Although the war, caused by economic and territorial issues between the Allies and the Central Powers of Austria-Hungary, Germany, Bulgaria, and Turkey had been ongoing since 1914, there was little evidence that concern over the war had reached this community. That is, except in the households of parents and relatives of men and women who were serving directly or in support of the US interest in the war.

Rollie's parents had a pretty large sized farm, maybe a hundred acres of land, maybe a hundred twenty-five, the Halls didn't know for sure. They were pretty much self-sufficient in that they grew most of their food, had a few mules and horses. Edward, who was one of Rollie's best friends told the family the Parkers also had a couple of dairy cows, a few cattle, a few of goats, and several hogs with pigs along with a passel of chickens.

The Parkers had already given Rollie a section of the land to settle on in order to start preparing for a family of his own. In fact, he was finished with the little two room house he'd built,

5

with the help of family and friends for his soon to be wife. It was conveniently located about two miles down the road and up a small hill from Clem and Cora Parker's farm house. Although semi-surrounded by a bit of forest land it was ideally located to overlook the Parkers' land and beyond. Edward had reassured Papa Frank his daughter would be in capable hands with Rollie.

The Hall family was obviously enjoying the tasty food so Lummie thought this may be an opportune time to ask for a little permission of her own. Since nobody knew, but Edward, at least so she thought, she just blurted it out amid the general chit-chat of her parents at the table.

"I think Rollie's brother Sammy is sweet on me," She nervously started.

Whatever Frank and Harriett were talking about halted when they heard the words "sweet on me" come out of Lummie's mouth.

"I kinda like him too." Continue Lummie since it was out on the table. Sensing the mannerism of her dad when dealing with an uncomfortable subject, she quickly added, "Papa Frank, nowadays some girls are already married at my age. Um not talking about getting married by next Saturday but I just want to know if yawl will let me see him. Papa, I like him, I do like him too."

"So, you talkin' bout seeing him like a girlfriend and boyfriend kind of seeing or are you just talkin' about seeing him at church of just walking down the road or something?" Asked Frank.

"Mama?" Lummie asked while soliciting help from her mother who knew of her interest in Sammy and his in her. She knew that her daughter liked the young man months ago. His interest in her just came to Harriett's attention almost a week ago.

Taking a long pause and looking at the faces around the table, Frank fixed his gaze on the only other person beside Lummie who seemed to know about this potential pairing, his wife. "Harriett?" He simply asked.

"Frank, Sammy's a nice young man; he just turned eighteen and is working with his daddy. He asked me for our permission to talk to Lummie. You weren't here that time he tagged along with his brother, who was here to see Versia. That's when I let him know . . . , that . . . , that, he had to talk to you too."

Frank turned his glance toward Versia and when their eyes met, his oldest daughter sheepishly looked back down at her food and continued to eat without comment. It was obvious she knew something was going on too.

"Frank, Lummie will be eighteen herself next year," his wife reasoned.

Frank sat back in his chair, looked up toward the ceiling as if the answer was somewhere in the rafters, and tried to sort out this development. How could this have happened without his knowledge, and worst yet, how come Harriett didn't tell him sooner about what was beginning to look like a done deal whether he approved or not. After all, the boy was a Parker and if they approved would see that he took care of his family if it came to that. Resigned to that fact, Frank began eating again but not before he told Lummie that she, Harriett and him would talk about this later.

"Now is not the time," he stated as he stuffed his mouth with a piece of a now cold molasses and butter garnished biscuit

Lummie smiled nervously as she glanced at the approving faces around the table. All that is, except Frank and the two youngest girls, Gracie and Lena. The little gigglers had found another potential couple in which to amuse themselves.

Rollie and Sammy Parker having hooked up the two horses to the supply wagon climbed up in and took their seats. Rollie was in the drivers' position with Sammy sitting next to him, wondering when he would be allowed to drive to the local town of Banks. "Get up there horses," Rollie ordered after making that tsk, tsk, tsk sound with his tongue that came from bringing the tongue to rest against the roof of his mouth three times. The horses understood it to mean move out, and they do so as Rollie guided them to stop at the family house front gate.

Clem, short for Clement, Parker was a tall dark skinned black man as evidenced by him bending his head down and sort of contracting the length of his body in order to exit his front door. He stood about five feet nine and weighed upwards of two hundred and fifty pounds. He looked back after stepping out into the yard headed for the wagon and yelled back for his wife. "Come on Cora. We gotta go."

Cora Parker, who filled in as the acting school teacher for black people in the Bradley County, Arkansas community was an attractive brown skinned black woman who carried herself in a most regal way. Some may even say it was because of her twelfth grade education by a convent of nuns in the township of Little Rock Arkansas. The fact that she never knew her mother or father, both of whom were slaves was both a blessing and a curse. The blessing was the fact she was raised as an orphan in the convent, and the curse being not knowing her family.

Sammy, the eighteen year old and youngest of the Parker's three boys jumped out of the front seat into the bed of the wagon and took a seat on one of the two bags of dry beans that would be used to barter with old man Purvis at the Banks-Gravel Ridge Country store. He was followed shortly by Rollie who tied the team reins to the wagons brake handle before taking a seat in the bed of the wagon.

Clem helped Cora up into the wagons seat, walked around to the driver's side, climbed up and grabbed the reins. In what seemed like one motion, he wheeled the team slightly to the left made the "Tsk, tsk, tsk" sound and shouted "Let's go horses, get up there Minnie." The team obediently followed instructions at the sound of Clem's voice.

The family, taking time off from their fields was off on their normal Saturday morning visit to town in order to trade with Skeeter Purvis, one of the few white owned stores nearby that would trade or do any kind of business with black people.

The Parker boys had loaded up the wagon with the trade goods of the day. A few items such as handmade quilts were given to them by other black folk in the community to trade for specific items in order to avoid having to go into Banks. There were other items such as canned field peas, sweet and Irish potatoes and a few normal sized watermelons. We say that because in this county, watermelons were known to grow up to one hundred pounds. The Parkers, unlike their neighbors on both sides, did not grow the number one crop of the county, cotton. They were, however, growing what was becoming a staple in the state, which is the tomato. They also needed additional seeding for their farm, which they actually could have gotten from Papa Warner.

The items they were looking for could not be found at Warner Johnson's store. Papa Warner, as his kids and most of the community called him, owned the only black owned store in these parts. He was located a little over a mile right outside of Banks along the main road to town. His store was on the right side of the road right across from his farm. The firm itself had to be well over eighty acres. They had to pass his store to get to Banks. In fact, the only reason a black person would go past Papa Warner's would be to get some service or goods he did not carry. The service he could not offer, or the goods he did not carry was rare indeed because he was like the Wal-Mart of the era.

The sign on the road read Banks, Arkansas, six miles. Seemingly the miles went by rather quickly as the family took in the farmland with fresh and newly harvested crops close-up and in the distant along the way. There was also the sight of densely wooded areas filled with tall pine trees waiting to be harvested.

They passed Papa Warner and, as usual, he was sitting on his stores porch watching the road for travelers, most of which, would either stop at his store or keep going to Banks. One got the feeling he was taking names and would remember those who drove the wagons that went by him. The feeling was correct. Clem knew he remembered who stopped to shop or passed him by. Once, Papa Warner asked why he didn't keep on going to Purvis Store in Banks. Clem had to remind him of the numerous times he drove directly to do business with Papa. He also told him that when circumstances called for him to do business with Purvis he would drive to Banks. After that, they got along just fine. That still didn't stop him from halfheartedly returning Clem and his family's wave as they drove past him a few minutes ago.

The town of Banks, Arkansas measured four square miles in size. The 200 plus people who inhabited the town was about eighty-five percent white, ten percent black and approximately five percent Indian, Orientals and Hispanic. It was the second major town, along with Hermitage, listed as such in Bradley County. Warren was thirteen miles away and the only Bradley County city listed while also serving as the county seat for the area. The story is that Warren was named after a freed slave. His owner-grantor, Captain Hugh Bradley, Bradley County namesake, was the leader of the early settlement party

An outsider may get confused trying to distinguish where a person lived. There were ten townships also known as divisions of a county. Each included unincorporated areas communities such as the Gravel Ridge Community. Banks was located in the township of Clay, within the surrounding Gravel Ridge Community in Bradley County, Arkansas. The county itself is some thirty-six miles long, north and south, in its longest place, and twenty-four miles wide, for an area of almost six hundred and fifty square miles or four hundred sixteen thousand acres.

If one had just arrived in Arkansas from living in a 1917 bustling city like Los Angeles, Chicago or New York City, you would expect a change in the small town's size as compared to the outskirts of the aforementioned cities. You pretty much understood that Saturday mid-day lifestyle would be more rural than urban.

Yet, you are stunned at the immediate contrast in overall activity. There are no grand or even small openings of an entertainment facility like the recent celebrated opening of New York City's Bijou Theater or even the Morosco Theater earlier in the year. Okay, so maybe that type of entertainment is wishful thinking. They must surely have a local baseball team here. You might wonder if they heard of the St. Louis Browns pitchers, Ernie Koob and Bob Groom no-hitting the Chicago White Sox on consecutive days last week. No evidence of a ball park nearby or even a field of dreams. They have horses, so maybe they know that the Preakness and Kentucky Derby were run a couple of days ago on the same day. On second thought, all horseflesh you've seen has been the working kind, pulling plows or wagons. There are no signs of an area breeding farm so far.

Placing yourself in the wagon with the Parker family and rolling through the town of Banks all you actually see is a unusually small country town with many of its people stuck in the last half of the

1800s following the Civil War. Their clothing, transportation, and town facilities indicate they have not turned the century.

There were plenty of reminders that this state was an integral part of the Confederacy that fought in the U.S. Civil War. And speaking to some of the inhabitants, if you were not certain of the winner yourself you might be convinced otherwise.

To give you an idea of the local pecking order, you were either white or not. If not, there were preselected social, and business lanes that were reserved for "your kind" as was the oftentimes southern designated label of non-whites. For their part, all inhabitants knew their lanes and pretty much stayed in their place. This was borne out as far back as laws enacted by the state aimed at blacks and other people of color after the civil war and near the end of the century. There were continuous reactions by whites that passed new local and state legislation to counteract the federal government's ratification of a new constitutional amendment. This ratification not only restored the franchise to all whites but guaranteed full civil rights to blacks officially ending the era of Reconstruction as of October 13, 1874.

Examples of one of the most egregious laws placed on the books as a way to separate the races were a Jim Crow law passed in 1891 segregating railroad coaches and waiting stations. A year later, Arkansas state legislators passed, and the Governor signed into law a state constitutional amendment implementing a poll tax that was meant to prevent poor people from voting. Although this law affected any poor person regardless of race, the current economic status of black people was such that a poll tax just could not be made a part of the monthly budget. Therefore, it disenfranchised the exact group of people for which the law was intended.

And just in case anybody missed the intentions of these and other laws and ordinances the Democratic Party adopted a "Whites Only" primary elections period. Needless to say, any candidate running for a public office would have to be a devout segregationist or they would not be elected.

The NAACP, established in February of 1909, had successfully fought against the so-called grandfather clause in court. The clause itself stated that a man could vote if his grandfather had voted. Obviously slaves did not have that right, so this affected all black descendants up to this era. The Supreme Court ruled in the Guinn vs. United States in 1915, that the grandfather clauses in the Oklahoma and Maryland constitutions violated the Fifteenth Amendment of the Constitution of America.

Skeeter Purvis' store came into view from a little ways up the street as the Parker's wagon rolled past another storefront along the way. This building stood out for several reasons. Not necessarily in any particular order, because of the oversized Confederate stars and bars flag raised to its highest point on the flagpole sitting atop its roof. There was just enough wind to allow it to flutter, occasionally waving at anyone who cared to look in that direction. There were signs scattered about on the buildings two windows on opposite sides of the door. Different size signs advertising food, other goods prices and assorted notices were tacked on a large sign board located to the right side of the front door. Looking in that direction, one could not help but notice the white men in front of the store. Two were seated while obviously playing some kind of board game that might have been checkers. The other two men were looking over their shoulders and sipping on some liquid inside of containers colored or covered in some way to disguise its contents.

That is until they saw the Parker wagon approaching the store. Their gaze quickly turned to the occupants of the wagon while tapping the game players to get their attention. They, along with this strange looking dog that had been lying at the foot of one of the men at the table, quickly joined in the intimidating stare down of the Parkers. The dog, which had the look of a mix of hound dog and some other kind of mutt, sat up, growled and then barked in the direction of the wagon.

Clem Parker quickly reminded his family members not to stare at the white men. "Keep yawl eyes on Mr. Purvis store," he said quietly. For Rollie and Sammy, their parents' timid way of acting around white folk was uncomfortable for them. The Parker boys had been exposed to a lot more education about the races and current matters. Their oldest brother was fighting in the US Army for the right of the United States to remain a free country. Nevertheless, the boys followed directions while understanding the ramifications of a confrontation with young white men drinking and having a habit of messing with colored folk just for the hell of it.

"Easy Bo, easy," one of the guys who were seated commanded the dog. The white men gaze was fixed upon the wagon as it passed by the store. There was no mistaken this store or whom it serviced. On a larger sign just above the wooden awning like structure that covered the entire front entrance to the store including its wooden board walkway was the words McBain's General Store. On one of the two poles that held up the wooden awning was attached a white face painting sign that could be seen from across the main street that read "Whites only" in black lettering.

Sammy Parker could not help but take one last look at the men who were still staring at them as they pulled up to the Purvis' store front. He quickly turned his head back to the front, as the wagon pulled around the corner of and headed for the back doorway of the store. They took their place alongside another wagon of colored people who were also there to do trade and do business with Mr. Purvis.

Ben "Skeeter" Purvis had operated his store for almost twenty-four years in Banks for the Gravel Ridge community. Going on fifty-five and looking every bit of seventy-five in the face, he still had a teenagers physic including the boundless energy of a much younger man. He moved here from Alabama to get away from his father who was a Calvary Officer in the Confederate Army serving under General James Longstreet.

Before and during the war, Skeeter's father, Samuel had over a hundred slaves in a large plantation around Mobile, Alabama. He went through more than a couple of overseers who left for various reasons or was fired because of dereliction of duty or other crimes against the estate. It became almost impossible to hold onto the majority of his slaves between the changeover of overseers, the fact his wife could not run the fields and that all able bodied men folk were serving in the Confederacy. The entire estate totally fell apart after the remaining slaves heard about President Abraham Lincoln's abolishment of slavery act with the House passage of the Thirteen Amendment on January 31, 1865. The Senate had already passed the amendment back on April 8, 1864.

Theirs was not the only local plantation that fell on hard times while their men were off fighting and dying for the southern cause. Twenty-eight percent of the entire population of Mobile and the surrounded areas were populated with slaves. So one can image the effect the amendment passage plus the loss of men folk in the war had on this Southern mecca's economy during the war. Having served as a significant port city on the Gulf of Mexico for the Confederate States of America, the city of Mobile itself fell into Union Soldiers hands after repeated attacks by the Union Navy on Mobile Bay in August of 1864.

Skeeter himself was born in 1862. He was raised, and many times nursed, by a black nanny because his mother, Henrietta, was a sickly woman who finally died of an overdose of laudanum in December of 1863. The nanny, whom everyone called Maggie, at one time nursed baby Skeeter and her own child. Her son, Tag, was just a couple months older than Skeeter.

After the war, his father returned home bitter about the outcome and especially finding his slaves had run off leaving just a shell of what once was a thriving entity that produced an exceptionally comfortable living for the Colonel. His views about the inferiority of blacks had not changed. He became more and more resentful as time passed and his fortunes continue to dwindle as there was no more free labor. Colonel Purvis, as he continued to refer to himself while insisting others to do the same, set about organizing the first Klan and Night Riders activity in the Mobile County area. Their entire mission was to intimidate blacks from voting, owning land, marketing crops or in some cases existing.

Skeeter was the only living child of the Colonel and Henrietta. His older sister died of yellow fever and famine during the early days of the war. As for himself, he could no longer take the bitterness and hatred for blacks by his father. The Colonel would go on and on telling young Skeeter how proud he would be when one day they could ride together and rid the South of all blacks. Finally, at age thirteen, he ran away from home looking for his nanny and her son, Tag. He would visit several Alabama Counties, working on farms and in towns for traveling money while continuing to look for Maggie and Tag. As he grew into manhood around the age of twenty, he began to travel up and down the Mississippi by steamboat working at his new profession of gambling. This led him to meet and marry his current wife, Gladys who was a dancer on one of the last steamboats he frequented. Mrs. Purvis, who is ten years younger than Skeeter, became pregnant but lost the child during their travels looking for a place to settle. She had kin folk in Arkansas so somehow their travels landed them in Gravel Ridge in the summer of 1893. Skeeter was thirty-one years of age. He had yet to locate Maggie or Tag.

He began working for a shop keeper name Lucas and was able to buy his store and house in town when Mr. Lucas decided to retire to the countryside and care for his wife who was becoming more and more depended on personal care. All in all, the gambling professions winnings saved, allowed the Purvis couple to set up a permanent shop in the town and make it successful up to this point.

By now, they have three grown children, Samuel Purvis, named after his grandfather in spite of Skeeter's hatred for the Colonel, Morgan Purvis, One of two local medical doctors and their daughter Beverly, who helps her father run the store. In fact, they have a wedding coming up this spring too. Samuel is marrying his sweetheart, Mary Warren in June of this year.

Clem told his family to wait in the wagon until he returned. This being a Saturday, the store was doing a brisk business with black and a few white folks. Even though most white folks shopped at McBain's, they also liked to buy certain items from Skeeter. Oh, there may be the occasional stare or warning by some whites when coming in close contact with blacks in the store at the same time. Overall, there are never any serious racial issues as cooler heads prevailed, especially with the possibility of intervention by Skeeter. The whites knew that Skeeter treated one and all people in a fair manner and accepted shopping in "mixed company" as they referred to being in proximity with another race.

Clem patiently waited for his turn and briefly conducted his trade and purchases, thanked Mr. Purvis, and walked back to the wagon. "Hey boys, I want you to unload those goods off the wagon and . . . Where is Sammy?" He asked.

"He went 'round the store and up the street to drop off those jars of jam I brought for Ms. Cameron. She supposed to have some clothes for me to wash and iron too," Cora answered.

"I told yawl to wait 'til I got back here before . . ." Clem did not finish his sentence before he saw Sammy appear from around the corner of the store almost out of breath while carrying the bag of dirty clothes sent by Mrs. Cameron. "What you running for boy?" His father asked. "Nothing daddy, 'cept that funny lookin' dog was barking at me from cross the road at Mr. McBain." With that, Sammy threw the bag of clothing up on the wagon telling his mom they were the clothes she was expecting.

"Good," Cora said. "Yawl help your father while I go in Mr. Purvis' store, there's some ladies things I wanna look at."

With a look of relief that Sammy was back safe and sound with no trouble, followed by puzzlement at how long Cora was going to be just looking at stuff in the store. Clem ordered the boys to help him unload the goods he had trading or sold to Mr. Purvis and load up the items he'd received in turn.

After exchanging pleasantries with the colored folk in the wagon parked next to his, he and the father of the family looked at each other with a knowing glance and wink as their wives finally came out of the store. The two men said their goodbyes to each other and headed for their family's wagon. "Let's go boys," Clem shouted to Rollie and Sammy who was talking to what appeared to be the son of the family in the other wagon. Shaking his head in amazement and some relief that she had not bought anything, Clem helped Cora climb onto the passenger side of the seat. He waved as the family pulled their wagon out first and left. "Ebe body ready?" he asked. With the family answering in the affirmative, the Parker wagon was loaded, and all were seated for the trip back home. Clem guided the wagon back to the main road through town, turning left from the side of the store after a model T truck had passed and all foot traffic was clear. They could see the wagon that left before them a few yards ahead of them.

"You know, I seen that guy up ahead before but can't seem to member his name."

"Why that's the Long family. You know 'em, Thomas and his wife Flo. We see them at church some time," Cora said answering Clem.

"Yeah Daddy, their son is named Robert and they got a daughter name Elsie," Sammy volunteered.

Clem heard his wife say they were likeable people too. She went on about where they lived in relation to the Parker family farm. Even though he was slowly being distracted by the sight of a tractor being driven by a man that was approaching them from the other side of the street. From a farmer's standpoint, this was a working machine which now had his full attention. He could see the unit must be brand spanking new because of how the light from the sun made it shine. It was surely motorize because it was moving on its own and had bright yellow wheels and a green housing body that covered the motor parts. The front wheels were smaller than the back wheels. In fact, the back wheels were large enough to reach the white man's shoulders, which looked like he was comfortable seated in between them and directly behind the housing body that had a steering wheel facing the driver to allow for guiding the tractor.

The tractor, traveling at a speed of about four to five miles per hour was so close Clem could see the model on the front, if only he could read. "Cora, what does that say on the front of that tractor coming yonder?" he asked. "Rollie, answer your daddy's question," she directed. "Fordson daddy, it's a model F Fordson." Sammy eagerly volunteered. By now the Tractor was in front of the McBain store, directly across from the Parker wagons while they both moved in opposite directions. All Parker eyes were on the tractor, except Cora, who even though her husband was driving the team, was making sure their wagon didn't run into anything or body crossing the road.

Nobody in the Parker wagon heard the funny looking dog barking at the Longs wagon as it rolled by for they were farther ahead. By now and in an instant, the dogs barking interrupted

Clem's thought process as he heard its master yell, "I said calm down god-dam it!" Too late, as the mutt took off running right between the tractors front and back wheels causing the driver to slam on his breaks trying to avoid hitting the dog.

"Get yo' ass back here Bo," The dog's owner yelled while running after his dog. By now the dog had reached its destination and was jumping up and down barking viciously at the people in the Parker wagon and seemingly specifically at Sammy who was just as startled as everyone else but could not hide his laughter at this funny little dog making all of this commotion.

All this sudden activity did not amuse the Parker's horses who didn't know what was going on, started rising up on their back legs and skittishly became unsettled even though Clem tighten up on the reins trying to calm them down. "Whoa team, come on Minnie settled down now." Clem ordered. Bo, the dog, was still viciously barking and jumping around. Suddenly, he tried to dash between the horses legs in order to get to the other side of the wagon where Sammy was sitting. In that instant, Minnie came down on his body with her front hoofs, several times instantly killing the animal.

The dogs master screamed at the sight of the horse stomping the dog. By now the other three young white men were standing alongside the wagon and directly behind their friend. The driver of the tractor had also run over to the scene.

Other onlookers were running up to the wagon and asking what happened? The dog's owner who looked to be all of eighteen or nineteen years of age was crying and yelling, "Those darkies' horses killed my damn dog. They killed him I tell you. What yawl going to do about it? They killed my dog for no reason."

The Sheriff, whose office and Jail is about four doors up from McBain's store saw the tail end of the accident while sitting on the bench in front of his office. He too had now reached the scene.

The young man turned to him, still crying and shouted in the Sheriff's ear, "These niggers killed my dog Sheriff. I want their ass arrested for murder, you hear me? Bo was my hunting dog. Now what am I gon' do?"

A few people in the crowd of a dozen or so smiled at the thought of Bo being a hunting dog, but you could tell they also thought this was a serious affair and wondered what the Sheriff was going to do about it.

"First of all Petey, Bo was not a bloodhound so let's clear that up right away. Did anybody else see what happen here?" The Sheriff asked the crowd standing around virtually ignoring the stunned but quiet Parkers still sitting in the wagon.

"Why Sheriff, that crazy dog ran between the wheels of my tractor trying to get at this wagon. Why, I don't know, but he came from off the porch of McBain's store over there across the street. Hell, I thought I'd ran over him until I saw him just a barking and jumpin' up and down and carrying on at the darkies in this wagon. That's all I saw," The tractor driver concluded.

"Well, did anybody else see anything or know what happen?" the Sheriff asked. "Yeah I saw it. These niggers stomped my little brother's dog. That's pretty much it, now we ask again, what you gonna do about that?" One of the men, Walt, who was obviously the dog owners brother and one of the men whom Rollie saw standing while looking over Petey's shoulder when they first passed by.

"Well here is the thing," the Sheriff began. "I, myself saw what happened when the dog reached the wagon. And Mr. Hendrix has confirmed the dog came from over at McBain's store trying to chase or attack the people in this wagon I guess. As far as that goes let me ask you Clem. I know you as a pretty decent darkie who minds his own self business. Do you know of any reason this dog had to try and attack you or anybody in yo' family?" the Sheriff asked, looking up at Clem who was still sitting in the driver's seat of the wagon.

"No suh," Clem answered.

"How about you boys up there?" The Sheriff asked of Rollie and Sammy.

"Sheriff Penelton, that dog was growling at us for no reason, when we first came into town. We ain't done nothing to that dog or even saw him before today. We just came in to trade with Mr. Purvis and were on our way home," Rollie answered.

"And how about you boy, you have anything to say?" The Sheriff asked of Sammy.

"No suh, 'cept that dog was growling at me too when I dropped off my Mama's jam at Ms. Cameron. She gave me a bag of clothes for Mama to iron, and when I left, I saw the dog again sitting over there with them in front of McBain's growling at me once again. I just took off running back to Mr. Purvis store," Sammy stated.

People around town and through-out the surrounding areas knew Sheriff Penelton to be a no nonsense man. He was not an absolute friend of colored folks, but he wasn't a Klan's man either. He just went about doing his job, so most people took him at his word. They felt that he would make the best decision in matters of the law which was why he'd been on the job over fifteen years.

"All right Clem, take your family and go on home. Petey, you and Walt get this mutt off my streets, and bury him somewhere. The show's over folks. Go on about your business now, you hear," The Sheriff stated as he watched each person take notice of his words and moved on, some with and others without comment amongst themselves. That is all except Petey, his brother Walt, and their friends.

"That's all right for yawl darkies," Petey said quietly as he picked up Bo's broken and lifeless body. "Yawl is gonna pay for this one way or another," He warned as the four of them watched the Parker's guided their wagon up the street and out of town headed for home.

"Did you hear me boy?" the Sheriff asked as finally Petey, his brother and their friends headed down the street in the opposite direction of the Parkers to find a place to bury their dog.

Gravel Ridge's First Baptist Church Sunday School teacher, Ms. Tennie Payne had completed her normal bible study subject for the morning. She was trying to calm the children down by having them read Genesis 18:19 in the bible that related to children. She finally read the verse, *"For I have chosen him, that he may command his children and his household after him to keep the way of the LORD by doing righteousness and justice, so that the*

LORD may bring to Abraham what he has promised him." with the help of some of the better readers aloud.

Ms. T, as they called her, was charged with about twenty children ranging from seven to sixteen years of age. She, turning twenty years old on April fool's day of last month, was still glowing at becoming engaged to Cicero Franklin Jr. She was holding bible study in a small study room alongside the kitchen in back of the church. Naturally, they could hear muffled voices coming from the congregation's main body. They could also hear the churning of the ice cream maker coming from the kitchen. Add that to the sweet aromas, mixed with other foodstuffs that permeated the entire church area, they could hardly contain themselves. The children were just too excited with anticipation of having ice cream and cake today.

This day was a memorable day of celebration. Not only because its little Gracie Hall thirteen birthday and the Long's little eight year old boy, Robert L. Long's birthday, along with a day of worship, it's also Mother's Day.

The ladies in the congregation are wearing their best Sunday-go-to-meeting dresses in anticipation of receiving compliments and maybe even small mementoes from their husbands and children. You can see the pride in their beautiful faces while singing along with the last hymn before the morning worship recess.

Meanwhile, the kitchen volunteers, led by the ever present Sister Hattie Payne, Pastor A.J. Payne Jr.'s wife and Ms. Tennie Payne's mother was directing her helpers to carry the main dishes prepared and brought by the parishioners ladies to the picnic area that ran alongside the east side of the church. The weather on this thirteen days of May was cooperating by providing a warm and cloud free sky at the 11:00am hour. There were six volunteers, Lummie, Versia, the Belin girls, Elsie and Lessie, along with Rollie and Sammy handling the delicate ice cream preparation and maintenance before serving.

All the Parker boys had to do was turn the liquid cream batter into ice cream. The process called for placing each of two round metal canisters, filled with the sweet vanilla ingredient mixture prepared by Sister Payne, into the center of an approximately twenty-four inch high medium, size tightly structured mini-half barrels. Rollie would operate one ice cream maker while Sammy would use the other one. The canister, fitted with a metal whipping unit attached to the canister's lid was surrounded by ice and salt in the half barrel which was required to cool its ingredients. Seated on the back porch of the church, Rollie and Sammy placed the churning gear units, which fit flush and tightly onto the square like metal prong of the canister's whipping unit. The churning mechanism was secured in place by hooking each end of it onto the metal loops attached to the barrel. The ice cream was actually formed by turning the long metal handle in a circular motion in order to ensure the cream was smooth and didn't become lumpy with the ice causing the mixture to freeze. Thus, by churning the ice cream mixture, they felt the cream becoming thicker inside the canister. It had been a little over twenty minutes since they started, but they also realized they were going to have to continue while others ate. They knew that when it became almost impossible to turn the unit's handle the ice cream was fully formed and ready for serving. The canister could sit in the barrel of ice for a while but would soon begin to melt as the ice in the barrel would melt too. "Don't yawl worry. We'll fix your plates and have them ready by the time you are finished making the ice cream," a smiling Versia lovingly told Rollie as she stepped off of the back porch of the church headed for the picnic serving area that was a buffet style event.

They had placed three picnic tables together, covering them with sheet like tablecloths for use as serving tables. The morning services ended, and people were lined up to be served. Most had not eaten breakfast at home in anticipation of this event. There were still three other large picnic tables with benches to seat some people. Others would have to find a seat in their wagons or somewhere to enjoy the festivities. Church members didn't mind the inconvenience because they're all together and enjoying this day of sunshine, good food, family and friends, which all in all was a sunny day.

As planned, Rollie got to eat the main dishes along with his fiancé Versia. Seated at a picnic table reserved for Gracie, the birthday girl, her sister Lena, Edward and the rest of the

Halls, they were joined by the Sammy and the Parker boy's parents. They, along with the entire congregation, including the table reserved for the Long family, joined in singing the "Happy Birthday" song adding "Happy Birthday to Gracie Hall and Robert Long, with special wishes to all the mothers present" to the lyrics. After which they all had a laugh at their creativity in added the Mother's Day line to the birthday song. They finished by having their choice from the assortment of prepared cakes and enjoying the ice cream that was beginning to melt as it was exposed to the bright spring sun.

After the brunch recess, meal celebration and clean-up, a few people had a hard time keeping awake during the first part of Reverend Payne's sermon. By now the 2:00pm sun was heating up the tin roof of the church. The open windows and door helped but, as usual, the inside of the church was beginning to heat up from summer like weather, although it was spring.

The Reverend had begun by directing the congregation to turn to John 16:21 in their bibles. He read the verse, *"A woman, when she is in labor, has sorrow because her hour has come; but as soon as she has given birth to the child, she no longer remembers the anguish, for joy that a human being has been born into the world."* He pointed out how crucial a role mother's play in a family structure. "She not only bears the burden—yet pure joy of carrying a baby for nine months—and bringing life to that child as it is born, but mothers have to nurture the young child. She has to be there to wipe the tears from the child eyes, perk them up when they are sad, and show them love every day so they can grow to be strong and caring individuals," he said. "All the while, reminding the child that he or she, in the case of a little girl. Yessssss," he shouted at the top of his lungs while pounding on the pulpit desk with one loud blow and continuing. "That the child is also a child of our God too!" The shouting of Reverend Payne's voice had the effect he was looking for. All of those people who were sleeping sat straight up at the sound of his voice and pounding on the pulpit.

Being a veteran preacher, while also understanding that anybody who just had a full meal with dessert and was subjected to a friendly warm environment would have a tendency to fall

23

asleep if left to their own habits, he wrapped up the sermon early. "And the church say Amen," was his last instruction to his members. "Amen," all replied as directed, with the exception of a couple of people who had fallen back to sleep.

With that, the preacher officially ended the services by advising all to have a blessed week adding his expectation of seeing all in this building next Sunday. As was the custom, Reverend Payne, Mrs. Hattie Payne followed by a couple of the deacons went outside to shake hands with those who exited the building. Normally people would allow him that courtesy of preceding the congregation's exit. Although a few were visible impatient, this Sunday would be no different.

The Halls climbed atop their wagon almost one at a time after saying goodbye. Frank to his next door neighbor, Gracie thanking some kids for hand written notes and small gifts she received, with Lena standing by her side. Versia to Rollie, Lummie to Sammy, Edward to, as his mother Harriett remarked, "Who is that young child Edward is talking to?" She never did receive an answer. In Frank's defense, he just didn't know but did recognize her family as the King's from up around Fountain Hill, Arkansas.

Frank drove the wagon onto the road with a couple of wagon teams in front of him and heading in the same direction. Some families, including the Parkers lived in the opposite direction and headed their wagons in that direction. Gracie and Lena was going on and on about the food and her birthday celebration. The horses were at a trot at the insistence of Frank who wanted to get home as quickly as possible.

"Thank you all again," Harriett said while thanking her family for the new hat she had received this morning before starting out for church services. "You welcome Mama," Gracie and Lena immediately answered followed by acknowledgements from the rest of the family.

By now they were pulling up to their front gate and were met by their own personal welcoming committee, Sadie and her three pups. As usual the nine week old dogs were doing their thing. They barked, turned flips from inside the gate. Thanks to Edward who locked them in before they left for church. Since her pups were safe from the danger of being stepped on by the horses,

Sadie decided to do a little welcome home barking on her own. "Whoa team," Frank commanded. The family was glad to see the dogs and home. It had been a long, yet pleasant day that turned out as promised. Yes indeed, it had been a memorable day for all concerned.

The morning of the day before the momentous day had finally arrived. Versia was so excited she barely could contain herself while helping her mother packing lunches. She repeated variations of what would become her name after tomorrows wedding. "Mrs. Versia Parker, Mrs. VP . . . Mrs. Parker . . ."

"Stop Versia, just stop that," her mother sternly ordered. "You are driving me crazy with that Mrs. this and that stuff. Anyway," she continued. "What's gonna be important to remember, is what's your husband going to call you. Hopefully he will always look at you with a lovin' smile on his face while calling you baby, honey or sweetie pie. Just, just remember this. A man wants a woman to be a whore in bed, a good cook in the kitchen, a good mother to his children, and a lady to all those other people because she is her husband's wife."

"But Mama . . ."

"All um saying here is being someone's wife, means you have a lot of grown-up wifely duties. It's a lot more to it than just having your husbands' last name," Harriett concluded.

"Oh Mama . . . I just know I love him so much, I can hardly stand it. That's all."

"Well, that's the best reason to get married that I know of, and I'm so happy for you," Harriett said as she hugged her daughter while also fighting back the tears.

Lummie, who had been watching and listening to this entire exchange smiled thoughtfully while closing the lid on her father's lunch pail. Harriett, wiping her eyes and noticing the expression on Lummie's face, smiled, and quickly interpreted her second oldest daughter nonverbal thoughts. She began by saying, "Even though he is Rollie's brother, we need to know more about Sammy. Your father did not hear of this little romance in your life until last week. So, if you two were planning to get married on Saturday too, forget it. There need to be a lot of talking and meeting between his mother, father and us before we cross that bridge."

A still smiling Lummie asked, "Can I still help Versia get her little house set up for the night after the wedding?"

At that instant, the front door flew open with Frank followed by Edward entering the kitchen area. "Okay, we got the team hooked up and ready to go. How's it going in here?" Frank asked.

"Versia is going over to the little house Rollie built for them. She hasn't done any cleaning in there since they put the roof on the place. She wants to get her little honeymoon cabin ready. Lummie asked to go along and help this afternoon," Harriett replies as Versia is nodding her head in agreement.

Frank sat down at the kitchen table to eat a semi-warm piece of ham and homemade biscuit sandwich for breakfast. Pausing in mid-chew, he asked, "How she gonna get over there? We're not going that way on the way to work. And where is Rollie gon be while she fixing the place up?"

Joining his father at the table, Edward grabbed another offering form the plate of sandwiches prepared for the family's breakfast. "Me and a couple of the boys are taking Rollie to the 'Hole in the Bushes' place for a couple of homebrews on his last night of being freedom," He added to the conversation.

"What do you mean last night of being freedom?" asked Versia.

"Yeah daddy, can I go? I ain't got nothin' else to do this afternoon. My chores at home will be all done," Lummie nervously asked her father.

"Edward, I said what you mean by being free on the last night. And what else are you and Rollie gonna be doing over at that, that 'Hole in the Bushes' place? I hear there are some fast girls that be hanging around there too," Versia said a little more loudly this time.

"Whoa people," Frank interrupted after taking a bite from his sandwich. First of all, how's Versia going to get over there and back home before dark? And Edward, you all better be careful down at that hole in the bushes place. You know there's a white lighting liquor still nearby and they also make homebrew around there close by somewhere. Why, the governments been all over them backwoods looking for that place. You don't want them to find it while yawl is there."

"I know daddy. We are gonna be careful. After all, we wouldn't want anything happen to my boy Rollie on his last night of freedom," Edward said while trying to assure everyone that they had it under control.

"Humph? Last night of freedom my foot, wait until I talk to Rollie," Versia said to nobody in particular and everybody in general.

"I also hear that Sammy will be there at the house to do the heavy lifting for his future sister-in-law," Harriett advised Frank while adding, "Versia and Lummie will walk halfway there, starting right about 11:00 a.m. this morning. Sammy is going to pick the girls up over by the road turnoff to Mr. McIntire farm to take them to the house and bring them all the way back home before dark."

"Yeah daddy, Sammy can sleep in my room with me. He is bringing his nicest suit so that he can drive his team to the church with us in the morning. We can even put some of our stuff in his wagon. Maybe Lummie can ride with him in the morning. And, and you and Mama get to talk to him about Lummie," Edward advised.

Realizing the plans were put in place to take care of any objections he would have, Frank agreed and added, "I guess it'll be okay for her to help Versia at her new place. After all, Lummie will be eighteen in a few months."

Harriett pleased with the outcome of the conversations and sudden realization there were family members missing, turned toward the girls bedroom. "Gracie, Lena!" she called out as she approached the bedroom door, "What you girls doing in there? You better not still be in bed."

As she reached for the door handle, the door flew opened. A smiling and giggling Gracie and Lena looked at their mom and replied in unison, "Here we are Mama."

"Were you two listening at that door to our conversation?" asked Harriett.

"Oh, no Ma'am," answered Gracie. "We were just coming out to eat.

"Hmmmm . . ." Harriett mumbled to herself while pushing the two girls to the table and telling them to eat fast because there is not much time. Daddy would be leaving to drop them off at Mama Halls place so they could go to school.

Versia and Lummie stood in the kitchen of the little two room house and smiled. Both could almost see the addition of rooms filled with children looking like their parents. They could almost sense them running in and out of their rooms, and indeed, the house while experiencing the gift of life provided by Rollie and Versia. They could hear them playing outside with the family dogs and various pets that make them squeal with joy and excitement. Yes, standing there in the middle of this small kitchen, both can imagine what the Parker family and this little house would be like in say, ten years.

For now reality sets in and they realize in their mind, it's just a cozy little place that needed a woman's touch to bring it to life.

Sammy helped to break their concentration by peeping in the front doorway asking if they needed him to draw water from the well. "Yes," Versia answered. "Girl we might as well get started."

The stove and kitchen table was bought or traded for by Rollie's Mama and daddy. The stove, rusty in some areas, had dried grease spots in others and needed a strong hand scrubbing. The table came with two chairs, which were in pretty decent shape. But the table itself was well used and needed a thorough cleaning to make it sanitary to prepare food and eat off of its surface.

The bedroom, adjacent to the kitchen, had no real door only, a frame at the entranceway. There was a bed that was just large enough for two people. It's a good thing that Rollie and Versia were not big boned or fat. Otherwise both of them could not have fit in it. For newly married lovers, it's perfect. The room had a large chest and a couple of midsized trunks for their clothing.

The entire house had two places for windows. The bedroom was one, and the kitchen was another. The glass had been installed in both areas, but the wooden shutters were closed and nailed shut to prevent someone or something from breaking the expensive glass. That is why the girls kept the front door open to let the little house air out.

Sammy had brought in two mid-size pails of water for cleaning and a smaller pail for drinking. Versia had made a fire in the stove admitting that cleaning the stove would have to wait until another day. For now, hot water was needed as she placed one of the larger pails of water on top of the stove.

"Sis, there is no use in watching water boil so let's clean up the bedroom first," Versia instructed.

"Okay, but don't you want to put some curtains over the doorway to the bedroom?" Lummie asked. "Maybe Mama has some old ones for now until we are able to make some."

"Hey ladies, Um gonna chop some more wood so it can last a day or so," Sammy said interrupting their conversation from the front doorway once again.

"All right Sammy and thank you for helping us," Lummie replied in a tone of voice Versia had never heard from her sister. Looking at the wide pearly white teeth showing smile she was flashing at Sammy, it meant only one thing. Lummie had it bad for Sammy. She don't know if its love yet but there is a huge attraction. And, from the look on Sammy's face the feeling is mutual.

For her part, Lummie caught Versia staring at her interaction with Sammy and volunteered without any prompting. "He is going to ask daddy if he can come calling on me when we get home tonight," She offered.

"Umm huh. Girl, come on here," Versia said almost laughing at her sister until she suddenly remembered how silly she must have seemed or looked when she realized how much she loved Rollie.

Sammy was busy chopping wood now, but felt someone was watching him from the woods. He was born on his father's farm and had lived and hunted in the surrounding woods since he was a ten year old kid. He had been taught to lie in wait for a deer or some other animal, so he was familiar with the still of the forest. Yet today, he had this feeling that someone or something was watching him, the house, or both.

He and Rollie were also taught that to carry their rifle when they are traveling in the backwoods or whenever they think they may need them. Walking in a nonchalant way, Sammy went back to his wagon, pulled his rifle from under an old blanket under the driver's seat and suddenly ran off into the wooded area.

Feeling that he was secure and in his element he made a half circle search in the woods that ran the same way on the sides and back of the little house. Walking in a stealth manner, he surveyed the area looking for any movement or clue as to whom or what was watching him. He didn't see anybody but manage to scare off a couple off a small doe he just happened upon while in the woods near the house.

Convinced the little doe must have been the source that caused that eerie feeling of being watched, he returned to his wagon, placed the rifle back under the blanket and walked to the doorway of the house to check on the girls. He found that they had not even noticed he'd left for few minutes. They were busy as bees, talking and making the little place a regular love nest for the expected newlyweds. He did manage to catch Lummie's eye. She flashed her pretty smile at him and he returned the gesture before returning back to his wood chopping chore. One other thing he noticed, it was getting late in the day and the sun was headed for its western setting in the sky. He figured it must have been around 3:00 in the afternoon. It was the only method of time he could rely on since he didn't have a watch.

With the chopped wood in place outside the house along with a good supply placed by the stove in the kitchen, the girls and Sammy sat down at the table. Problem number one, it was now too dark to head home. The girls had gotten so busy talking while preparing the house, in spite of Sammy's help and warnings of the fast approaching night; they found themselves working past sundown. It simply was not safe to travel the roads at night for the youngsters.

Problem number two was Frank Hall would probably want to kill Sammy for letting this happen, maybe not literally but certainly in a figurative manner. He most surly would not trust Sammy to take his Lummie anywhere, especially away from home.

Neither Harriett Hall nor his parents would be happy about this day's development.

While problems one and two could not be helped now, problem three, getting situated to spend the night, they all agreed, was something they had better work on now. Sammy bedded the horses down for the night by tying them to a tree near the well where they were originally placed. By now the moon and stars were the only light in the sky which still shone minimal light on the ground. It was so dark; Sammy barely could see his hand in front of his face. Feeling around, he retrieved the rifle from the wagon, once again feeling as though he was being watched. He thought he saw a flicker of light coming from a spot in the woods on the side of the house. He stared at the spot for a minute with no evidence of the light or any movement from anything. He returned to the cabin securing the door after entering.

Realizing there was no food in the house, they accepted the fact that there would be no supper tonight. They talked for a while longer and figuring it must have been about eight O'clock, they prepared to go to bed. The girls took the bed and Sammy made himself as comfortable as could on the floor in the kitchen. They turned the oil lamps out in the bedroom and kitchen, settling down to sleep for the night.

After what seemed like a couple of hours of sleep, Sammy began to toss and turn as if trying to avoid the disturbance outside the house. It wasn't so much the strong odor of automobile gas that by now permeated the inside of the house, or the smell of smoke that crept through the crevices of the structure, it was his horses sounding an alarm that made him set up from his pallet. Immediately realizing the house was on fire, Sammy ran to awaken the girls. Smoke was beginning to fill the house. He could still hear the neigh and nickering of his horse team moving around while trying to get break free from the tree. "Turn them goddam horses' loose," he heard a familiar voice shout at somebody on the outside. "Turn 'em loose I said," the voice continued.

"Wake up, the house is on fire. Let's go," Sammy shouted. By now all the commotion and smoke had their attention. Sammy, with the girls' right behind him ran to the front door and found that someone had placed something on the door that prevented it from being opened from the inside. With that bit of news the girls became terrified that this was deliberate, started screaming followed by coughing as the smoke became thicker. They could all hear the horses run off down the road still pulling the wagon because somebody had either cut them loose or they broke free on their own. It was also getting hotter from the fire burning that absolutely surrounded the house. In the darkness, an oil lamp was accidentally knocked off the kitchen table, breaking and spilling its contents onto the floor. The fire began to penetrate the structure causing even more panic.

Sammy grabbed a pre cut log, ordered the girls to grab his shirt as he headed for the backroom window. Versia pulled Lummie in her direction as she latched onto Sammy's overalls strap. When they got to the back window, she put Lummie in between her and Sammy with the intention to get her out first. Using the log, he gently broke the glass to keep it from shattering and began pounded on the shutters. On his last swing before forcing them open he drew the log back and unknowingly struck Lummie knocking her unconscious to the floor. Versia, who still had a hold of Lummie's hand, fell backwards, flailing her other arm and knocked the oil lamp off the big chest. The force sent it against the far wall spilling its contents. The fire immediately spread a trail to the lamp meeting with other hot spots now spreading throughout the house.

With the last swing of the log forcing the shutters open, Sammy turned back to see Versia struggling to her feet trying to locate Lummie in the chaos. He grabbed her, picked her up and forced her through the window. She was whispering through a choking voice to get Lummie as she passed out falling to the ground outside the window.

Barely able to breathe or see much except the fire and smoke, Sammy called out for Lummie. He heard two extremely loud piercing screams of one in pain coming from his right. He turned to see a wall of flame as that entire side of the house in the bedroom was openly burning. Just as suddenly, there was no sound from that area or sight of anybody. He tried to call Lummie's name but was so choked up he could no longer utter a sound. With his last ounce of strength he climbed out of the window, using his feet and legs to push himself away from the outside window frame. His aim was to avoid hitting Versia who was lying motionlessly on the ground beneath the window. The last thing he felt before losing consciousness was his shoulder blade pop as his body and head hit the ground.

Accompanied by one of his friends, Charles, from the Hole in the Bushes party, Rollie got home a little after eleven p.m. They'd ridden their horses to and from the aptly named get-together. Getting off their mounts, they noticed the sky to the south of the house illuminated from the glow of what must be have been a fire. He reasoned it had to be coming from his new house and immediately woke up his father and mother. Clem Parker had managed to complete a pay-on-time and trade with Skeeter Purvis for a 1915 REO Speedwagon last year. He made the final payment on his last visit to town. Clem climbed in the driver's side with Cora setting next to him in the front and off they went into the direction of the house with Rollie and Charles following on horseback. They tried to leave Cora home, but she was having none of that. They held out hope that the Versia had left for the day but was concern because Sammy had not returned home.

Unknowingly to Sammy or Versia, the fire engulfed the entire house bringing the tin roof down to settle over the debris in less than an hour. The light from the fire could be seen for miles which explain why so many neighbors, black and white, in spite of the midnight hour was drawn to the spot to see what was going on. A fire in this southeast part of Arkansas region with all of its wooded areas and prime Yellow Pine Arkansas timber near causes considerable concern among all local inhabitants.

The Parker truck along with Rollie and Charles were the first to arrive at the site of the still smoldering debris. Finding the two survivors, they were able to immediately revive Sammy who was in so much pain from a broken shoulder. Crying softly, he kept calling Lummie's name and finally was told by his father that she did not survive the fire. He reported to his family that the fire was deliberately set and he recognized one of the men's voices. He just couldn't put a face with the voice at this time. No he did not know how many, but there must have been at least two because of one of them ordered somebody to "cut the goddamn horses loose."

Clem told him they found the horse team, with the wagon intact on the way up. They'd brought it back with them to the site. Yes, he answered to Sammy's question if Versia was alive. "She's not able to talk about what happen but she is awake. Rollie is over there talking to her now," he said.

"She says she is feeling fine and not hurt. But she is also in some kind of shock at losing her sister. Her family has to be told. We gonna take you and Versia back to the house in the wagon team and wait for the doctor to come see you both. How do you feel baby?" his mother asked.

"Mama, I tried to help. I just . . . ," with that he just broke down crying.

"Don't blame yourself, Sammy. We will contact Sheriff Penelton in the morning. We gon find out who done this," Clem added.

Rollie had taken the REO Speedwagon and was headed to the Halls place with Charles riding along as shotgun. It was about ten miles or so drive in the dark of early morning over country roads, through farmland and sparsely wooded areas. They had to be careful and on the lookout for a stray cow, deer, or some other type of animal that might be crossing or simply standing or sitting in the dirt road. While the noise of the vehicle may scare some animals away, it may very well attract others. That's another reason Rollie brought his rifle with him.

Arriving at the Halls, Sadie and her pups had already sounded the alarm after spotting the vehicles headlights coming up the narrow road towards the house. Already on edge, yet figuring the girls had stayed at the little house in spite of promising to be home by dark, they were devastated to hear the news. Edward, angry at himself because he felt he should have gone to check on them, was trying to calm Gracie and Lena down who heard the news firsthand as they were listening to Rollie inform Frank and Harriett of Lummie's death. Harriett screamed even though she was relieved to hear Versia survived. Frank could hardly talk, he just kind of stared as his teary eyes gaze went from Rollie, Charles, Edward, then to Harriett and finally Gracie and Lena telling them to get dressed in a whisper. The rest of the family was getting fully dressed as Frank, grabbing his shotgun, ran out the door to help Edward hook the horses to the wagon.

Even though there was a makeshift half wagon bed on the back of the REO speed wagon it was not a truck as we know trucks of today. It simply would not be able to carry the Halls, plus Rollie, the driver and Charles in the passenger seat. It was about eleven or twelve miles to the Parkers house so the trip would take some time anyway.

Edward, who also placed his hunting rifle in the wagon, climbed onto the drivers section of the Hall's wagon team with Frank sitting beside him. Gracie and Lena took their places in the bed of the wagon alongside and extremely shaken but quite Harriett. They all pulled out to the sound of Sadie and her pups barking as if they wanted to go along with them. The REO led the way with Rollie driving and Charles in the passenger's seat of the vehicle. The only remark heard in the still of the night as they turned onto the dirt road leading to a main road came from Rollie who yelled to Charles above the sound of the vehicle, "I sho' hope we got enough gas to make it." His friends answer was more disconcerting than Rollie's sort of wondering statement. "Oh shit!" He replied.

How could this happen? Who would do such-a-thing? It was all that Frank could think of on the drive to the Parkers. His intention was to check on Versia and then go up to the burn site to see if there were any clues as to who would deliberately set a fire with those three kids in the house. It had to be white racist. No black person would do such a horrible thing to one of his own people. Not unless they were crazy in the head. "Who in the hell would do-such-a-thing to people?" he heard himself screaming into the dark night air.

By the time they arrived at the Parker house, the front yard was scattered with other visitor's mode of transportation. There were a couple of wagon teams, another truck, a tractor and a 1911 Abbot motor car which belonged to Dr. Morgan Purvis. The nearest medical facility that would accept black folk with serious injuries or illnesses was located in Little Rock. Dr. Purvis, Skeeter Purvis' middle son was one of two medical doctors in the local area covering about thirty to forty miles. He was the only one who would make a house call to black folk and was always a welcomed sight in time of need or otherwise.

Walking through the door, Harriett, with her husband holding her in his left hand and the shotgun in his right could not contain himself. "How's Versia Dr. Purvis?" he asked. The doctor, who was exiting a bedroom that held Sammy and was about to check on Versia answered. "She is fine but still in shock. I figure you are her relative or parent?"

"Yes Doctor. We're her mama and daddy," answered Harriett. "What about the Parkers boy, Sammy?" she continued.

"He's . . ." Cora Parker started to say while motioning for the doctor to go on and check on Versia. She grabbed Harriett's hand and guided her and Frank to the kitchen where they all sat around the table. Clem was already seated drinking a cup of coffee. "He has a broken arm and a good size lump on his head but he is fine," She finally concluded.

"Just who in the hell set that fire, do you know and . . . and why?" Frank asked Clem who understood the urgency of the other angry father's question. Shaking his head back and forth, he began to verbally frame his answer, painfully aware of Lummie's mother sitting at the table.

"The Sheriff will be out to talk to your girl Versia and Sammy this morning. They don't know who done it either. My boy did hear one of the voices of men but can't remember where or whose voice it is. I can't tell you how sorry my wife and I are about your little girl. We gonna do everything we can to help you get through this and find the bastards that did this," he answered.

Meanwhile, Rollie was listening to a disturbing diagnosis from Dr. Purvis. "Now . . . now Rollie, before you go in there remember she's still in shock," He warned. "Why she is not even sure where she is right now. So you got to be patient with her. In time, and I don't know how long it will take, it just depends, she will come around."

Rollie, not sure what to say or think, went into his fiancé room. Versia stared at him with an expressionless face as he took a seat next to her bed. He wanted to take her into his arms and console her but, despite the doctor's warning, was taken aback by her gaze that seem to look through him instead of at him. He asked how she was feeling, and received no response from her. He could not help but ask her if she knew who he was, and again received no response. He gently tried to hold her hand, but she recoiled at the idea of him touching her. After a few minutes, he left the room confused at his future wife who didn't recognize him.

Versia parents, after listening to the same warnings from Dr. Purvis, were next to visit their daughter. The girl seemed concerned at the visible tears on the face of Harriett. Yet she did not show any recognition of or even acknowledge the man and woman standing by her bedside were her parents. She did respond to them calling her by name. The sadden parents hugged their daughter at least the best they could without her contributing to their embrace and left her room. By now, Harriett was openly crying with both parents almost overwhelmed at the thought of losing one daughter in death while hoping for another's quick return to reality.

Sheriff Penelton had arrived at the Parkers farm a little after eight in the morning. The front yard was filled with the same vehicles and horse teams that were there since the earlier morning hours. Walking up to the front door, he took notice of Dr. Purvis vehicle. Rollie answered the door and announced his arrival to all. Not looking to waste time, and with the Doctors concurrence he entered Sammy's room. In spite of being medicated from having his arm popped back into his shoulder, Sammy was awake and coherent. The problem was that he could offer no more evidence of who committed what was clearly an act of arson and murder than that of a familiar voice in the night. The Sheriff told Sammy, along with the Parkers and Halls that if they found out anything more about the perpetrators identities to let him know. He was there all of a half an hour before heading for the fire's site to continue his investigation.

After thanking everyone for coming and saying their goodbyes to everyone including the Doctor, the Halls and the Parkers returned to the kitchen table. Cora served up more coffee as they began to discuss how to go about retrieving Lummie's remains from the burn sight. There was also the concern of when and if they should take Versia home. They knew they were going to postpone the wedding. How long and until when was an open end mystery that depended upon the full recovery of Versia.

Although the town of Banks, along with the white people it and surrounding areas' culture were not changing, black people in the Gravel Ridge community, the State of Arkansas and all across the South was awakening to new opportunities as a result of World War 1. In spite of Americas late entry into the war in April of 1917, there was upwards of 500, 000 black southerners who took part in "The Great Migration".

This was not an act of kindness by the north. This was a case of labor required because of the war and the pool of supply exhausted by using those European immigrants that were available and white women. Northern business recruited mostly by word of mouth and looked to black Americans to fill the void. Blacks could almost hear them asking, "Anymore like you down home boy? Tell them to come on up, I got a job for them."

Blacks in the south have always said good or bad news spread fast in these parts. The good news of blacks being hired and the wages they were paying in northern factories spread like wildfire. Those who were already there were sending word back through letters and verbally while visiting family in the South. It prompted even more, especially young blacks, to bolt close families and friends for a better life. This caused a social, cultural, and political landscape fundamental transformation in cities like New York, Pittsburgh, Chicago, Detroit and Cleveland. And as one would guess, the area losing these workers, i.e. the South felt it too. Although they may have been slow to realize it.

Once the exodus was actually witness and felt by the white landowners, they brought out the conspiracy theory against the south and outright lies. They claimed that northern businesses were luring unsuspecting blacks to a brand new life of urban misery. Oh, there were cases where a family did not get the job they thought was there. By the time they got there it was filled or for other reasons. Some of these new arrivals would get some blowback from older black residents for their unsophisticated behavior and backwards thinking. Racism was not confined to the south and they found resentment from a lot of white workers who felt threatened by their presence on the jobs. Neighborhoods became crowded, and some living conditions were substandard. Yet when the migrants compared the life they left to the city life of simple things like indoor plumbing, and new appliances, even though they may not be able to afford them right then. When they took into account the paved streets and all the accompanied lifestyle versus dirt roads and a constant threat of violence for family and self-there were no comparison.

For black people and the nation as a whole, this was like a breath of fresh air. Culturally the southern blacks had a refreshing impact on new music, cooking, and arts in the city. Most had family members who arrived first and was sent for when there was a job opening in the factories. At first arrival they lived with family until able to strike out on their own. Those older family members had already assimilated into the black fabric of the cities. So much so, that as time passed the only time blow back was felt from current residents was when the new arrivals got the same job a resident family member applied for. An otherwise somewhat bumpy migration at first was becoming seamless as far as the current and future residents were concerned.

The migration had slowed somewhat by the spring of 1919 and for almost all points and purposes World War 1 had ended. For the Parkers, the war ending last year as they received notification that their son Clement Jr., was killed in action. The family took it hard but was proud to say their son fought and died for the freedom, and that freedom meant African-American freedom too.

A lot of the vets returned home or was about to return home. All had new pride in themselves and their country in spite of the Jim Crow laws still on the books. Most all felt and even vowed to fight for what was rightfully theirs in the homeland and nothing more. They certainly did not have that same timid way of approaching or fear of white people as did their parents' generation. This was something the southern white self-elected ruling class immediately saw and increased their intimidation tactics to meet this new challenge.

The fall of 1919 brought about the powder keg that blew the lid off the world of Sharecropping.

According to the Historical Text Archive on *Revolution in the Land: Southern Agriculture in the 20th Century* in a section called [2] "The Changing Face of Sharecropping and Tenancy":

Late in the evening of September 30, 1919, black sharecroppers were holding a union meeting in a church in Hoop Spur outside of Elaine, Arkansas. Tensions were high and they had posted guards at the door. When two deputized white men and a black trustee pulled into view, shots rang out. Who fired first is still debated, likely unknowable, and perhaps not that important. What is important is what transpired afterwards. One of the white men was killed, the other wounded. The black trustee raced back to Helena, the county seat of Phillips County, and alerted officials. A posse was dispatched and within a few hours hundreds of white men, many of them the "low down" variety, began to comb the area for blacks they believed were launching an insurrection. In the end, five white men and over a hundred African Americans were killed. Some estimates of the black death toll range in the hundreds. Allegations surfaced that the white posse and even U.S. soldiers who were brought in to put down the so called "rebellion" had massacred defenseless black men, women and children. Nearly a hundred blacks were arrested, and in sham trials that lasted no more than a few minutes each, sixty-something black men were sentenced to prison, and twelve were slated for execution. A massive effort on the part of the NAACP and others, including a prominent black attorney in Little Rock, ensued, and by 1925 all the men were free. But planters had established that blacks had best not organize, even within the law, for racism would bring whites of different classes together to put them down.

Elaine, Arkansas is 95 miles or so from Banks and the Gravel Ridge Community. There was and is sharecropping going on here with the same cotton and other crops. This atrocity could have happened in Banks. It could have touched the Hampton, Hall, Davis, Belin, Green, or Childs family's in more ways than one.

One thing it did do immediately was to get the communities' attention all the way up and through the release of the twelve men in 1925 that were slated to die. It effected the returning GI's and Sailors in an embolden kind of way. It did not deter them from their newfound resiliency. Its effect on the old folk was in a grief-stricken way. People like Edgar, Rollie, Gracie, Lena, and most community children of non-voters and some former slaves the same way. They got angry. From that anger grew a quiet resolve. They personally avowed separately and among themselves not to be intimidated by white people tactics any longer. They also struck a bond with each other, to always be there for each other no matter what.

It was said that the tipping point of common sense came when a headline appeared in the Arkansas Gazette on October 3, 1919. It read **Negroes plan to kill all Whites**. *Slaughter was to begin with 21 prominent men as the first victims. "We just begun" was to be the password. Blacks had armed themselves and planned to kill every white person in sight when plot was exposed.*

Needless to say, this was a major reason younger black people were angry. They were simply tired of being blamed for everything. There were a lot of whites who was also angry at the way some in their race conducted their business with black people. So it was not like African-Americans did not have allies in their fight for equal justice and Civil Rights and all that came with it. Each day, more and more people from all walks of life were stepping up to the plate to voice their opposition to these types of tactics.

CHAPTER 2

Gracie's Sixteenth Birthday

Thomas Woodrow Wilson was in the last year of his eight year term as President of the United States. It was July, mid-summer of 1920, the seventh month of a new decade that would become known as the Roaring Twenties or the Jazz Age. Prohibition on the sale of alcohol was more than a year into practice. The sale of liquor and other alcoholic beverage ban set by the Eighteenth Amendment to the Constitution and enforced by the rules of the Volstead Act was not enough to prevent the thirst for a large number of Americans. The era of bootleggers along with Chicago/New York style gangsters were just getting off the ground. Discovering what an opportunity the liquor ban presented for anyone who was willing to take a chance on quick and easy money was now in vogue.

In fact Hot Springs, Arkansas (Approximately 84 miles from the Gravel Ridge community), a national resort town with its hot spas and ideal location would become a yearly getaway for such famous gangsters as Al Capone and Charles "Lucky" Luciano to name a couple. The local Indian tribes called what is now Hot Springs "Valley of the Vapors". They literally believed the natural hot springs had healing powers. The town had already become famous lately for the ever growing Bathhouse Row.

Besides the current illegal gambling spots, one could visit Oaklawn Park in the city and bet on the thoroughbreds. Sometime during this same era, Capone imported local "Hot Springs" moonshine to his Chicago nightclubs.

Yet all that did not matter to this little community of Gravel Ridge in Bradley County or the small town of Banks. Bradley County was as were many surrounding counties, a dry county. Efforts to limit or prevent the sale and consumption of alcohol had been prevalent in this neck of the woods since Arkansas territorial period. Bootlegging had always been the norm in this community as long as anyone could remember.

The hot button issue for the locals at this time was getting in the ground the late summer and fall crops. The bulk of planting season had just ending and the area schools had reopened for the summer. There was as there had always been up to this point, plenty of work for Frank over at old man Jennings. The three hundred acre farm was about seven miles from Halls. The farm on his left was another white family named Sampson with the Parkers farm to the left of the Sampson's. Mr. Jennings' land also had about forty acres of pine trees that were thinned and cut at the proper time for wood for the farm and individual sales. The Hall Family was lucky that an excellent working relationship had been established over the years with Lee Jennings and his family. Times were hard, and in some areas, getting harder for all.

A couple of months ago, one of Frank's horses broke his leg by stepping in a gopher hole. Frank shot the horse on the spot. The girls and Harriett, after helping with the seeding of the Jennings fields, were on their way home in the wagon with Frank. The good news is that they were only a half a mile from their house. The bad news is that left them with one horse or a "half a team". Frank could borrow a horse from the old man, but for now, he was saving his money to buy another horse. Or maybe his luck will change, and he will "come by a horse some other way," as he likes to say.

Gracie woke up to the sound of her mother's and father's voices speaking in almost hushed tones. Although it was dark, she figured it must have been close to four O'clock in the morning. She heard Mama Harriett tell her father to be careful as he rode his horse bareback through the woods and through other farms to the Jennings place. There's a lot of growth in those woods this time of year where snakes could hide.

"Aw Mama H, you'se worry too much. Besides, if I want to get to work and make us any extra money then I need to leave now so I can get there early and leave at noon time. There is still some work to be done even tho' Mr. Jennings planting season is over," Frank Hall responded to his wife.

"I know, I know. I just . . ." Mama Harriett voice trailed off. "Shhhhh . . . you are going to wake up the children."

"I'll be back right after lunch to finish planting our sweet potatoes," Frank said as he went out the door. Little Gracie could hear the creaky front door being closed after her daddy went through the door into the pitch black early morning. Although it was a summer day on this 13th of July, Little Gracie could still feel the cool morning air rushing throughout the cabin immediately upon the opening of the front door. Considering the draftiness around the windows, underneath the back door and the small holes in the houses structure the cooler air is constantly present. It just adds more to it, stirring it up at the opening of the front door. By the time the sun is shining around mid-morning all will be aware that it is an Arkansas summer in full bloom. Gracie looked forward to that time of the day, but for now, she knew she better get more sleep as she would have to get up to do her chores before school time in about an hour.

No sooner than she fell back to sleep she was awakened by the sound of that damn red speckled rooster. You would think he would wait for the sunrise, but the Hall family's bird is always a little early. He acted as if it's his job to wake up all the roosters in the Clay Township, Bradley County vicinity so they can crow in unison at first light. *Daddy was right, Red* (as the bird was called) *must think he is top bird in the county*, she thought. Darn that bird, one of these days I'm going to wring that stupid birds neck and put it in a pot with some dumplings and serve a feast to my family," she heard herself say out loud.

Mama Harriett voice interrupted her thoughts by shouting, "Are you chillen up?" They could hear their mother rustling pots and pans on the wood stove in the front room. "Come on now, its gon' be a busy day, so you better get moving, up and outta that bed. This is a school day."

Gracie smiled at the thought of her sixteenth birthday last May 13th. Some girls her age were already married. Her brother, Edward first met Ruth King at the Halls' church. That was the day of Gracie's 1917 thirteen birthday celebration. Ruth was much too young for romance back then. Nevertheless, Edward, at twenty years old, married the fourteen year old girl six months later and moved to her parents' farm in Lawrence County, Arkansas. She thinks they are living in Powhatan or Denton. Just couldn't be sure of which because both are close together in Lawrence County.

Even though that John Hampton boy was sniffing around her at school, Gracie was a girl who had her own ideas as to when she would marry and what kind of woman she was going to become. She felt a duty to her parents to stay with them as long as possible considered how the older children had left the Hall household. For she, a keen observer of human nature and outstanding instincts on how to survive as a southern Negro young girl in this day and age saw the happiness coupled with the underlying sorrow in her parents faces as each child left home.

It was a couple of months and three years to the day that Lummie was killed in the Rollie Parker house fire. No one has ever been held responsible for starting that fire. A couple of years ago Versia, who had slowly returned to her 'right mind' as they called it, met and fell in love with a new beau, got married and moved to Hot Springs, Arkansas. It was where her husband James Boswell was born and raised. Rollie waited a year for his fiancé to remember or display some kind of affection for him. It got so bad that they could not even carry on a conversation about how it once was between them. Finally, tired of unreturned love, he took up with another girl. They are expecting their first child in the fall which means they will probably be getting married too.

Add the circumstances of Lummie's death to Frank and Harriett's quiet suffering and, well, Gracie was the oldest child left at home and was not going anywhere anytime soon. She knew their parents needed help with the chores since the older children were no longer in the area. Although lately, and almost

45

every night up through the wee hours in the morning, her body send signals that she is growing up fast. She calls them funny feelings. In reality, they are sexual urges. Nevertheless, she is not going to get married just for the sake of being married. "Mr. Hampton will just have wait if he wants me," she says softly as if she didn't want anyone to hear her innermost thoughts. Giggling while trying to manage a serious expression of thought on her face she continued a little louder, "But I do like him."

"I know you like him," Lena said. The sound of her sister's voice in the dark surprised Gracie who thought she was still asleep in spite of their mother calling for them to get up. "Come on, we better get up, or mama will come chase us outta here," The younger sister urged.

Dressed and ready for school, having put food in the chicken and hogs' pen, the two girls sat down at the kitchen table to bowls of homemade grits. By now they had become accustomed to being the only other members of the family living in the house as both young girls tried to act more responsible for their personal responsibilities.

In fact, one of Gracie's premonitions, as her mother calls it, came true this morning. A few months ago, she thought she was daydreaming as she sat in school. She saw a vision of her and Lena sitting at the kitchen table eating while her mother was cooking. The eerie thing about it was that she was now going through the scene in real time. They all were in the same exact spot, saying word for word what she envisioned. Finally, the scene ran out. Gracie, clearly shaken at the event called out her mother's name.

Her mother, somewhat startled at hearing her daughter scream out her name, asked, "What's wrong?" Gracie went on to explain to her and Lena that this scene she envisioned months ago had just played itself out. Her mother reassured her as she had done before that some people have this type of gift from God. Some have intuition, others like Gracie, can see the scenes, and hear the talk long before it actually happens. There is no need to worry, no, you can't bring them on yourself, and they happen naturally, she told the girls.

"It was another premonition, baby. You will be alright," Harriett said in summation.

After the morning chit-chat, helping with the dishes, receiving the day's agenda and their lunch pails from their mama, Gracie and Lena left for school. It was about four miles away, and the only way they were going to get there was to walk. Taking a shortcut through the woods was not an option as both girls were scared of snakes. They could stay on the little dirt road for a mile or so but would have to cut across the local farmlands for a couple of miles to cut some of the distance down. If they hurry they will meet a couple of the other kids on their way to school. They may meet John Hampton and one or two of his cousins. By that time the walk will become fun as they play games on the way.

About a mile down the dirt road, the first school travelers they meet are ten year old Curtis McFarland, his eight year old brother, Ernest, and their seven year old sister, Christine, all headed in the same direction. Their mother, Hattie, as she had every school day this summer was standing by the road with her children.

"I guess by now you girls must expect me to be here. If yawl don't come along, I'll have to walk them there myself. That's our house up the hill there," said Mrs. McFarland pointing to a house about a quarter mile up a small dirt road. "You tell your mama, I'm gonna make you girls a sweet potato pie for walking my chillen to school. You hear?"

"Yes 'um," the girls replied in unison while smiling at the thought of a treat just for them.

"I'll be right here this evening when you 'all get out of school. Okay?"

"Yes 'um," the girls answered.

As the children continued on down the road while occasionally looking back at Mrs. McFarland going up the hill, Gracie said, almost under her breath, "This is like a babysitting job."

"I ain't no baby," came an instant reply from Curtis, who was also in charge of carrying his brother and sister molasses pail that contained their lunch.

They all walked briskly to an area along the two line log fence line where they climbed over the bottom log to cut across a freshly seeded field. "Don't step on the rows or we gon' get in trouble," Gracie ordered.

"Here, follow me," Curtis told his siblings while taking the younger Christine's hand and carefully walking between the rows.

Finally, having walked through the seeded field at almost a ninety degree angle, they climbed through the fence and onto a dirt tractor trail, more so than a road. The sun, which had lit up the sky just before the girls left home, was peeping over the horizon promising to a host a warm day. One could see for miles across these newly planted fields as long as there was no foliage in the way. About a quarter mile up ahead they could see three boys looking their way. They seem to be walking slowly enough so the girls could catch up to them. They could not make out the faces, but Gracie knew one of them was John Hampton. A knowing glance from her sister Lena validated her thinking, which was followed by that nervous feeling in her stomach every time she thought about him, much less talk to him.

"Shoot! Why are they stopping?" Gracie asked Lena while simultaneously waving for them to keep going on their way.

"You know, I told you he . . ." Lena replied before she was cut off in midsentence by Gracie who half whispered, "Don't say nothing in front of the little kids."

"Everybody knows that boy like you Gracie," Curtis said with a teasing smirk on his face.

They finally caught up with the boys. It was Dempsey Davis, his fourteen year old younger brother, Mansfield, and their cousin of course, that fourteen year old John Hampton boy. Just the fact that he was two years younger than Grace caused all kind of confusion in her mind. He's just a kid, she always thought to herself. At least she and Dempsy was the same age. But then, she didn't have these feelings or a strong like for him as she did for John. There was just something about this kid.

"Hey, Gracie, hi you feeling this morning?" John asked.

"Did your mama pack your bottle in your lunch pail?" She asked sarcastically. Instantly feeling sorry for her snippy words as she saw the sad affect it had on him, she quickly added in her kindest voice, "I'm fine, John. Hi you do this morning?"

The entire scene made little Curtis sick to his stomach to hear and see all this mushy stuff going on. The kids talked and joked around for a few minutes more until they all reached the top of the little tractor dirt road where they could see the schoolhouse down the other side of the hill.

It was a fairly new one room school house with windows around each side allowing for sunlight to brighten up the inside of the room. All first through the eighth were located in the one room. The older kids would help the younger kids study and keep them occupied while the one teacher would ensure that all was busy learning something. No one left their seat without permission. There was no electricity or running water. The one outhouse was for the girls. The boys were asked to go outside in the little wooded area along the back and pick a spot for relief.

The Arkansas school system, as was the rest of the country, was segregated because of the Plessy vs. Ferguson case ruling by the US Supreme court in 1896. The ruling stating black and white students should go to separate schools and those schools should be equal. "Separate but equal" became law in name only, especially in the South. The local Arkansas school systems, already short on funding, built many more one room school houses that supported grades 1-7 and 8-12 grades for whites than black people. Various private organizations and individuals stepped in to fill the void to build the same type schools in heavily concentrated African American areas. The local schools systems were more than happy to admit these private funded schools into the systems because a large building cost had been avoided.

The Rosenwald Fund was one such private funded organization that was founded on the premise and established beliefs of Booker T Washington. Washington, the principal of the Tuskegee Normal and Industrial Institute, now known as Tuskegee University, championed the mantra of 'self-help for black people' in the late nineteenth and early twentieth centuries. Unlike the NAACP, who directly challenged segregation, Washington did not discount this as one method of changing the status quo. He believed the most prudent way of overcoming economic and social blight for his race was through education. He found that he was not alone in his beliefs as he attracted financial support from black and white Americans. The overall feeling was that this method, as long as it was done in black schools, would be less confrontational to a mass of white people.

Julius Rosenwald, a philanthropist and part owner of Sears Roebuck and Company was most noted for his contributions to the building of such African American schools in the rural South. He was first approached by Washington in 1912. It was well known that the two men had a general respect for each other along with similar goals in educating black people.

Thus, Mr. Rosenwald's fund contributed to, supplied grants, and fully funded, in some cases the efforts of local black and white educational officials, in placing young black children in newly built schools in southern rural areas located near their homes. It should also be stated that one of the stipulations of receiving a Rosenwald Grant was that blacks had to contribute cash and in-kind donations of material labor. Another stipulation for receiving Rosenwald funds was that the participating county school board had to provide their support of the project. They were to take ownership of the new school property along with the maintenance of the building. In other words, the school itself would have to become part of the local public school system.

And as noted at the outset, rural communities, short on funds and without the support to build schools for blacks, gladly accepted the terms. Reportedly, the Fund was instrumental in getting four to five hundred schools built per year from 1920 to 1928, mainly in the South. The Fund itself totaled approximately $356,000 to $414,000 per year.

This little school, Gravel Ridge, was part of the Oaklawn and Pleasant Hill School System and happened to house about thirty-five students when everyone was present. Those kids who wanted to continue pass the eighth grade would have to go all the way to Warren, Arkansas. Warren was thirteen miles away from Banks, and a few more from the surrounding Gravel Ridge community depending on where you were standing at the time. If that happened, they more than likely would move in with a relative or somebody who lived in Warren.

Just as the girls, McFarland kids, Davis boys and John Hampton started down the hill heading for the school's front door, Mrs. Tennie Franklin was ringing the bell to announce that class would start in exactly fifteen minutes from now. Mrs. Franklin, Gravel Ridges Baptist church Pastor A.J. Payne Jr. and Sister Hattie Payne's daughter, finally married her fiancé, Cicero Franklin Jr. She was six months pregnant with her first child due in early October. All the kids in class still called her Ms. T, as did those who knew her from church. One could tell she was with child even though her belly bump was not as pronounced as one would think. However some of the kids in the class, especially some of the boys, whispered at one of last week recesses that she was growing bigger by the minute. Ever since then she has had to remind some of the kids to look into her eyes while they are talking to her and not at her stomach.

All the kids had settled in their assigned seats within their grade level and alongside their younger classmate. The older kids were charged to act as a youngster's tutor by helping them with their work as part of one of their own assignments. It was a complicated arrangement that in practice worked out rather well.

The only disturbance occurred about thirty minutes into the school morning. Just like clockwork, Robert Long, who practically lives next door to the school, was late again. Gracie, his same age group and grade, was visible annoyed because all the children seated at her bench-table had to get up to let him take a seat next to his younger class ward. "Cuse me, excuse me, 'cuse me," he said as he made his way past Gracie, her ward and four other students before settling down next to his ward who could not keep from giggling at all the commotion. Gracie rolled her eyes as he looked back her way after taking his seat.

"Robert Long, you got one more time to be late. Just one more time and you gonna be sorry," advised Ms. T.

Meanwhile back at the Hall household, a couple of their neighbor's family oldest men were helping Harriett to plant the last seeds of sweet potatoes in one of the sections on the small farm. She wanted to finish before twelve noon and move on to other pressing chores. Today, it was the only help Harriett could get considering everybody else in the area was watering, hoeing, and taking care of their field or gardens. The planting season was pretty much over except for certain vegetables normally planted in late June and early July. The Halls had one more section to complete after this one. It would have to be a late plant for that section.

Her nephew, twenty-four year old Edgar Hall, son of her brother-in-law and his young twenty-three year old bride, Viola, had already offered and gave their services in planting and hoeing during the early planting season. They filled in when Frank could not get time off from working on the Jennings farm.

It was also convenient that they rented a house from a family that moved to California a few months ago. The house was no more than a city block from Frank and Harriett. Since Edgar's father's family, as well as his bride's family lived in Warren, they were lucky to have the young couple and their five-year-old little girl as neighbors and family. Edgar wanted to own a farm one day, so he chose to live in this area rather than Warren. He and Viola wanted this for their family, which they expect would expand. His daughter, Mae Ellen, was born on August 10, 1915, four years before he and Viola got married. Their parents were a little uneasy that a marriage did not take place before the child was born but supported the wishes of the youngsters to wait until they became more settled and had their own place. Mae Ellen was a cute and smart little girl who was well aware that she was the star of this little family. She had taken to Gracie and Lena as if they were her big sisters. She thought they knew everything about anything.

Although the young Halls were off working in their own little garden today, they would join the older Hall family for a fish fry this evening.

Harriett was looking forward to it. She was also glad to have the young couple around since two of her oldest children had married and moved out of the area. The fact that Viola was a "fair to good seamstress" as Edgar put it, made her companionship even more important. The both of them could exchange thoughts on Harriett's quilting and Viola's dress making ideas.

Running from farm to farm was more than a notion, but Frank Hall was grateful that old man Jennings was able to arrange his work schedule these last few days of the planting season. It allowed him to put in a couple of small crops on his own. It was especially rough since his son moved. Gracie and Lena was helpful enough to his wife but they could only do so much. To pay someone to help out was simply not in the cards as they did not have the money to pay anyone. So any help from his young nephew, Edgar and his wife, was a bonus. The family would be able to share their foodstuffs and other items they raised or bought as payment. The newlyweds and their little girl were just settling in as farmers and were being help by Viola's family too.

Frank could hear Sadie and her full grown offspring barking as they spotted him coming up the road approaching the house. As he led the horse to the fenced-in barn and dismounted he thought, *one day I'm going to get a saddle for this horse. That's a pain in the butt forever it seems he concluded,* while trying to loosens his underwear from the crack in his booty.

This would be the first time he planted sweet potatoes on his land. He, having become somewhat of an expert on sweet potatoes for the Jennings, surveyed the two cardboard boxes to see if the contents were still in planting shape. One box contained sweet potato slips with the other holding about a dozen starter plants. Trying to be careful as not to break off any roots stemming from the slips, he put each box in a little kid's wagon and pulled it to the planting site.

This promised to be a long warm summer and it was perfect weather for planting. Mr. Jennings gave the slips and starter plants to Frank as a working bonus. He knew if they were planted right, properly nurtured and watered, he would reap a fine harvest in October.

Harriett and the others saw Frank and waved as he continued on to the planting site. This was not only a planting of love for family servings, it was one of the staples of their diet and used at almost every main meal. They were especially great for making sweet potato pies, a favorite of the entire family. Convinced that he had planted a crop that would bring about a good harvest, Frank headed back toward the barn. By now, his wife and helpers were already finished and back at the houses doing other chores. With a quick glance at the sun's position, he reasoned it to be about four O'clock. *Not bad for a half days effort* he thought as he walked along.

Reaching the barn, he put the little wagon in the corner and walked over to the well to wash up for the rest of the day. They always kept a small bucket and a bar of homemade soap on the bench next to the well. A person could draw fresh water, pouring it in the wash bucket, take care of their personal hygiene on the spot and walk to the house feeling fresh and clean. Frank did just that and asked Harriett if she needed help upon entering the house.

"Sho' honey, would you clean that mess of bullheads and catfish over there in the corner?"

"Why yessum, I sure don't mind cleaning fish for my supper." He answered as he took the pail and sat down at the table to finish the job.

A little later on, Sadie and the pups began to announce more visitors. Harriett took a quick look out of the window spotting Edger, Viola and little Mae Ellen walking towards their house with Gracie and Lena. There was also some other boy with them. She could not make out who he was because he didn't look familiar. She smiled as she thought it was so wonderful to see four young family members walking along laughing and talking about who they were and what plans they had for their future.

"Frank look at this, here come the girls with Viola and Edger. Do you know who that boy is that's with them?"

Grabbing an old wash rag to dry his hands after dipping them in the fish guts water pail, he positioned himself next to Harriett so he could see.

"Noooo . . . , I can't say that I do. Whoever he is, he must not be a stranger to the others because they all seem comfortable with him. Um finished anyway, let me get rid of these fish guts, wash up and I will be right back."

As he turned back toward the table, Frank playfully kissed Harriett on the cheek, while rubbing a hand on her butt. "Stop you old fool." A blushing Harriett retorted.

"Um just letting you know that I got more than eating fish on my mind, woman." Frank said with a wide smile and wink of his eye going out the front door. "So you just be thinking about that tonight, you hear."

Harriett's only reply was a warm welcoming smile at him. She knew that would be enough of a signal for her man.

By now, Gracie and the others were coming through the front gate. Harriett couldn't hear Sadie barking anymore, but those other pups of hers were. They make more noise and are even nosier than ever. Even though she was still in the kitchen and could not see the dogs, she knew those three picks of the litter were still turning flips, wagging their tails and running around the girls and anyone who come through that gate. Edward named the three, Moe, Zoe and Oh No. The last one born was called Oh No because he couldn't seem to turn the complete flip. He would always stumble, yet that would not keep that dog from trying. As usual Sadie retreated to her normal spot on the front porch to lie down with her head on her front paws. She would roll her big brown eyes while watching the show. It's as if she is trying to say, *yawl is using way too much energy.*

It was a Friday meal of southern fried catfish-bullheads, fried potatoes, fried corn with fried okra, biscuits and molasses with leftover black-eyed peas and cornbread. Viola had baked a peach cobbler for dessert. It was her specialty.

Frank said grace, after amen; all began to serve themselves from the platters and plates on the table.

John Hampton thanked Ms. Harriett for allowing him to eat with the family. He thanked Mr. Hall for letting him visit Gracie as he intimated that he had walked her and Lena all the way home from school. His visit was twofold as he was also coming by to visit Edgar and Viola. Yes, his family knew of the visit because they wanted to see if the young couple needed anything as they were very good friends of Viola's parents. Yes, Viola and Edgar was expecting him this evening and was prepared for him to spend the night. It also helped that little Mae Ellen liked him too.

Even though Frank heard the boy when he said he walked Gracie home from school, he still asked, "Aw John, how do you know my daughter Gracie?"

"We go to the same school," both Gracie and John nervously answered in unison.

That got everybody's attention. Clearly something else was going on between these two children. Up until now, no one at this table, except Lena, knew how Gracie and John felt about each other. Whether planned or not, the secret, if that was what it was intended to be, was now out in the open.

Frank glanced at Harriett for some indication that she was aware of what seems to be a budding love affair between these kids. Harriett's blank expression toward Frank was an acknowledgement that she had no clue about this development.

"Johnny", she began . . . .

"'cuse me Ms. Harriett, but its John. John Hampton," the young man confidently stated with a sheepish smile.

"John", she corrected herself, "Gracie is sixteen. How old are you?"

"Ma'am, um fourteen, but everybody says I act much older."

By this time, Frank had heard enough. He cleared his mouth of food, put his fork down on the table, leaned back in his chair and began . . . . , "You just a kid, tho' you look older too. Who are you boy? Where are you from and whose child are you? Who yo' kin folk? Where do your family live and how do they know Viola? And furthermore, where do you plan on sleeping tonight?"

"Daddy?" Gracie said in a mild attempt to calm Frank down.

John, eager to answer the questions began to do just that. "Sir, my name is John Hampton, first son and child of Sallie and David Hampton, Sr. from right here in our Gravel Ridge Community. I got me four more brothers at home, Lemon Davis, seventeen. Monroe who is thirteen, David Jr. who is seven and Van D (Peach), who will be five years old next month."

"They call my daddy Sambo. Somebody said some white man started calling him by that name. Not sure, but he don't seem to mind. My grandpa is named Monroe Hampton Sr. and grandma is Jane. Her last name before she married my grandpa was Trotter. My mama's last name before she married daddy was Davis. I got lots of relatives hereabouts but Gracie ain't one of them," he concluded, looking at Gracie with a smile.

By now, everybody was quietly eating and chewing softly in order not to miss a word while anxiously awaited Frank's response. John, much to their surprise was not through.

"Mr. Frank, I know um a young boy but my daddy says I have to grow up fast 'cause um second oldest. We are farmers with a house, land and some stock over by the Oak love Gravel Ridge School. We are in the back woods off the old highway road to Banks and down around Lanark. I do like your Gracie here, and I'd like your blessing to call on her from time to time if she don't mind and you'll let me."

"Well, if you are asking to take her out. My first question would be, take her where? Since you don't have or may not even be old enough to have a job and you walked over here. Shoot! You don't even have the right courting tools to ask a father to see his daughter. Why . . ."

"Frank, I don' think he's asking to take her out anytime soon. I just think he want yo' permission to stop by the house every now and then," Harriett added while trying to calm the conversation down.

"Is that what you mean boy?" Frank asked while trying to accommodate his wife's not so subtle way of asking for calmness.

"Yes suh." John agreed.

"Yes Daddy, that's what he means. Like eating together at the church socials and coming over her to visit and stuff like that," Gracie eagerly added.

"Boy, I'll say this. You are one lucky son-of-a-gun, you must have already impressed my wife and daughter to have them speak for you. But let this be my first and last warning to you. You do anything, and I mean anything to hurt my little Gracie here, um gon' hurt you bad. You hear me boy?"

"Yes suh." John answered.

Edgar and Viola who sat through that entire exchange without saying a word looked at each other, John, Gracie, Lena, and Frank. They could not hold back their wide smiles at what they had just heard. For Edgar, it brought back memories of him courting Viola.

"Ms. Harriett, would you show me how you get your biscuits to turn out so light? Edgar says mine are always so heavy."

"Sure girl, but mostly it's just practice and more practice." Harriett responded.

"I guess you right. They are heavier at times than others."

The supper conversations turned to more general chit-chat and less inquisition of young Mr. Hampton, which made everyone feel at ease.

Viola, Edgar and May Ellen had said their goodbyes to their host and hostess, along with Gracie and Lena and were preparing to walk back down to their own house for the night. All eyes were on the hand waves and awkwardly nodding of head by Gracie and John while they said good night to each other. John tuned toward the door after saying good night to Mr. Frank and Ms. Harriett. He complimented the cooks, including Viola for her peach cobbler. Standing, he looked much older than fourteen in posture too. He had a slender build yet strong hand shake. He seems to like wearing a ball cap that he placed back on his head before walking out on the porch with the others.

The fact that he walked and talked like a man was not lost on Frank as he watched them walk down the road toward Edgar and Viola's. A sly glance at Gracie's face told him all he needed to know. This was a relationship that was going to grow so everybody better get on board. He laughed out loud as he thought of the nerve of little Mr. Hampton.

Gracie and Lena ran into the house, started to clean up the table and washing dishes so they could turn in for the night. It had been a long day for them too.

"What you laughing at?" Harriett asked with that teasing voice that reminded him of his promise to her earlier of lovemaking long after the girls are asleep.

"Just thinking . . . , baby, that boy is way too serious. But then enough about him, let's go in and settle down for the night."

It sounded like Lena was asleep as soon as her head hit the pillow. Gracie was awake long enough to imagine what a life might be like with that Hampton boy. She also could not imagine her leaving her Papa and Mamas house in the near future. They needed her here more than she needed to be married to anybody. She prayed that John would wait and not be too anxious to run off together and leave home. Besides, Papa had laid down the law. Don't look for our little love affair foolishness to turn into something serious for a long time, he advised and John had agreed. Gracie smiled as she thought of how persistent John would be from his words and the look of determination his face. "If it happens, I think I'm going to have me a strong man," she said to nobody in particular but specifically talking to herself.

Now she could hear Lena giggling beneath the covers. "Girl, go to sleep."

"I am sleep." Lena lied.

Both girls could not help but hear the huffing and puffing going on in their parents' room. Neither one made a comment but if you could see their faces, you would see two girls blushing and holding back major giggles as they tried to ignore the distraction. Finally, the entire household was asleep. You could tell that all was quiet in and around the house because there wasn't even a sound from Sadie's pups.

The summer passed without incident. That is, nothing special happened. The crops flourished and furnished a great harvest for all in the area. For the Halls and everyone in the county, the canning of tomatoes, peas, beans, and other vegetables was bountiful. Food had been put up for the expected long winter including storing of fresh hunted game, fish, pork bacon, and hams. For that matter, everything on the pig was edible, from the rooter to the tooter, as the old folk say, was stored in their farms or a neighbors smokehouse.

The smokehouse was a necessity in these rural areas because it was used to smoke and store meat that could be stored up and over a year. Some would even contain a wood burning stove where hams, sausage and other meats would be smoked for many hours. Others didn't need the stove; they were used for the same reason and secure enough to prevent animals from getting inside. The meat would be packed in salt or sugar for preservation.

The Halls did get together with Versia and her husband John Boswell over the Christmas holiday. They came up by train from Hot Springs for Christmas day and stayed until three days before the New Year's. It was an unexpected surprise to both her parents but a welcome visit that made the holidays so much more special. They all missed Edward, and talked about him so much that "his ears must be ringing," or so Harriett said. In the end, Mr. and Mrs. Boswell promised they would be back sometime before the end of summer or around Thanksgiving. "John works in the Arlington Hotel at home. He's got to be back before the New Year's Eve. It's the largest hotel in Hot Springs, and it's hard for him to get time off." Versia told the family.

"Yessum, we will be back though," John added.

With that said, hugs and sloppy kisses were given and received by all involved. The young couple, still without children, climbed up on the wagon and was being driven to the town of Banks by Edgar and Viola. Versia and her husband would be able to board the train going back to Hot Springs from there. The wagon team belonged to Frank, all except the one horse that Mr. Jennings let him use for the winter. It wasn't a cold day, but the air was brisk. More importantly, the dirt roads was clear and dry and snow was not expected until three or four days past January 1st. Viola and Edgar were only too happy to do it because they were going on to Warren to bring in the New Year with their parents. It would give their folks a chance to see their grandchild. That's why little May Ellen was bundled up so tight in order keep warm on the long wagon trip. Frank knew that Edgar was an excellent driver and would take very good care of the horse and team.

About a week later, his trust was rewarded when Moe, Zoe, and Oh No started barking at something. He looked out the frosty window and could barely make out his team coming up to his front door. And sure as heck, it did not make Sadie's dogs any difference because it was winter. They did their job by announcing Viola and Edgars return.

It would be over a year and closer to two years before Versia and John would see or visit Harriett and Frank. They all kept in touch by writing but the fact that now both were working at the Arlington, it became almost impossible for the both of them to get time off, much less together. The fact is they were more concern about keeping their jobs rather than getting time off. John had graduated from being a cook's helper to a full time cook. His off day was Mondays. Versia was a maid who cleaned rooms on a daily basis except Wednesdays.

Two winters had passed, and the summer of 1922 had arrived. Nationally, it was a year where Federal spending reached $3.29 billion, unemployment was at 6.7%, and the cost of a postage stamp was two cents. In fact a dollar bill in 1922 would spend like $13.05 in the year of 2013. The average house at a cost of $8,024 would be $104,691, a car would cost $355 versus $4, 632 today and an average wage of $991 per year would be $12,930.

Warren G Harding was serving as the 29th President of the United States. A Republican from Ohio, he was a self-made newspaper publisher. President Harding advocated an anti-lynching bill to curb violence against black people. The legislation was blocked by a prominent Republican and the politically stout of Democrats entitled the 'Solid South'.

The term 'Solid South' was given to the southern part of the United States Democratic Party candidates from 1877 up through the passage of the Civil Rights Act of 1964. At the time, the vast majority of local and state officeholders in the South were Democrats. This was accomplished through many ways in which voter intimidation, suppression and outright denial had its presence felt and realized by African-Americans through-out the southern states. It was common knowledge that a majority of whites in the South targeted the Republican Party for its favorable stance on political rights for black people during the Reconstruction. There was no doubt of the Solid South's willingness to embrace Jim Crow laws and racial segregation.

This was a bright sunny late June Saturday morning. The little town of Banks was hustling and bustling with activity. And as usual, the décor of the town itself and the mood of most non-black inhabitants and local visitors was that of a year before reconstruction, like 1864.

Frank drove his team to Banks, with Edgar, Gracie, and Lena who was now all of sixteen years old herself. They left Harriett and Viola to their home chores of the day. Seven-year-old Mae Ellen also stayed with her mother helping out wherever she could. He parked in the back where everyone with a wagon team conveniently could unload and load their wagon with goods from Skeeter Purvis store.

Gracie had finished the eighth grade in school and stayed an extra year to help out her sister and the younger kids when she didn't have chores at home. She had begun to let Viola have her way with her homemade dresses. The fact is Viola was beginning to earn money from the community for making and enhancing ladies and young girls' dress ware. She often used Gracie, whose petite body had all of a young woman's attributes in abundance and located in the right places, and Lena whose petite body seems to be following her sister's lead, as her personal models. According to the local young men folk, Gracie was already ripe at eighteen. Her girly shape was hard to hide even in the long flowing house dresses both she and Lena wore today. By now, she was also enjoying the attention of a couple of guys in the community. This time the object of her attention was Sammy Parker. Or maybe, it was the other way around. Nevertheless, Sammy was now a robust twenty-two years of age, the son of a successful and well respected family in the community and had not been genuinely interested in anybody after Lummie died. Better yet, in his mind, and others, murdered.

Rollie, who left his wife Willa home with the married couple's two year old son, Rail Jr. had also driven to town with his younger brother Sammy. They parked their wagon next to the Halls.

Frank and Edgar were already half way loaded before the Parkers arrived. Considering they had further to go back home, it's no wonder they were there ahead of Rollie and Sammy.

Gracie and Lena, who finished whatever little shopping or exchanging they had, were talking to Dempsey and Mansfield Davis, cousins to the Hamptons. The Davis boys were on the other wagon parked behind the store. They had this tall slim young man with a funny first name with them. His name was Colrolus Strong. He was paying quite a bit of attention to Lena, and she was enjoying his advances. They too finished with their shopping and loading duties turned and watched as Sammy approached them.

"Hi everybody, you look pretty Gracie." Sammy remarked.

"Is she the only one pretty around here?" Lena kiddingly responded.

"Well no . . ." Sammy started. Everyone just broke out in laughter.

"All right, yawl got me", he smiled. "Gracie, would you walk with me around the corner to Ms. Cameron house? I got to deliver this laundry from my mama and pick up some more dirty clothes."

"Oh, I don't mind, but let me let daddy know where I've gone to."

With that, she ran into the store, re-appeared just as fast and motion for Sammy to join her. They both disappeared around the corner heading for the main street. They were walking along talking about this and that when they noticed, as always the same group of guys sitting in front of McBain's General Store. That was the store that had the largest confederate flag in town flying atop its roof on a tall flagpole. It was also one of the buildings in town that posted a 'whites only' sign.

It was Petey and Walt Sampson with a couple of their friends. Petey was playing checkers with one of the guys while the other two looked over their shoulder. It was common knowledge that regular patrons could buy homebrew beer and moonshine at McBain's. It was also clear to the human eye that the four men were drinking out of private containers. Given their body language, one would surmise that alcohol of some sort was their drink. They gave Sammy and Gracie the old 'just don't walk on this side of the street' smirk, said something under their breath and returned to their checkers game.

Having dropped off the clean laundry and accepting a small clothing bag of dirty men dress shirts for washing and ironing, they entered the main street walkway on their way back to Skeeter's. Sammy was so involved with their conversation that neither one of them noticed anyone on the street.

Passing McBain's from the opposite side of the street was not a given this time. Walt, who always seemed to be the instigators in these matters, got Petey's attention by poking at him. "What you want?" a clearly annoyed Petey asked his older brother while looking up from his game. "Here they come again walking like they don't have a care in the world." Walt answered.

"I see that dog killer's son. I'd know the family anywhere," Petey remarked loudly enough to ensure his voice traveled across the street.

The young couple looked toward the men for a second, instantly returning to their conversation while ignoring them and walking on. A satisfied Petey, more interested in his game then taunting a couple of niggers made a move on the checker board. "Gotcha!" He told his opponent.

Walt's attention was on Sammy and this other girl whom he had not seen before. Not satisfied that they were on the other side of the street, he walked to the edge of the walkway and yelled "Hey boy, I think its way past the time you shoulda replaced my brother's dog."

Sammy immediately stopped talking mid-conversation and walking simultaneously. He jerked his head to the right, looking to see which of the men were talking. Walt pleased that he gotten his attention continued.

"I know Nigger . . ." Walt continued yelling "It's been five long years since yo' folks ran over Bo, almost in the same area of the street. But yawl had time to save your money and get Petey here a another hunting dog just like Bo was before yawl killed him."

"What are you doing? Nooooo . . . Sammy," Gracie urged as Sammy walked into the street and directly toward Walt. He strolled as though he was in some kind of trance. She ran after him, grabbing at his arm in the middle of the street in a frantic attempt to stop him from approaching the men in front of McBain's.

"Sammy!" Gracie shouted as he turned his head toward her for just a second, which was time enough for her to see the rage in his eyes and the scowl on his face that warned something bad was about to happen. "Stop Sammy, stop," Gracie shouted again as she walked briskly alongside while tugging at his arm. He did not stop as his footsteps were deliberate and his laser like gaze was on the face of Walt Sampson. The commotion was now attracting others who were close enough to hear Gracie voice. One of which was Sheriff Penelton whose office is four doors past McBain's. By now he had become observant of what was going on. He looked up and over his glasses while holding a cup of coffee in his right hand and a newspaper in his left. He put the coffee and paper down on the bench as Sammy and Gracie reached the edge of the walkway and directly in front of Walt and the men.

"You gotta a lotta nerve, boy, coming over here. Nigger, what's wrong with you?" Petey angrily stated as he stood up and joined in the conversation.

"Sooooo . . ." Walt continued. "Are you gonna pay a little bit a week? Do you have a dog already to give to my brother? We just need to know the plan boy. What's your plan to make things right?"

"You . . . , you was one of them." Sammy, trying real hard to control his emotions began, "You were there. Walt, it was your voice I heard that night yelling to somebody who was with you. Who was it Walt? Was it you Petey?"

Gracie could not believe what Sammy was saying, yet if anybody could remember what happened the night of the fire when Lummie died, Sammy would.

"Say what? What's going on here?" Sheriff Penelton, who walked up, interrupted and asked anybody who could provide an answer. Walt and Petey stopped talking, neither of which expected this subject to be brought up, now or ever. They looked as though they had seen a ghost and was literally shell shocked at Sammy's accusation. Meanwhile, the two men behind them gathered up all of their containers and disappeared by walking around to the back of the store.

"Sheriff, I want to put in a complaint against Walt and Petey for the charge of setting a fire and the murder of Lummie Hall. It was Walt's voice I heard that night while the fire was burning. He yelled at somebody. My guess is, it was Petey, to, 'Turn them goddamn horses loose. Turn 'em loose I said.' There is no doubt in my mind that the voice belonged to Walt."

"Nigger, you crazy? You don't know what you talking 'bout." Petey yelled at Sammy.

"That's right, you're Cora and Clement Parkers younger boy, Sammy?" asked the Sheriff.

"Yes suh."

"You, Petey and Walt come on down to my office. And you young girl, who do you belong to?"

"Frank and Harriett Hall suh, Lummie was my sister," Gracie answered just as the other two men, Bob and Clarke, who was with the Sampson boys, came back around the corner without the containers. "My daddy is down at Skeeter Purvis store. Sammy's brother is down there too."

"Girl you go on back down there with your folks and tell Rollie Parker to come to my office. Better tell your daddy, Frank to come too. Break it up folks and go on 'bout your business. Go on now, you hear? Let's go fellas." Talkative Walt had nothing else to say at this time. He, along with his brother, Petey turned to walk to the Sheriff's office, telling their friends they would see them later. Gracie took off running back to Skeeter's store.

Sammy, a little bit calmer now was seated in front of Sheriff Penelton's desk. The Sampson boys were in another small room, behind a closed door. They were not under arrest. Once again Sammy gave a clear statement of the facts including the facts of what Sammy saw and heard that night of the fire. He didn't add much more than that he'd said five years ago other than actually naming the owner of the voice he heard that night. By the time he finished signing the additional statement, Rollie and Gracie's dad Frank, had made it to the office

The Sheriff explained the 'Complaint process' to Sammy with Frank and Rollie listening. He then put them into the same room that the Sampson boys were in and asked Walt and Petey to come into his office. Although they tried, Frank and Rollie could not hear any outside discussions in their room.

The Sheriff asked Walt and Petey if they understood the complaint process. They didn't, so he elaborated for clarity on their part. Once that was done, he advised them of their rights as the accused. He specifically asked each man where they were at the time of the fire. Neither one could answer.

"Sheriff it's been 5 years. I don't know where I was that night." Walt answered.

"Me neither Sheriff, but I can tell you one thing for sure, we were not at the Parkers' place setting a fire," Petey added.

After another fifteen to twenty minutes round of questioning by Sheriff Penelton, and getting the same results, Walt and Petey Sampson left the office without any arrest, suspicion of arson, or any other charge. They were told they would be called in if there were any other revealing information on the case.

Shortly thereafter, having explained the lack of evidence other than the sound of a voice to a clearly upset Sammy, he left with Rollie and Frank too. The three men walked back to their wagons in silence. Clearly all were thinking of that horrible night and the way that Lummie died in the fire.

"If the law won't do nothing, I will," began Sammy. Um gon' kill that son-a-bitch and his brother too."

"Now wait a minute, son," Frank advised. "Two wrongs don't make a right. You need to Let God hand out his punishment. We are Christian folk; there is no need for that kind of talk."

"It's already been five years and they are still walking around, alive and enjoying themselves." Sammy answered angrily. "They gonna pay for their sins alright. Cause I'm gonna help God out. An eye for an eye . . ."

"Sheesh . . . here come the girls," Rollie pointed out to Sammy almost under his breath. He grabbed Franks hand and shook it while saying goodbye and thanks for everything. "Say goodbye to Gracie and Lena, Sammy. We got to get on home," He said, afterwards climbing up to the driver's seat of his wagon.

"You all right Sammy?" Gracie asked. "What did the Sheriff do? Did he arrest those white boys?"

"No, Gracie, nothing like that. He needs more evidence than a voice in the night. Say goodbye to the Parkers. We have to get on home too. It's getting late," Frank said while answering for Sammy.

For his part, all Sammy could say to Gracie was, "I'll see you later. Bye." With that he climbed up on the wagon besides his brother, backed the team up, and headed for the main street. Both men looked back at Frank, Edgar and the girls seated in their wagon and coming up right behind them. They waved goodbye as they rounded the corner.

Both wagons rolled on the down the street past McBain's where other white men were seating with containers, playing checkers and laughing at each other's comments. They looked toward the wagons without any word or curiosity, just smirks if they to say, *it's just some darkies leaving town. Good.* There was no sign of Walt, Petey, Bob or Clarke.

Both wagons passed Papa Warner's. They recognized his silhouette off the background of his store. They could tell it was him in his familiar rocking chair that sat on the porch. He needed not worry because his parking area seemed filled with potential customers. Papa gave his familiar halfheartedly wave to those parties in both wagons as they passed him heading for home.

Rollie and Sammy waved to the Halls again as they peeled off the main road headed for their farmhouse.

"Daddy, I still miss Lummie," Lena later remarked in an almost hushed tone, while they too turned off the main road headed for their home.

"I know. We all miss her, baby girl," Frank responded after a minute or so. Gracie seated in the wagons bed on top of a sack of grain reached out to comfort her sister with Lena holding on to her tightly as if to ensure she would not leave her too.

The wagon moved slowly down the small road. If by chance, you would meet another wagon coming from the opposite direction, one of them would have to pull over and let the other one go by. That is, if there was enough clearing to do that. Otherwise someone would have to back up or stop at an earlier clearing to let the oncoming wagon go by. This little concern somehow weaved throughout Gracie's thoughts. Nobody else said a word. If was as if the entire incident had reawaken feelings that all involved thought were buried. Gracie, who was also beginning to have premonitions, was deeply concerned. First because she really did not know what to think of these small advance warnings about something that was going to happen in the future. Her mother had told her to keep them to herself unless it involved a real threat of life or death. She convinced her it was a gift from God that should be used for the good of people and not in a vindictive way. Secondly, and more importantly, she did not see this new revelation of who started the fire turning out in a favorable way for the Parkers or the Halls. She could not see what was going to happen but she felt deeply something was and she was not sure who would be involved. Her thoughts were interrupted by Sadie, Moe, Zoe, and Oh No.

People got so busy with their daily lives, working hard, getting married, having babies, enjoying the summer, a successful harvest, seasonal fall, soon followed by another Christmas which seemingly all of sudden rolled around again. Worship and celebrating the birth of Jesus Crist was always the Christmas theme. New Year's Day quickly passed and the winter lasted a little longer but eventually gave way to spring and then summer began. Another year had passed, and 1923 was in full bloom.

The Roaring Twenties were becoming an era where the rich were getting richer and the poor getting poorer. The gangsters of the era were becoming more infamous for their brand of violence. Al Capone was on the run in Chicago. A newly elected city government caused him to move his gang's headquarters to Cicero, Illinois outside of the city limits. He and his cronies were still frequent visitors to Hot Springs.

By now the automobile was becoming the choice of transportation by not only those who could afford it but those, including blacks, who found ways to purchase or barter a vehicle for their family or farm use. Although trains and boats whenever convenient were still used for the long haul, the nation was using the quicker mechanized trucks to transport goods and services across the country and within the various states. So it was inevitable that trucks, tractors and other mechanize tools for farming would find their way to Arkansas. Now a visit to Warren or even Banks, one could see more than enough evidence that these type vehicles were becoming a part of this area daily existence.

There was also progress by black people in the form of entertainment. Bessie Smith "Queen of the Blues" recorded her first song entitled "Down Hearted Blues". The Cotton Club opened in New York's Harlem with all-black performances to white-only audiences. The Nicholas Brothers, Cab Calloway and Ms. Lena Horne was among the performers.

The NAACP, individuals and their supporters were taking on the rule of Jim Crow laws throughout the South, winning some legal battles and causing others to be highlighted for the nation to see. At least the intention of these laws and actions were made clear to the public at large.

Along with progress came the usual backlash. Whether through rumors, false senses of threats to whites way of life, or downright hatred, there was one organization that would set the wheels of terror in motion. The second Ku Klux Klan movement in U.S. history grew by gathering more wide spread support, also stirring widespread controversy. Along with their growth came repeated and more credited violence against non-whites.

Blacks lost a supporter of African-American civil rights when President Warren G. Harding suddenly collapsed and died in California while returning from an Alaska trip. Although his administration was filled with scandals, he always came down on the side of fairness for children, common laborers, and federal fiscal responsibility.

This particular summer also brought a swift courtship and pairing for Lena. Colrolus Strong, the young man, now twenty-one years of age first met Lena in Banks. That was the day that Sammy identified Walt Sampson as the voice he heard the night Lummie was killed. Colrolus was not only a fast talker but a fast mover too. He and Lena had been talking on and off for a while before showed up at the Halls door this past spring, asking her father to see his daughter from time to time. Frank, aware of the Strong's who went to his same church, gave his blessing. Gracie and Lena was surprised because, after all, Lena was his baby girl and last child.

It did not take long for Mr. Strong to ask for Lena's hand in marriage. Lena, seventeen and still the giggle kind, was in love too. Colrolus' family owned land on the other side of the railroad tracks further down in the woods off the road to Banks. It was another one of two houses already on a small piece of the property built by his father some time ago and was the type of place his son wanted. He loved horses and owned six at the time. He trained them and others in the area for pay. He also had a few hogs and chickens. This impressed Frank so much that he and Harriett gave their blessing for Lena to get married. The date was set for late September or early October. Gracie was happy for Lena although kind of sad. It meant she would be the last child to leave her Mama and Papa's house if she got married.

Lo and behold, Lena and Colrolus Strong dot married on October 7 of the year. It wasn't a big celebration except for a special dinner at the church after the marriage. Lena's move away from the house affected Gracie more so than it did her parents. They were not only sisters, they were very close friends. Yet, she knew that Lena would be happy and that was what life was all about, being in love and happy.

The Halls were seated at their table for the Christmas dinner of 1923. Edgar, Viola and little Mae Ellen were there. Harriett, Viola, Gracie with the new bride Lena helping could be proud of the feast they put out for family this day. Frank cut a small Christmas tree for the festivities. He placed it in the corner, just behind the front door. The little tree quickly became Mae Ellen's favorite as it looked a lot like the one in her house that she helped decorate. Other decorative signs of the holiday were scattered and hung throughout the two bedroom house with its extra-large kitchen and dining area. All had to be careful when opining the front door, because it swung open in the direction of the tree and small presents under it.

Versia and her husband, John Boswell arrived the day before from Hot Springs. John drove his brand new 1923 Ford Model T Tourer. Everybody loved this new automobile thing-a-ma-jig. Colrolus told the family him and Lena was looking to buy a truck for their little place. They still worked at the Arlington Hotel. For two years, they saved tips and part of their wages to buy a house. Since they've yet to have kids, they paid the full $370 price for the private transportation the automobile afforded them. They carefully checked the weather for the next few days because the dirt road outside of Hot Springs to Banks could become a hazardous drive. They surely didn't want to get stuck in the middle of nowhere. The cool rather than cold weather is and predictably was great with no rain, sleet or snow in the forecast.

They held hands around the table, with Frank saying grace followed by amen in unison. The happy chatter began while serving up pork chops, chicken and dumplings, corn bread, green peas, roasted duck and dressing, sweet potato pie, peach cobbler, lemon and chocolate cake, with a side order assortment of vegetables.

They talked about when and if the Boswells were planning to have children. Surprising to Frank and Harriett, the answer was no time soon. They teased the new bride, and Lena tried to be the little lady but couldn't help but go into giggle mode a few times. Mae Ellen smiled broadly because she thought it was appropriate while trying to follow Gracie and Lena's cue. She was very aware that she was the youngest person in the room and felt if no one notice her she could sit and listen to grown folks talking. Colrolus just smiled with the look of a new husband. They talked briefly about their plans for their place. Frank was glad they were only about a two and half miles away from his house.

They revisited yesterday's conversation and comments on the move of Edward, his wife and three kids from Lawrence County, Arkansas to Cleveland, Ohio. At least Harriett and Frank got to see their first grandkids before they moved. Edward got a job in a factory and is doing well in the year they've been there. The kids are in school, and all is great. They hope to reunite for an Arkansas family reunion in a couple of years if not sooner.

They wished Viola continued success at becoming the community's local seamstress. There were also congratulations on the lease with an option to buy of the 15 acre property they formally rented. Versia and John were looking to move in a house in Hot Springs by next year. John was thinking about opening up his own restaurant one day. He doubts if he will ever become a chief at the hotel. Versia may get a raise next year.

Frank finally paid Mr. Jennings for the horse he borrowed to take the place of the one that broke its leg in a gopher hole. Once again the Hall crops provided a successful harvest. Yeah, Frank would still have to work for old man Jennings. The items planted by Edgar and Viola turned out perfect. Thus, it was a terrific canning season for all. Everybody agreed that the meal was sumptuous, everything tasted great, everybody looked great, and then there was this statement from Gracie.

She had listen quietly to the table conversation and decided to let the family in on her secret. "Last Sunday at the church social, John Hampton asked me to marry him," She said softly while never looking up from her plate of food.

"What did you say baby?" her mother asked.

All eyes turned toward Gracie. Those who heard it, including Lena, could not believe what they heard and was anxious to have her repeat it. Others who was not sure what was said, was curious too.

"John Hampton asked me to marry him by next spring."

Silence, and then came this question from her father. "How old is that boy?

"Daddy, he will be eighteen this coming Feb and I will be twenty next May. And . . . and I love him so much. I do, Daddy. I can't help it. I love him. I don't want to leave you and Mama but . . . , I love John, and he loves me," Gracie responded, moist increasing in her eyes with every word.

Frank glanced at Harriett who had a smiling and sympathetic expression of love on her face. He had to admit he felt the same toward a daughter who was well past her community's marrying age. A grateful Frank understood why she stayed with her parents, helping out wherever she could after his son, and Versia got married leaving home.

"Well, you tell that boy to stop by and see us. We want to see how he is doing. I haven't talked to him in a long time," Frank responded with restraint.

"The few times I have seen him, he has been a well manner boy. So if this is what you want to do than I'm all for it," Harriett added.

"Thank you Mama and Daddy, I been worried sick on how you two would take the news," She answered as she got up from the table, ran and hugged both parents in appreciation.

"Yes Gracie, but I want to see him too. And I would like to meet his mother and father," Harriett added.

"OK, I will get yawl together." A now beaming Gracie promised.

"Have you said yes, yet?" Lena asked.

"No not yet, I wanted to ask Mommy and Daddy first. But John knows what my answer is gonna be."

"Congratulations to my little sister. I am shocked. I just thought you would stay home a little longer," Versia said while hugging Gracie.

"Yeah, good luck little sister-in-law," John added.

"You have our prayers and blessing," Edgar stated.

"May you and John be as happy as me and your sister is," A smiling and almost stuttering Colrolus volunteered.

"Where you going to be married and do you want me to make the dress?" asked Viola.

"The dress, yes. You . . . , Where? I don't know yet. We want a small wedding. And there is a lot to do, a lot to do before the wedding. Whew!" Gracie said slumping in her chair while looking exhausted but excited.

During the rest of the dinner, Gracie could hardly contain herself. Her thoughts drifted back and forth from the present, past, and future. No, she had not given John an answer because at the time she didn't know the answer herself. She was torn between leaving her parents, which she thought at one time were her duty for life, and getting married.

She also knew that her dad, and possibly mom thought she and Sammy Parker would end up married. However, she and Sammy both knew his one love was Lummie. The tragedy of how that love affair was brought to an abrupt end before it actually began has turned him emotionally unreachable. At one time, they spoke briefly of being a couple but even he realized that his heart died with Lummie. Since she cannot climb out of the grave, the only possible closure to that connection is to get justice for her killers. He now knows who they are. He doesn't know how yet but he does know he will be a part of the solution. Until that issue is resolved he is no good for love to anybody. They vowed to remain friends and left it at that.

Then there was the fact that she and John had never spoke of where they would live, how they would earn a living, did he like children, would he like to have children of his own and so on. The reason being is that they have not been a couple anticipating marriage. John has mentioned it several times, as far back as her seventeenth birthday. The problem was that Gracie had never seriously thought about it until she blurted out his proposal request at today's dinner.

There is no doubt in her mind that the both of them are in love with each other. It's just that logistics and circumstances have not let them talk about a possible future together. Well, that all changes today because the cat is out of the bag. Her family knows how she feels and has approved. Another problem is Gracie has never met John's parents.

"Oh my lawd! What are their names?" Gracie blurted out loud.

"What did you say Gracie?" Asked Versia.

"Nothing, nothing, I didn't say nothing." *Well that, me and John has a lot of taking to do before we get hitched;* she thought while smiling as most of the family looked at her like she was crazy.

"Oh Mama, it's just Gracie acting like herself. You know how she does . . . she's just nervous, that's all," Lena added while laughing along with the rest of the family.

CHAPTER 3

Gracie's Engagement—A Community Development for Entertainment

I t was the last Sunday of 1923. Gracie sent word through Viola that she and her parents wanted to see John. He was to stop by as soon as possible. Understanding it was necessary, he made arrangements to stay all night at his cousin Viola's house. He could go to church with both Hall families the next day. That would put him at her house on Sunday after services. It would be the first time since a week before Christmas that Gracie and John would see each other. That was when he proposed. He ended up getting to Viola's after nine pm on Saturday. Edgar and Viola convinced him that it would not be smart to call on Gracie at this time of night. Frank might wonder what prevented him from calling on his daughter at a respectable hour, like before supper. John agreed it was best to wait until Sunday.

The roads were still pretty dry from the snowfall before Christmas. A chill was in the air but it was not real cold. Frank pulled his wagon team to a stop in front of the young Hall's house. His entire family was bundled up tight and wearing woolen scarves wrapped around their faces for the approximately four mile ride to the church. It didn't matter, because if one was paying attention, you could still see Gracie's eyes light up when John Hampton, following Viola and May Ellen, came out of the house. Edgar made sure the door was secure, since he was the last to exit and climb up on the wagon. John sat across from his intended. Beside the morning greetings, there was hardly any conversation on the way to church.

Once they arrived, took their seat with Gracie seated next to John, they all waited patiently for the pastor's sermon of the day. Various church members, including the pastor's wife, Sister Hattie, made announcements of upcoming events. The choir sang a couple of down home spirituals that lifted the spirits of the congregation even more so than a normal Sunday. And, of course, the collection plate was passed around. John, an ever-so-often visitor to this church ever since he began chasing Gracie, surprised the Halls by placing a dime in the plate. Finally, the pastor began with an opening prayer. After which, the Reverend A.J. Payne did not disappoint. He started out slowly talking about the massacre at Elaine, Arkansas that happened in 1919. Since the US Supreme Court had sent the case back to the Arkansas courts for illegalities at the initial trials, the lower courts might set free the remainder of the twelve men who were sentenced to die.

He went on to stress to anyone thinking that God do not answer his prayers by quoting from James 1:5-7, "If any of you lack wisdom, let him ask God, that giveth to all men liberally, and upbraideth not; and it shall be given him. But let him ask in faith, nothing wavering. For he that wavereth is like a wave of the sea driven with the wind and tossed. For let not that man think that he shall receive any thing of the Lord." He went on to stress again, that one must have faith in God first and foremost. He highlighted his point by stating "God might not be there when you think you need him, but he is always right on time."

Reverend Payne, in full preach mode by now, brought up other current incidents that applies when a person think his prayers have not been answered. No matter the subject, he always returned to the theme. "We are on Gods schedule and he is not on ours." He shouted. It was a short but effective sermon lasting about forty minutes.

There were a couple more songs by the choir followed by the pastor dismissing the congregation for the day, advising them to have a great week. There would be no refreshments in the picnic area today. This was not picnic weather. Everyone said their goodbyes, wishing the pastor and his family well before headed for home. The ride back seemed a little longer because they all were looking forward to a warm fire and Sunday afternoon dinner.

Edgar and Viola asked to be dropped off at their house. They were obviously giving John and the Halls a little private time.

Gracie and her mom got out of the wagon at their front porch and gate. Frank and John continued on to the barn to unhitch the horses, get them settled, wash up and head inside for a good hot dinner. John was surprised that Frank didn't ask him any questions in the barn.

Both men walked to the front gate where Sadie was lying on the porch. Her offspring, Moe, Zoe and On No didn't do too much barking. However, they did check out the newcomer by giving him the sniff test. After that, they returned to a warm spot under the house where they could curl up.

The table was set. All the men had to do after entering the house was to sit down. Frank led the meal prayer followed by all saying "amen." The serving was accompanied with normal chit-chat about what was being served and how it tasted by the diners.

Then, of course, the topic of the day was brought up by Harriett when she asked John, "What do your parents think of you getting married to our Gracie here?"

"Well, Ms. Harriett, they have not met Gracie yet, but are going on my judgment because they know me."

"You seem to be pretty high on yourself too." Frank added.

"Well, I just think I got good folks to look up to. They gave us boys a good talkin to whenever needed and the strap when words did not get through our head. They always tell us if we are doing something wrong and help us figure out the best way for everybody. People around here, say they did and are still raising us good."

"So where do you two plan on living and how are you gonna feed yourselves?" Frank asked. It was the very question this meeting was based on and he really did not know the significance of the question to Gracie. Why, because she didn't know the answer.

"Well suh," John paused before continuing. "My folks have a small house on our land not too far from the big house as we call it. They always felt that the first one who got married would live there and farm the two acres behind it. The big house is a few miles from our church, Oaklawn Methodist. That's the church that is down the road from yawl's church."

Gracie was the first one at the table to breathe a sigh of relief. The second was her mother. Frank was pleased but wanted to check this out with John's father. So, the next test would come when the parents of these two people had a conversation.

The remaining meal conversation centered on general conversation about local politics, KKK activity in and around Warren and other cities in Arkansas. John himself was pleased with the way the meal and conversation went.

At the end of meal, John had time to spend with Gracie. The Halls allowed her to walk with John down to Edgar and Viola's while delivering a sweet potato pie sent by Harriett.

"I guess you know my answer is yes," Gracie stated, with the two of them walking pass the sniffing at her fiancé ankles by Moe, Zoe, and Oh No until they closed the front gate of the Halls.

"Yes, and you made me the happiest man alive. I always dreamed of us being married and having a family. I know we have not talked about it much."

"The only thing I hate is leaving Mama and Papa. They will be by themselves. Who's gonna read things for them? Everybody else is grown up and gone off to be with their new families and stuff."

"Well, lots of Negro people their age can't read or write and they get by. They will be alright. They got cousin Viola and her husband not far from them. It's not like they don't have other neighbors and friends to be there for them."

"I know, but it's not me. Mama and Papa haven't taken to their kids leaving home to well."

"Gracie, I love you like no other," John said while stopping to emphasize his point. For her part, she managed to allow and anticipate his next move. John, who initiated the contact, kissed her. She almost dropped the pie in her one hand while the other arm was wrapped around her fiancé aggressively returning a kiss that almost took her breath away. Now this, they both thought, was a serious kiss. Oh, there were the schoolyard and church ground smacks on the cheeks. A few very brief kisses on each other's mouth while in fear someone was watching or would catch them. But this, well, afterwards, the both of them silently realized this was their first kiss. It also confirmed the idea of marriage between the two.

The rest of the way was spent holding hands and smiling at each other as they arrived at Edgars and his wife's front door. Yes, the sweet potato pie was intact.

John walked with deliberate steps as he waved good bye to Viola, Edgar and little Mae Ellen the following Monday morning. He had a few miles to walk but did not mind because the thought of marrying Gracie Hall filled his mind along the way.

Just because he put up this front that he had it all together didn't mean he did not have anxiety about taking such a bold move in his young life. The fact that he could count on his family, including his older brother Lemon, to find his way if he ever became confused, was a relief on his mind.

He'd often spoken to his parents about Gracie since he was fourteen years old. They knew she was the primary reason that he would attend the Gravel Ridge Baptist church instead of his own. The two churches themselves were no more than three-fourths of a city block apart from each other on the same road. In fact, they were on the same side of the road. Yes, they were aware that he had very strong feelings for, and indeed, in his mind was in love with his sweetheart. They were not aware that he asked her to marry him.

That was the major source of his anxiety. It was way too late in the game for this kind of conversation with his folks. This was why he was in such a hurry. That conversation with his folks was going to happen today. At certain spots, he even ran in order to get home. He needed to tell them before they heard it from somebody else. *"Cause if they did, there would be hell to pay,"* he thought to himself.

By the time he reached his church's area, he was able to hitch a ride from his cousin, Dempsy Davis. He and his brother, Mansfield, just happened to drop off a load of firewood for the church. They drove their family's two horse team wagon down for the delivery. Their folks, Oliff and Lula were the next farm over from the Hamptons. They all talked sparingly along the way with John seemingly becoming more and more nervous the closer he got to his house.

Finally reaching the turnoff to the big house, John jumped down, thanked the Davis boys and ran up the almost quarter mile incline leading to his front door. He bolted up the three steps to the porch, to his front door, opening it to find his mother peeling Irish potatoes for a stew or something, he wasn't sure. He just stood there for a moment, practically out of breath.

"What's-a-matter with you? Is somebody chasing you or something?" Sallie Hampton asked with a concerned expression. She started to get up, but John immediately let her know that everything was alright.

"Nobody's chasing me Mama. Um okay. Daddy 'n 'em in the fields?"

"Yeah, him, Lemon, Monroe, and your cousins are down there thinning out the timber by cutting down them dead tress for firewood. I think old Oliff is gonna take some down to the church. What are you running for? Did you have a nice visit with Viola? I know you got to see your little sweetie pie, didn't you boy?

John could not help but smile sheepishly as he sat down at the table across from his mother. "Yeah I saw her. Viola n'em all right, they do just fine. I caught a ride back with Demp and Mansfield from the church. They'd just dropped a load off. Mama, I got to talk to you and Daddy," He added in a most serious voice matched by his facial expression.

Eleven years old David Jr., followed by his younger nine years old brother, Peach (Van D), burst through the front door. Each boy was holding a small croker sack bag in their hands. "Mama, here is the field peas and salt pork from the smoke house you wanted," David Jr. said.

"Okay babies; sit those bags over here by me. Yawl go on out to the barn and get that bucket of chicken feed and sprinkle some around the barnyard for the chickens. Don't you throw too much out there, you hear?"

"Okay Mama." Both boys answered. "Hi John," they yelled almost in unison with young Peach bringing up the rear as they ran out the door. They carefully close it to keep the morning chill outside and in anticipation of hearing their mother give the order.

Sallie Hampton stood about five feet five inches, round shaped semi-dark skinned face, piercing light brown eyes with dropping eyelids that looked as if she could use another nap. She was an imposing looking black woman for her time. She kept her black hair comb back in a bun. There always seemed to be a serious look on her face because she had seen and even heard of a lot more in her thirty-nine years in the South. Ironically, David had her all of her facial features except his face was slim in lieu of full. He had most of her expressions, which amounted to three or four different looks depending upon the situation. She had little trust in man and things she could not see, feel or touch. She was always deliberate with her words. Yet she was a gentile woman, especially with her kids and family members. She also knew her boys. Something was troubling John and she wanted to know what it was and right now, not after her husband got home.

"John . . . , baby, you got something you want to tell me? Cause you look like a young man with something on his mind. Boy you look like you gonna bust with whatever news you have. What's going on baby?"

"Mama, I wanna marry Gracie Hall in the spring. I asked her and she said yes. I wanna move into that little house down there by the creek. Yawl always said the first one who got married could do that." John blurted out, no longer able to keep his thoughts from his Mama.

There must have been a full five or ten minutes of silence before his mother spoke. She just sat there and looked at him. Every now and then she would peel another potato, drop it in the pan and look up at her second oldest son, with an almost I can't believe what I just heard expression on her face. It was a new expression that John had not seen.

For John's part, he sat there, sweating like a greased pig. He had to go to the outhouse but decided against it because of that look on his Mama's face. He was going to take it like a man, whatever the answer from mama or his father would be. He and his sweetheart were going to get married if they had to work and live with some other people in the area.

Finally, Sallie looking John in the eye started to say something only to hear, "Mama, um sorry I . . . ," John interrupted. His mother held her left arm straight out with the palm of her hand open as if to say, don't speak.

She composed herself and stated, "you, your daddy, and me gon' have to talk about this when he gets home. 'Til then, you go on 'bout your business and chores 'til we can get together . . . around lunchtime or this afternoon."

Then she asked, "Do the child's mama and papa know about this proposal?"

"Yes ma'am."

"They said it was okay with them?"

"Well, I think they are okay with it, but they want to talk to you and Daddy."

"Oh lawd! Git on outta here and tend to your chores John. We'll talk later."

Around 1:30 or so, Sallie could hear the family wagon team coming over the ridge to the big house. She walked out on the porch and could see her husband David in the passenger seat with Lemon driving. She could tell that Munroe was squeezed in between her husband and oldest son, Lemon. The wagon itself was full of firewood.

Her mind was filled with thoughts of John, barely turning eighteen next month, getting himself married. Not that he was not a responsible young boy, uh, man. He surely was mature for his age. She wondered if the girl is in a family way and that may be why he thinks he need to marry her. Naw, Sallie felt he would have told her if the girl was pregnant. She felt she knew Gracie, although they had never met, in fact, had never laid eyes on each other. Yet John had described her in considerable detail many times. There is no doubt in her mind that her son was deeply and sincerely in love with Gracie. Come to think of it, knowing her son, he would walk through hell and high water to protect his Gracie from whatever threat came about, be it man or animal.

That she was sure of, because she knew her son. He is loyal to a fault when it comes to family or friends. So in the end, she had just reminded herself of who she was thinking about. Her son was a man and had made a man's decision to take on the love of his young life as his wife. So as his mother, she will support this marriage, because she knew John Hampton as a deep thinker who doesn't make rash decisions. Now, she has to remind his father that his son is now a grown man.

John, who heard the wagon coming too, had walked up from the barn reaching the driver's side. David, sometime lovingly called Sambo by family and friends, eagerly by some white folk, jumped down from the passenger side. He asked Lemon to unload the wagon and pile half the firewood outside the back of the barn and the other half just outside the barn yard closer to the big house. He also asked John and Monroe to give Lemon a hand.

"If the two little ones ain't doing nothing, ask them to help you out." He ordered. Since every name he mentioned was standing there listening they all rode or followed the horse team around to the back of the barn.

David (Sambo) senior was a wiry five-foot-seven inch man. His legs look longer then they really were. His oval face was marked with what has become known among family as the Hampton high cheekbones with a ball shape at the end of his nose. His dark brown eyes were piercing, actually revealing where his sons got theirs. His eyebrows almost met in the center of his face. He wore a cap that covered his receding hair line. He walked with a deliberate gait as if he was in a hurry to get somewhere. He gently touched Sallie on the shoulder as he went into the house. She turned to follow him.

Once inside, after pouring him a cup of hot tea, she told him of Johns plans for marriage. He was surprised when she first brought is up but after reflecting on a few conversations he'd had with John, he, like his wife, knew their son. David agreed with his wife that they would have known if he was not serious about the girl. They both agreed that the best thing that they could do for the young couple was to let them move into the little house by the creek and farm the acreage behind it. That would keep them close and farming would provide them with a means of support.

John, more so than anyone else, when told at supper, had his folks blessing, breathe an enormous sigh of relief.

"I hoped yawl would support me daddy. I also know that maintaining that place is going to be a lot of work. I ain't stupid, so um sure we will ask your help with tools, wagons, mules, plows and stuff to help us along. You don't have to worry, because some of that stuff we are going to buy for ourselves." John stated for the record.

The supper conversation turned to what tools, farming equipment, seed, and seedlings would be needed for opening the ground and planting before the first spring arrived. Some neighbors would help, but most of the stuff and labor help would have to come from family.

After Lemon and the rest of his brothers congratulated him and told John how anxious they were to meet the new family member, it was an accepted fact. John was getting married and the Hampton men would have another woman in the family.

"She will be good company for you mama." Lemon remarked.

"Umph," was the only reply Sallie could give at the time.

There was talk of buying 'one of those tractor machines' to help out this planting and harvesting season. The family all agreed and maybe next year they could buy a truck. "That would be nice," David senior added. "Let's pray on it."

Still at the table, they all clasps hands again while David senior began, "Father God, we thank you for giving us good crops and health last year. We pray that you keep watching over the Hampton farm and house during this New Year. We pray that our son and brother, John, will find happiness with his new bride to be. And if you can find a way and the time, would you please help us to get a tractor machine to help with the planting and harvest. In Jesus name we prey, and all the Hamptons say," And all did say, "Amen."

"Can we have some cobbler now?" Asked little Peach. Now we really know how he got his name. Mama Sallie began dishing out the leftover pie.

Meanwhile, approximately eight to nine miles away, Gracie was eating supper with Papa Frank and her mother in almost silence. She, with a heavy heart, had a sad look on her face. Her eyes were moist, and she clearly was not having a good time of it.

"What is wrong with you girl? Do you want to get married or not?" Harriett asked.

Frank who was just as concern and could not understand what was wrong with Gracie stop eating anticipating an answer.

She could not hold back the tears. "Mama I am so sorry. I don't want to leave you and Papa alone."

Harriett relieved to hear the reason for her daughter's mood, got up, slid her chair next to Gracie and wrapped her arms around her shoulders. This brought the full waterworks and sobs. Mama, um sorry, I don't want to get married. I'll wait."

This almost started Frank's eyes to become moist. "Girl, you don't want to get married?"

"There was a time when we didn't have any children," Harriett, still holding a sobbing Gracie in her arms began, while her eyes began to tear up too. "Your papa and I will get by. Your daddy is fifty-two and I'm fifty-three. I've brought five children into this world through pain you have never felt. Frank and I have raised yawl from the silly years to the grown years. We been through . . . , well, I ain't got the time to tell you what all we have been through raising you girls and Edward. We made do with no child in the house and a house full of children. We've suffered; I watched my mama and papa suffer through the South's war hangover."

By now, with just the thought of those years, tears were rolling down Harriett's cheeks. They were getting into Gracie hair, which after being felt by Gracie made her stop crying. She slowly turned her head upward to look into her mother's eyes as she continued to speak. "We had night riders run us off of land we legally owned. We've found friends, relatives, and close loved ones hanging from trees. Some for stuff like looking in the eye of a white woman or some white person lied about what a colored person done. They would track them down like dogs, shoot, or hang them of little of nothing. God only knows why a race of people can be so . . . so mean. And it's still going on. Look what happened to Lummie?"

"Mama I didn't mean . . ." Gracie tried to interrupt with no success. She looked at her papa who also had that faraway look in his moist eyes.

"We go to church to thank God for the week before, pray to God for the week coming up. We try to get along with anybody, but some white folk just got the devil in them. I know you don't want to leave us alone. But baby, we been alone before. God helps us through it. We turn our troubles over to God or otherwise it would drive a person out of their mind, as it has for a few. One of the things you are learning is that there is something no one can take from you. That is the love you receive and give to your husband and family. Nobody can tell your heart who to love or who to fall in love with. It can happen anytime and you are damn lucky if it happens to you and that love is returned. That is, some say its luck. I say it's God's will." She concluded looking into her daughters eyes.

"That's right little girl." Frank added, "If you sure you love John Hampton and you are sure he loves you too. Then that's it. Go and be with the man you love. Your mama and I will be just fine, happy for you and all our children."

Gracie, wiped her eyes, straightens up her hair, face and half whispered to both Frank and Harriett. "Thank you. I so love you both." She stated "I'm gonna make you proud of me., cause I do love John and want to marry him."

She had never heard her mother speak that way of the past. It's not something the older generation likes to talk about. Oh, there are some stories but by and large they don't dwell in the past. They've always talked about the present or future.

Maybe, just maybe she was about to see one of those premonitions, as her mother called it, come true. Several times within the last year, she had seen herself in a little house in the country cooking breakfast. A man she thought was her husband came out of the bedroom walked up behind her and kissed her on the cheek. He would say "Morning sweetie pie." and take a seat at the kitchen table. She never saw his face because she turned to take the bacon from the skillet. By the time she would turn back around, the scene would end. Although the man has not revealed himself up through this day, she hoped and prayed the man in her premonition was John Hampton. Gracie knew her future was now blessed by God and her parents. Her mama and papa would not be alone. That's all she needed know. She was now at peace with her decision.

Nevertheless, the next few weeks reminded all there was a reason for concern and safety of all blacks in and around Arkansas towns like Banks and cities like Warren. Since this was a time of prosperity for well-placed and semi-rich white folk, it was a potent breeding ground for the Ku Klux Klan. Poorer and even poor whites felt that any economic gains felt by America belonged to real Americans, the white race. They were beginning to pay attention to these self-sufficient nigger community enclaves with the help of the Klan all around the country, especially in the South.

They began to notice blacks were buying used and new automobiles, tractors, and other farming tools. They were raising crops on land given to them by their ancestors who no doubt got it from those who were once their masters. It did not matter that it was once considered land that no white person wanted in the first place. Why some even had money of their own and purchased more southern land.

Some blacks were reaping the rewards from successful cotton crops that were not on sharecropping land. The land was being divided up among their children with their new wives and other family members. They had their schools where they learned to read and write, their churches where they congregated and worshiped a white Jesus Christ. They raised pigs, chickens, had cows, mules and horses. They ate the food they grew, animals they slaughtered or hunted and found no need to buy goods from the local white farmers. This was unsettling, not to think of the fact it upset the balance of nature in the general pecking order. This all boiled down to one thing as far as a lot of whites and especially the KKK was concern, they were prospering more than whites in the United States of America. They were also forming organizations like the NAACP with its communist leaders, according to the KKK. They were going to court to protest laws put there to keep them in their place. Next thing you know, they will be marrying white women.

The KKK was pushing all the right panic buttons belonging to a lot of white southerners. They reminded them of "The Red Summer" of 1919. This was a time when whites physically attacked black people in over thirty-six cities throughout the United States. They were taking decent white folk jobs. Their soldiers returning back from World War 1 thought they deserved equal treatment in housing and such. Blacks had forgotten their place and were fighting back in cities like Chicago and Washington, DC. Another prime example took place right here in our own backyard of Elaine, Arkansas, they would say.

The Klan began having recruiting meetings in the backwoods of white supporters' land. Evidently the winter months did not prevent these types of rallies as long as the weather cooperated. One of the local meeting spots was on the Sampson farm, right next door to Clem Parker, who, in their eyes, was a prime example of an uppity nigger. At night, the Parkers could see the light of burning crosses and other fires from the gatherings across the horizon from their bedroom windows. Besides the host and hostess, old man Harvey Sampson and his wife, Clara, their sons, Petey and Walt, along with the boy's friends Bob, Dickson, Clarke and a few others joined up at last week's meeting. After the indoctrination ceremony, they lit the giant symbolic cross, shouting a few organizational slogans, piled into their mode of transportation and went home convinced they had or was doing some worthwhile. The objective was to turn the tide of nigger success.

Besides the obvious targets, they preached one hundred percent Americanism and demanded the purification of politics, meaning America is for white folk, everybody else can get out. They enforced their way of life on other whites who are depended upon a fellow Klansman for goods or services. They used local elected officials to intimidate whites who helped black people. Violence on blacks rose in the local communities including legal arrest and overly long time sentencing for minor crimes. There were sporadic burnings of farm houses and other properties and isolated mob initiated hangings of blacks for perceived, or on the word of white woman, transgressions against themselves or other white men.

This all resulted in the black communities being on high alert. During the day, it wasn't easy for a white face to show up in most of those backwoods farms, schools, and churches without being seen, sometime for miles away. The nights brought about some anxiety but, once again, and this was especially true for the Gravel Ridge community, they would have to travel a considerable distance across the fields, through sporadic timberland and thickets, and along narrow man made roads to get to most of the black people farms and homes. Even the law didn't relish chasing a known criminal back in those backwoods. Therefore, you could say the environment, was Gods way of evening the score. This theory would be severely tested in future springs and summers.

These threats did not reach Papa Warner Johnson's store, farm or any of his holdings alongside the road to Banks. His place was easily accessible to the night riders. Papa, never one to take chances, posted guards by his store and farm houses during the night. He used his family members, cousins, and friends for that duty. After a few weeks, it became evident as he cut down on the guards; no one was going to bother his property. It was rumored, because some white man relayed the news, they had orders to stay away from Papa's store. He was the only black man who owned a store in the area and purchased a lot of goods and services from white distributors in Banks and Warren. Therefore, no one was to cut off that source of income to white wholesalers. This was a way to collect money from blacks indirectly and not have to deal with them face to face. Hell, it was a win-win against the KKK for Papa and the white wholesalers, and ironically, a source of amusement for black people. The only ones who were not laughing were the areas open targets, sparingly as they were, of the KKK.

Late February and early March had already allowed planters to put seeds in the ground for their early crops, such as collards, turnips, mustard greens, corn, potatoes, garden peas, and a variety of vegetables. Cotton fields, the number one crop, would be prepared with the seeds planting beginning mid-April. Therefore, the entire community was alive with work in anticipation of harvest time and all that it brings.

For now, in the middle of March, and in anticipation of the coming events of this spring and summer that would include weddings, births, deaths, and celebratory parties for this community, the 'Hole in the Bushes' place was adding a dance room and band area to its modest building. This was in response to the lack of entertainment venues for black people in the surrounding area.

Thirty-six year old Henry Strong Jr. and his thirty-four old wife Carrie had run this place for almost seven years. Its location was not selected by accident. Bradley is a dry county within an entire state that wants to be dry. When Henry J, short for Henry Jr., who is Colrolus Strong's (Lena's husband) cousin, wanted to open a restaurant specializing in bar-b-que and fried fish in Banks, they would not allow it. That was in the summer of 1917. He had just returned from the war and gotten married. They put all kind of legal obstacles in his way, saying he needed a special permit to serve fried fish. He would need a license for this, that, and whatever else he had in mind. They were not going to allow a black couple to open a business in the town of Banks.

If he wanted to open a little picnic stand where he served food, invited the locals to play music and dance that would be fine. The location could not be in Banks or alongside a road leading to and out of town. It would have to be on private property back in the woods somewhere. To their surprise, and almost everyone in the community, that is exactly what he did.

It wasn't until a couple of years ago you could reach this place by automobile because there was no real road. Most customers arrived by foot or horseback. This little mecca for black entertainment was so isolated you could literally get lost trying to find it. That is why the name, the 'Hole in the Bushes' stuck because behind the bushes and trees is where it is located.

The land was donated by Henry Strong, Senior. The loan for the building material that the Strong's were not able to cut came from his silent partners, Papa Warner Johnson and his wife, Dora Johnson. Both men were black Masons and their wives were in the black Order of the Eastern Star (O.E.S.). Each organization called for helping any member achieve their dreams by contributing your time, money and expertise. All members are expected to return the favor, no matter how large or small. One cannot overlook the fact that when finished, this will be the only black club south of Little Rock. Therefore, it promises to be a bread winner for investors.

Papa was also responsible for a private road crew who worked to clear and widen the road that ran up to a well travel road linking to the main road to Banks. They put down gravel in some places where flooding might occur. Since the facility was behind a very small creek, they had long ago built a bridge where a horse, wagon or person could get across. They decided to upgrade the bridge to allow for automobiles and trucks. They also cleared more space for customers to park their vehicles.

The idea of the addition pretty much tells the story by virtue of the type of rooms being added. The dance floor will allow Henry to charge for gala events such as a dance with one or more singers and their bands providing the entertainment. The stage or other area will be there for the band. The dining area is also being enlarged in anticipation of more people to enjoy the home cooked cuisine of Carrie and her helpers. Henry's father, who is also a Mason, got hold of another two gas run generators to help out after the addition.

Colrolus Strong sipped on a cup of freshly brewed hot coffee as he watched his bride of five months dished out his portion of three scrambled eggs she'd prepared for their breakfast. "Here you are Mr. Strong," She said, no longer giggling but smiling while thinking of the love they made last night. Each had a chicken wing to go along with the biscuit they shared, both left from yesterday's supper. Lena, still a blushing young bride, had a certain air about herself that revealed the happiness she felt being married to the husband she lovingly called Mr. Strong. Colrolus would cringe every time she repeated it because it seems so formal, especially in the presence of other people. "After all," he pleadingly reminded her, "we are married now, and you're Mrs. Strong. Please, please call me Colrolus, honey, husband, anything but Mr. Strong." Lena, having called him that ever since they'd met, and all through the brief courtship promised she would try to address him another way. True to her word, it sounded as though she would start this morning.

"Honey, why do you have to go over to Henry J's this morning?"

A smiling Colrolus replied, "Sugar, you 'member me telling you that my Uncle Henry wanted me to keep an eye on his son and lend a helping hand. That family raised me after my parents got killed in the house fire. I looked to Henry J while I was a little tike. He's more like my older brother than cousin."

"Yeah I remember, Uncle Henry got hurt in that fire trying to save your mother, bless her soul. I 'member 'cause the fire was started by night riders after they hanged your daddy."

"Yeah, I was six years old then. I just got out 'cause my mama told me to run into the woods and hide. She pushed me out the front door while those men were hanging daddy. She shot at the men in the KKK getups. I saw one of them fall from one of the shots. The house was already burning, but they returned such a heavy volley of firepower at mama standing in the front door. She ran back in and shut the door. That's when Uncle Henry and his two brothers rode up on horseback firing and the cowards scattered and ran back into the woods toward their horses." A still choked up Colrolus recounted.

By now this incident, especially the building fire, resurrected memories of how her sister Lummie died, the effect the entire ordeal had on her family and the Parker family. She wiped tears from her eyes and quietly said, "Some white folk are lower than dogs. They just crazy." She took a sip of her coffee as her husband continued the story.

"Uncle Henry said they found three bullets in mama's upper body when they finally got her out. His brothers had to drag him out because one of the main beams in the ceiling fell on the back of Unc's feet as he knelt down to grab Mama. That's why he can't walk today. It broke his ankles and smashed his feet in such a way that he can't put no weight on them to this day."

"What did they want?" a visibly upset Lena asked.

"They wanted our land. Oh, they said that daddy had said something wrong to some white woman. Unc. said they never did find out who the woman was . . . , and of course the men were never identified, so there were no charges. The rumor mill gave them all the answers they needed. A white man, whose land butted up against Unc's, who really owned the land, wanted the spot our house was built on and surrounding land for hunting and fishing."

"Damn, so that's it."

"Yep, that was the reason. They still didn't get the land." Getting a handle on his emotions, Colrolus began to answer Lena's initial question. Henry J and I have got to go see Papa Warner 'bout some Hole in the Bushes business. Unc wanted me to go along, to make sure Warner Johnson don't get his feet in too deep on the ownership side of the place 'cause of his investment. You see, I got a lot more book learning than Henry J."

"Seem like everybody know how Papa work if you ain't careful."

"That's right sugar," Colrolus agreed while kissing Lena goodbye and heading for the door. "Papa is a good man and does a lot for this community. But, he always likes to be in charge. We just want to keep him as a very silent partner with a very small amount of ownership and right of say on how things are gon' be run."

"Uncle Henry got the right man on the job. I know that much," A smiling Lena yelled after her husband who climbed his long tall frame onto his saddled riding horse, pulled back on the reins, turning the animal toward the Hole in the Bushes place.

"Thanks sugar, see you later on this evening." He replied as he urged his horse to pick up the pace. "Come on Batty, we late, let's move." The white stallion with the white main and tail immediately obeyed, breaking out in a gallop to travel the little under a mile trip to Henry J's place.

Lena turned and looked down at one of Colrolus hunting dogs. He called him Dog. This one always curled up or laid down on the porch; waiting for a command from his master before he would even roll over. "Why can't you be more like Moe, Zoe, or even Oh No.? You don't let us know if anybody is coming or anything. Mark my words, you hear. We gon' get to know each other before long," She advises before entering the house and closing the door behind her.

Batty, with his owner aboard, arrived at Henry J's in full gallop. "Whoa, Whoa Batty," Carrie heard Colrolus say in his best horse trainers voice. That's a Strong for you. They only know one speed, and that's in a hurry, whether going or coming, she thought. She was cleaning tables in a screened off the patio dining area of the place. This area was not affected by the addition going up on the other side of the eatery. One of three men was closing up the open end of the addition by putting in a window. The other two were putting up the inside walls over the vertical wall beams. You could hear the hammering although the sound was somewhat muted from the closing of the wall.

The horse stopped on command and looked at Colrolus as he dismounted, walking toward Carrie as if to say, you didn't think I was going to run through that house did you?

Carrie and Colrolus gave each other a glad-to-see-you embrace. She told him Henry was saddling his horse. They both took a seat in the dining area, exchanging pleasantries about the amount of work remaining before the grand re-opening on the targeted first weekend in April, and other things.

"How is that new bride, Lena, doing?" she asked.

"Why, she's doing just fine, Carrie. She told me to tell you Hi, so . . . , Hi!"

Carrie had to laugh at Colrolus, now smiling from ear to ear. "Boy, you so crazy. Here comes Henry now."

They turned their heads toward the walkway leading from the storage house and saw Henry J leading the brown bay roan stallion, with two black socks right above his front hoofs. The horse's main was a dark brown color with a tail to match. He had a black marking almost in the shape of a diamond between his eyes that went down and spread across and around his nostrils. Like Batty, his coat was almost shining against the sun. It was also a beautiful animal and a gift from Colrolus.

Carrie, always with the jokes according to anyone who has met her remarked, "Hell, now I can't tell which is the best looking, the horse or Henry."

They both broke out laughing, "Whoooo Carrie, shame on you girl. You know that horse look better than Henry J."

For his part, Henry saw them both laughing so the ultimate night owl asked, "What's so funny this early in the morning.

Closing the screen door behind him and following Carrie to the gate, Colrolus playfully teased, "Why Henry J, I was just telling your wife that horse is prettier than you, that's all."

Henry, checking the documents that Carrie brought out to him, putting them in a saddle bag double pouch and securing it to his horses' saddle while going along with the joke, finally said, "And I bet she said the horse was better looking too, didn't she. I know she did. Didn't she?"

"She sho' did. Boy you sho' do know your wife." Colrolus answered with everybody enjoying a big laugh. So much so that Batty decided to join in by bobbing his head up and down and neighing as if he understood the entire exchange of words. That brought even more laughter from the three.

Henry kissed Carrie goodbye, climbed up on his horse, Sand, answering yes to Colrolus question of did he have everything he needed for the meeting. "Come on Colrolus, let's go," Henry said still smiling.

"You boys take care now. See you later." A waving Carrie shouted as Batty and Sand, with the men secure in the saddles, galloped across the new Hole in the Bushes new bridge toward the main road leading to Banks.

After crossing the bridge, she heard Colrolus get in the last word just like he normally does, this time saying "Bye Carrie. See ya when I see ya."

While riding along the main road could not help but notice the different type traffic along the way. Every four or five minutes a motorized traveler would pass from the front or rear. There were all kind of vehicles going and coming including tractors and trucks turning in and out of turnoffs to various farms along the road. Some heading into Banks and others headed toward Lanark, in the opposite direction. Both men acted like kids in a candy store singing the familiar song, "I got to get me one of those." It didn't matter if they were looking at an automobile, truck, or tractor. They finally galloped up to Papa Warner Johnson store realizing had it not been for their sightseeing they could have been here earlier.

Papa was sitting in the same old rocking chair, in his normal spot while watching the morning traffic. For a Thursday before the weekend, his parking lot had a couple of delivery trucks from Banks and Warren. There were only a couple local shoppers. A few of his ever-present family members were getting into their daily fields of specialties.

Anybody who knew Papa understood; he and he alone acted as the Chief Operating Officer of his business. He made the decisions on any expenditures, cost of sales and services, who would be serviced, and which of his family members would do the service. He and his wife Dora had nine children, ranging from twenty-four through ten years old. They all worked on the farm or businesses in some capacity. His oldest child was a girl, twenty-one year old Carlee, followed by Edna, now nine-teen. His first son, eighteen year old Joel Johnson, had been groomed since he was twelve as the future leader of the entire enterprise. He, more so than the others, not only retained the book learning but possessed natural leadership qualities. He ran the various field work crews needed to fill in where there were not enough family or cousins to complete all of the work.

Papa, or more succinctly his family members, was literally the jack of all trades for black people in and around the Gravel Ridge community. He acted as the undertaker by making coffins. He was a syrup maker, barber, blacksmith, horse team or plowing reins, and shoe repairer. He was fast becoming an automobile-truck-tractor repair shop.

Dora was the areas professional beautician with a wide range of customer in Bradley County. Some regulars came from as far away as Hot Springs and Warren. They ran what would now be considered a small but effective laundry and dry cleaning business on the eighty acre farm across the road from the store.

Papa Warner had more land; some say upwards of 100 more acres, than the farm across from the store in and around the community. He owned timber lands. He grew cotton, corn, any kind of vegetable that one can grow in the area, all kinds of beans and peas, cantaloupe and watermelons. He has a persimmons and apple orchard. Of course, he had the horses, mules, cattle, hogs, goats, chickens, a tractor, wagons, and new additions, a truck and an automobile to work his enterprise.

In other words, Papa Warner Johnson was the closest man to a capitalist, far ahead of many white men in the area, as any man in county. One had to be aware that talking business with him could be worse for black people. With him being aware of them playing dumb when negotiating with white folk. It was against this backdrop that Henry J sat down on an old peach crate next to Mr. Johnson. Colrolus took a seat on the porch in front of Papa with his back leaning against the corner beam holding up that end of the porch.

"Hi yawl boys do this morning?" A younger looking forty-five year old graying at the temples Warner Johnson greeted. He had on a country workingman's wardrobe of the day, a pair of blue fading loose bibbed coveralls with the shoulder straps sitting atop a dark blue well-worn shirt. His ankle high boots had a looped strap in the back of the footwear to provide the wearer with something to pull in order to put on each boot. They looked almost brand new. He smoked an old corn cob pipe that wasn't lit at the moment. Yet you could tell by the brim of his dark blue cap with the "Lucky Strike" cigarette logo that smoke had discolored that one little area of the cap.

Colrolus noticed the only difference between Papa's coveralls from his and Henry J's was the colors. His was a faded blue, Henry's, a newer blue and Colrolus coveralls were light gray.

Henry asked Papa if they should talk somewhere else, like behind the store.

"Naw, we good right here. You got something for me to sign?"

Henry pulled the agreement from the pouch and gave it to Papa who began to read the four page document.

"I see your daddy had these papers done by that black lawyer in Little Rock." He noted.

"Ah . . . he just wants to make sho' there is a piece of paper that tells each of us what we agreed to."

"Yeah, I know," He said while continuing to read.

"The 15% share of profits after expenses is the same amount we both agreed to," Henry pointed out, once more interrupting the reading of the document.

"Yeah, I know," Papa repeated while glancing annoyingly at Henry.

"You can see that . . ." Henry started again.

At this point, Papa clearly annoyed at the interruptions asked point blank, "Do you want me to sign this agreement?"

"Yes suh."

"Well then, shut up and let me read the darn thing."

"Oh, all right . . . , sorry Mr. Johnson"

Colrolus smiled at Henry J's impatience. He'd heard the man was remarkably thorough. This scene only reinforced that reputation. Papa took his own sweet time and started to read the agreement from the beginning after his cousin's interruption. Finally, he spoke after satisfying himself that he understood each word in the document.

He began by stated his family was not in and had no intentions to get into the entertainment business. He reiterated conversations that he and Henry J had from the beginning. He was aware that local singers would be able to show off their talent at the place. He also hoped, along with Henry, that the big club and radio stars would eventually find their way to our little area and have someplace to perform for our people. They all agreed that gospel music had its outlet in one of many churches in the area. Whereas blues or secular music needed a venue in these parts to grow and in that respect they wanted the Hole in the Bushes to be that place. The fact they served good food was icing on the cake.

"Me and yo' daddy go way back. Um doing this as much for the community as for myself. Yo' daddy knows that's how I do business 'round here. You and yo' wife been running that place for over seven years. You should know what you doing by now. If yawl don't, shame on me. Either way, my hands are full with all that I do. That's why, I agreed to put the cash and some materials up for yo' improvements. I'll sign both copies, and then you sign, giving me a signed copy. You tell yo' daddy, I am still Warner and we still friends. Ain't nothing changed." He said before directing a question to Colrolus.

"After the signing is finished, are we done here, young pup? You his bodyguard, ain't you?"

Colrolus and Henry J smiled with Henry adding, "Naw, he just came along for the ride.

"That's right, and I want to buy a couple of things. Can I get a couple bottles of that soda pop you sell? I want grape and orange . . . and a peppermint stick for my wife too. She still got a sweet tooth," Colrolus asked.

"Sho' you can. You just make sure I get those soda bottles back, you hear? Otherwise, you will owe me for 'em." He pulled another empty peach crate from next to his rocking chair and placed it in between him and Henry to use while signing the agreement. Henry signed each copy, passing each one to Papa. He signed both; passing one copy back to Henry J. Colrolus felt this was the perfect time to go get his soda pop and candy, disappearing inside the store.

He heard Papa call for his thirteen year old son, Frank Johnson who ran by Colrolus as he finished paying for his pop and candy. He followed the boy back outside to the porch in time to hear his instructions.

"Papa, you called me?"

"Take this paper, and hold on tight, take it up to the main house and give it to Joel. Tell him I said read it and put it away for safe keeping. You hear, tell 'em just what I said." He instructed without repeating himself.

"Yes suh," with that Frank took off running toward the main house across the road.

Papa had one more instruction. This one was for Henry. "You make sho' I see the details of income and expense every quarter, that's every three months during the year and how you got your profit number. Finally I want my 15% on time, every time it's due."

The sound of screeching tires on the road caught everyone on the porch by surprise. Papa, Henry, Colrolus along with a couple of shoppers exiting the store immediately looked toward the road.

"Um all right", young Frank Johnson yelled back at his daddy while still running to deliver the paper Papa gave him.

It looked like the second auto, behind the Sheriff's auto, skidded as it maneuvered to turn into the stores driveway, avoiding hitting a sprinting Frank Johnson, and continue following the lead auto. The first auto driven by Sheriff Penelton came to an abrupt stop in front of the stores porch. Both cars caused enough dust flying everywhere almost making one forget it is still the middle of March and winter. Both riding horses and a team of horses were spooked; its lucky Henry and Colrolus tied them to a post securely.

With the dust settling and the animals calming down, Papa bellowed out at the sheriff, "What the hell is wrong with you? You'll almost hit my boy with those machines. What's going on?"

"Warner, we are on our way to the Parker's house. You seen their boy Sammy?" The sheriff answered. The white deputy riding with the Sheriff got out of the vehicle and stood guard so he could watch all traffic leaving or coming into the stores driveway. This, while the two white men who were riding in the second auto took different paths around the stores building. One man taking the time to make sure a wagon team was not carrying anybody while waiting for its driver to return, who had just exited the store at the start of the commotion. He was still standing on the porch. Meanwhile, the two deputy sheriffs both met each other in the front and went inside the store with pistols drawn. After a brief couple of minutes, they came out with no one in custody.

"Why no, we ain't seen the boy round here. What you want him for?" Papa, not knowing for sure if anybody saw him, yet speaking for everybody answered.

"Murder, God dammit! Seems there was a shooting up around those woods at the edge of Parker place. We're on our way over their now."

"What happened Sherriff?" Papa asked.

"Walt Sampson's dead and his brother, Petey is on his way to the hospital. He's been critically shot too. Word is Sammy is the shooter. Um trying to find him before someone else does. Whose horses are those, Warner?" Sheriff Penelton asked any of the four men on the porch and no specific person in particular.

"Those are me and my cousin, Colrolus here, Sheriff." Answered Henry J. Colrolus nodded his head in agreement.

"That's my team over there, Sheriff." The fourth man on the porch beside Papa and the Strong's said while pointing to the wagon that the deputy had already checked out.

"All right, all right, we gotta go. Listen Papa, and the rest of you too. You' all better tell that Sammy that he is in danger out here. He needs to come on in and give his self us if and cooperate if he wants any help from the law. You tell him what I said now, you hear?" Was the Sherriff's last warning or instruction, considering how anyone might take it before he got back in his auto.

Before turning the vehicle toward the road again, he shouted. "We'll stop by again on our way back to town." He then took off with the second vehicle behind him. Both made a left turn on the road in what looked like they were heading for the Parker Farm.

"I wonder what happen to Rollie, or where he was," Henry J said.

"I wonder what happen period," Papa added.

By that time, young Frank Johnson had returned from the main house and told his daddy he gave the paper to Joel as instructed. His daddy ripped into him about running across that or any road these days because autos move faster than a horse pulled wagon. His son smiled and said okay and went back into the store to continue his chores.

Henry J and Colrolus mounted their horses, thank and waved goodbye to Papa Warner and rode off toward the Parker place. Rollie Parker and Henry J were friends, and he was concerned for Sammy, Rollie, and the family. Either way, Henry J was going to find out what happen, who got shot and why.

CHAPTER 4

Sammy's On the Run–Gracie & John Hampton's Wedding

"**M**e and Elmo was just tipping along daddy, trying to sneak up on a squirrel or rabbit. All of sudden shots rang out. I don't know . . . , maybe four, five maybe even seven. I don't know. It all happened so fast. One bullet hit me with such a force it spun me around before knocking me down."

Clem Parker was listening to Sammy recount the events as they occurred while attended to a bullet wound to his shoulder. There was not much blood because the bullet went straight through the muscle part, never touching an artery or bone. "This boy must be part cat, having nine lives and all. Thank God." Clem said.

Meanwhile, his oldest son was almost in shock staring at his Cousin Elmo's body pressed against a pine tree. His face was turned toward Rollie with a shocked yet resigned expression. The body was motionless while his right arm was positioned as though he was trying to hug the tree. The left dangled at his side. His knees were slightly bent while both his feet were on solid ground at the base of the tree. The back of his jacket, soaked with his blood, revealed he'd been shot several times in the back. Such was the force which pinned him to the tree. It looked like he just dropped his rifle from his right hand while grabbing onto the tree itself.

"Rollie, Rollie," Clem called. He held down a semi-shocked Sammy, cleaning his wound with water from a canteen he instinctively grabbed as he ran out of his door. He looked over towards his nonresponsive son and called out again, "Rollie dammit, check on those two bodies over yonder in the bushes."

Doing as his father asked, he walked about sixty feet from his cousin over to a clump of revealing bushes that was between two tall pines. He peaked over the three to four foot shrubbery and saw Walt Sampson lying in a pool of blood. The lower front area of his throat was still seeping blood. It was where a bullet hit, instantly killing him. His rifle lay halfway across his body, looking like he fell backwards as soon as he was shot.

To his left, on the other side of a tree, lay a crumpled up Petey. He moved every now and then letting one know he was still alive. Rollie backed away from the scene, returning to his father's side just in time to hear his brother scream in pain.

"What happened daddy?" Rollie asked.

"Nothing, he's alright. I just poured a little gunpowder in his wound and lit it with a match to seal it. I ain't no doctor but this boy is going to live." He poured a little water into Sammy's mouth.

Rollie reported the scene by the bushes to his father. His father was visibly shaken and immediately concerned about the possible ramifications of a white man dead and another seriously wounded that still may die.

"After I fell, I heard 'em daddy," Sammy continued. "I heard one of them crackers scream 'yah hoo! We got them niggers.' It was the voice I heard in the woods the night Lummie died. They were running towards us. I couldn't even see Elmo, but I grabbed my rifle and fired about three quick times at the shadowy outline of the one in the middle. That's when I heard Petey Sampson yelling to his brother, asking if he was hurt. I could see him walking toward where his brother fell. That's when I opened up on him. I must have fired four more shots and heard him fall too. There was somebody else with them, but I never saw him. He ran off in the trees somewhere; he may still be out there."

"Nobody else is over there but Petey. I think he is still alive," Rollie volunteered.

"Shhh . . . , Shhh," Clem cautioned. "Rollie, I want you to put Sammy on your horse and get him out of here."

"But daddy, what . . ."

"Shut yo' mouth boy and listen," Clem said almost in a whisper, though clear enough that Rollie could understand his instructions. "Sammy, Sammy you hear me boy? Are you alert and okay to ride?"

"Yes suh."

"I want you to get yo' ass on that horse and gone likety-split down by Sambo's house. His son Lemon and dem boys will take care of you down there. You got to get out of here. Nobody's gonna admit them white boys fired at yawl first. We'll get word to you with what's going on. Now, do you hear me boy?"

"Yes suh."

Clem quickly hugged his son after helping him to his feet. "Take your rifle with you."

Rollie walked his brother to his horse, which was tied to the wagon his father rode up to the site. "What am I gonna do, Rollie?" Sammy asked.

"You do like Daddy told you to do. Don't ride back by the house. Go through the woods and use the side roads a much as possible. You'll be alright. I'll see you soon, now git outta here?" Rollie slapped the horse on the backside, and it took off with Sammy holding onto the rifle and still feeling pain in his shoulder. He slowed the animal down as he entered another clump of trees to make it harder for someone to track him.

Riding Rollie's horse, Paint, made Sammy even more nervous and cause to be extremely cautions. Almost everyone knew the brown and white pinto that Rollie appropriately named paint. You could stop counting at three if you were adding up the number of pinto horses in Gravel Ridge. The other two were Paint's parents owned by Colrolus Strong. Getting use to the pain, he maneuvered the animal through the woods, alongside but out of sight of people working in the fields. He finally came upon the direct shortcut along the back roads to Sambo Hampton's.

Rollie rejoined his father. They walked over to Petey who was still crumple up, moaning in pain on the ground.

"Who is that moaning back there? Why it's Mr. Sampson's boy. Petey are you hit? Are you alright?" Clem asked.

He could not see the men standing over him, but he knew they were not white. "Naw, I ain't alright. I been shot, and I think my brother is dead. Can yawl go get my daddy and tell him to bring a doctor?"

"Okay, we'll get you some help."

By that time, Clem heard autos coming to a stop right next to his wagon team outside the densely wooded area. He told Rollie to stay with Petey while he went back to the wagon area to see who was in the autos. He was shocked and relieved to see Sheriff Penelton get out of one of the vehicles. His relief was brief, Harvey Sampson, carrying his rifle, came from around the other side of the vehicle.

The second auto had two deputies and another individual that looked like the one they called Bob. He ran with the Sampson boys, Clem correctly thought to himself.

"Damn Clem, what happened up here and where is your sons Sammy and Rollie?" the sheriff asked without any other kind of a greeting.

"Um not sure Sheriff. We just got here a few minutes ago ourselves. Rollie is in the trees over there with a couple of bodies."

"Yeah, this is about where it happened, Mr. Sampson. This way . . ." Bob reported. He also carried a rifle and took off into the woods toward the shooting site. Old man Sampson, the Sheriff, two of his deputies and Clem followed them.

"Oh my god, Petey, these niggers shot you?" old man Sampson asked. "Where is yo brother?"

"It was that Sammy boy again daddy. I can't feel my legs daddy. I don't have no god damn feeling in my legs, and I can't get up!"

"Son, that's 'cause you been shot. Let me take a look at ya." Harvey Sampson took a brief look at the bullet holes in Petey's stomach and shouted. "Sheriff, he's been gut shot; we got to get this boy to Banks or a hospital."

"Ron," the sheriff motioned to one of his deputies. You and Al put this boy in the auto and take him to Doc Purvis clinic in Town. Doc will fix him up to transport him to the hospital in Warren."

They tore off his shirt and told him to hold the shirt, already soaked in blood, over the wounds. The bigger deputy carried the smaller Petey in his arm to the auto. Once there, they made him as comfortable as possible before driving off back down the hill, pass the Parker house, onto the road and to Banks.

Meanwhile, the old man walked over to his other son, who was lifeless. "He looked up a Clem and the sheriff with such a rage it took them aback for a minute. "Somebody is gonna pay for this. Yo son is a murderer and is going to die for this. Bob here says they fired upon them while my boys were hunting up here."

"I don't know who fired the first shot, but that don't look like what happen up here," Sheriff Penelton stated. He looked at the early afternoon sky and his watch. He asked everybody to sort of stay still for a while. He directed the remaining deputy who had joined him after the other two left to follow him and take notes.

They pointed to a little area on the other side of Walt where there were spent rifle cartridges. The grass was still matted down like someone had been standing there. Sheriff Penelton looked back to his left at a direct line of fire where Clem's nephew was still pinned against the tree.

"Is this where you were standing Bob?" he asked.

Bob, not sure how to answer the question, didn't. He looked at Mr. Sampson as though searching for instructions. Sampson said nothing; he just glared at the sheriff. The sheriff, never a patient man, walked up to Bob, patted both left and right pockets. Finally reaching in Bob's jacket pocket, he pulled out a couple live shells. He picked up a couple of the same type spent shells, putting both live and spent in the same vest pocket. He wrote down the model and kind of rifle belonging to Bob.

"Again, is that where you were standing Bob?" He asked as he pointed to the area of the matted down grass to the right of Walt.

"I guess so. I can't be sure. It all happen so god dam fast. We just returned the fire. We didn't know who was shooting at us." Bob blurted out while occasionally looking at old man Sampson for guidance.

The sheriff and deputy then walked over to Walt's body; examine his rifle, writing down the make and model, placing spent and live shells in a small brown envelope. He tagged the envelope Walt Sampson.

They repeated the same scenario at the area where Petey had fallen. His rifle was still there. The Sheriff advised Mr. Sampson to retrieve the weapon.

Then they walk over to Elmo's body. His rifle was on the ground with no expended cartridges. The sheriff noted and wrote down the four bullet wounds entering his back, three below the shoulders and one just above his waistline. The deputy carefully patted his jacket pocket finding shells and took two, placing them in another small envelope. They wrote down the make and model of the rifle.

The last area to examine was the spot behind a tree next to and to the right of Elmo. One clearly could see the grass matted down as if someone was lying down instead of standing up. There were several spent cartridges but no rifle. The sheriff looked over his shoulder, which gave a good line of the fire area to where Petey and Walt were found. He took his flashlight and survey the area but could not come up with anything except the presence of someone lying down while firing. He put a couple spent cartridges in a separate envelope and asked Clem if he knew the model and type of Sammy's rifle. Clem cooperatively provided the lawman with the information requested.

Finally, the sheriff summarized what he thought happened. "This morning, closer to noon time, there was a firefight. It looks like it occurred between the Sampson boys and their friend Bob and Sammy Parker. The evidence says that everybody in the Sampson party was shooting at the Parkers with only one person returning fire, and we assume that was Sammy. As for who shot first, I would say the body of Elmo Parker gives everyone the ultimate clue. It looks like the first shot came from the Sampson's, killing Elmo and possible wounding Sammy. I need to speak with Sammy to clarify what exactly happened. Until that time, the case is still open. Clem, you tell your boy, he needs to get his ass up to my office to give me a statement so I can hopefully close this case down.

That led to an outraged Harvey Sampson, who practically turned blood red at the sheriff's summation and handling of this incident thus far. "By Gawd, I don't know what in the hell you trying to pull here Penelton. This ain't over by a long shot. And another thing, you better hope you find that nigger before I do, cause I ain't promising there is going to be enough left for him to give anybody a damn statement. That boy killed my Walt, and he is gonna pay for it, you hear?"

Not afraid to let anyone who is in charge, Sheriff Penelton shot back at Mr. Sampson. "I know you know this Harvey, but let me remind you anyway. You are standing on Clem Parker's property. So the first question, I asked of anybody involved here is why they are on this property. Bob here says they were hunting. The Sampson's got plenty of good hunting grounds on their property. So I say, hunting what or should I say who?"

Sampson, through talking with the sheriff advised Clem that he was on his way home to get a wagon after which he would return to pick up his sons body. He refused to be helped by Clem with his wagon or the sheriff. He also refused to ride back to his house with the Sheriff even though he was picked up and brought to this location by the sheriff.

"Like my dead boy," he added. "I've walked these parts of the woods many times, and it didn't matter whose property line I crossed long as I was doing no harm. I think that's just what they were doing. One of mine is dead and maybe another one dying. This will not stand, I tell you that. Come on Bob."

The two men walked off leaving Clem, Rollie, the sheriff and his deputy shaking their heads at what they just heard.

Finally, the sheriff broke the silence, "Hell, Bob is lucky I didn't arrest him as a material witness or much worse. I'm just trying to keep the peace. Clem that should underline what I told you earlier. You have your boy Sammy turn himself in to me before some of Sampson's friends get to him. It's possible we can close this out without the entire county in an uproar about this incident. But you got to know, some people 'round here is gonna be hot as all git out."

"I know suh. I'll try to find Sammy and bring him in myself."

Meanwhile, the deputy examined Elmo's back to see if the bullets could be extracted. He was able to get one. He, with Rollie's help took him down from the tree. The deputy was then able to get two bullets which were imbedded into the tree. He showed the sheriff who told him to tag and bag them.

"All right, you can take your nephew Elmo Parker's, body home now. I'm going back to town; turn in my report to the council and newspaper. That way people can see there is another side to this story other than the one that Harvey Sampson and Bob is gonna be spreading."

Clem asked the sheriff just as he was headed back to his car, how had he heard about and where the incident happened so fast. "Somebody called me on the short-wave radio in my office. Bob was standing next to the caller because I could hear him screaming in the background, saying "That Sammy boy just shot him down. We weren't doing nothin', he said. I figured we better get out here ahead of the mob.

"Thank you Sheriff Penelton. I appreciate yo' help"

"Just trying to keep the peace, boy, that's all, I'm just trying to keep the peace in my county."

By the time the sheriff got to their car, Henry J and Colrolus had ridden up, dismounted, tied their horses to Clem's wagon and was looking for the Parkers.

The Sheriff saw them and asked, "Have you seen Sammy yet?" The men shook their head no so he pointed toward the area they would find Clem and Rollie. He and the deputy left going back down the hill toward the road back to Banks.

Henry and Colrolus helped Rollie and Clem carry Elmo's body back to the wagon in an old blanket. The Parkers told the Strong's what happened along with the plan to get Sammy out of the county. They knew they were talking to two people who would not relay this information to any white person or loud mouth black person for that matter. All four men agreed Sammy would have to leave the county, if not Arkansas all together.

Lena often used these after church socials to sit with her parents and catch up on family news. Weather permitting, food brought by parishioners were served buffet style. Families sat and ate at the picnic tables in the back of the church. It was the thirtieth day, the last Sunday in March.

The Sampson boys shooting happened eleven days ago. The last anyone heard, Walt was still dead. That was a little humor for those around here that knew him well. Petey was still in a hospital in Little Rock. He was bedridden and the prognosis for him ever walking again was null and void. It was a difficult conversation for the entire gathering; even the pastor mentioned it in his remarks. He led a prayer for the community, victims, Sammy Parker and his family.

At the Halls table, Colrolus reported that Sammy was still safe and within the county. There were a few people in the community intimidated by known KKK members, but it did not lead to any real confrontations or violence. There was a pertinent question lingering at this table, especially among the womenfolk.

Lena put it up for discussion by asking, "Gracie, how is the wedding plans going?"

"You know there is no planning without you. There is not going to be a big to do wedding. We planned to get married by the justice of the peace in town. John's daddy is going to put up the bond. We planned on marrying May fourth. That's mostly it."

"Where yawl gonna live?" Lena persisted.

"We are going to live on the Hampton farm. Their place is up the hill a ways from the Oaklawn Methodist Church. There is a little house that was built for the first child who gets married," Gracie responded.

"It sounds nice, Gracie. Ain't you happy? 'Cause you seem a little sad." A smiling Colrolus added.

"Oh, she so happy she can hardly stand it," Harriett chimed in. "She don't want to leave her mama and daddy by ourselves. But we told her not to worry. Look at her, she is happy than all git out."

The evidence of Gracie's smile confirmed her state of mind on this subject. All that's left was for her to say it, which she admitted. "Yes, I am very happy to marry John."

Talk turned to planting as it always does this time of year. Viola and Edgar was through planting their gardens and field area. They were now helping Harriett and Frank put in their crops.

111

Colrolus and Lena was also finished with the early crops with the help of his Uncle Henry's family. As far as Gracie knew, her John and family were taking care of their planting requirements.

At the end of the meal, members cleaned up their area, said goodbye to friends, family, climbed into their mode of transportation and left for home. It had been a fantastic month for putting in crops in anticipation of a great harvest in a few months. Except for frayed nerves in anticipation of repercussions for the Sampson's shooting incident, it had been a fantastic month.

David 'Sambo' Hampton and his wife Sallie were enjoying a morning quiet time cup of coffee. The three younger boys were going about their chores while Lemon was planting the last of the sweet potato seedlings in a small field nearby the little house. John, continuing work on the little house, was putting wall shelves in the kitchen area with the help of Sammy Parker.

Speaking of which, the Hampton's guest was hot. They'd hid him out in the little house that John and his new bride would occupy in a couple of months. Even though he was not in the big house, he was still on their property and was wanted for questioning by the law. There were little clues of his possible presence, like Rollie Parker's horse, Paint, grazing in the back of the barn with the other stock. What about the sudden activity in and around the little house itself? The clues of and actual presence of was a nagging concern for Sallie.

There is no doubt about the closeness of the black community in Gravel Ridge. Residents are acutely aware of their living and working environment. In other words, they know where they stand with a local white person in any given situation, and that is secondary to "Mr. Charlie's" agenda. Most, especially the younger blacks are not afraid of Jim Crow laws. They will fight any way they can to earn the right to survive, to thrive in the land of United States of America. A land constructed with the help of, and some time on the back of their ancestors. World War 1 was not that long ago. For those who served, it produced black men with more education and awareness of their rights as a free born Americans. As noted before, that is exactly why the KKK is worried about this new black man.

However, for older blacks, specifically women, who are like women of all colors, want to see their children grow up, have children and get along with other kinds of people so no harm will come to them. They do not like to put the nuclear family's lives and property in jeopardy for other family members, much less for an unrelated person.

No one had to tell David what was on Sallie's mind this morning. He too was from the old school of thought. Even though he now agreed with the younger generation methods regarding race relations. The problem was crystal clear in both their mind. They are harboring a black man who killed a white man and critically wounded another to the point of paralysis. He had been there for eight days and counting. If Sammy was seen or caught on the Hampton property by a white person, albeit KKK and old man Sampson, or even Sheriff Penelton there would be hell to pay for all involved. The reasons why it happened would not matter, only the fact that it happened. Local restless white people wanted to know what was being done about it.

"I talked to Clem Parker the other day. I let him know his boy was rested and well enough to travel," David began. "He's supposed to send somebody by tomorrow whose gonna help that boy get up outta here."

"Um sho' glad to hear that. 'Cause I was beginning to worry that somebody might see him or something." Sallie responded.

"Well the boy hasn't had the sun shine on his face since he been here. John says he is getting stir crazy staying inside all this time. Hopefully it will all be behind us after tomorrow. See you later," David finished his coffee, grabbed his rifle, a lunch bucket with a bacon and biscuit sandwich, pulled his cap down tightly on his head and exited the door.

It was a good day to finish plowing that little section over by the trees that overlooked the entrance to his property. For the small black farmer, most new crops were attempted on a trial and error basis. Getting detailed instructions from other planters, they would plant a small sampling before expanding the next year. This was the second year for this particular tomatoes field project. They had planted about five rows of tomatoes, using a mixture of seeds in odd rows, and seedlings in the even number rows. There was still extra space that could be used after plowing five more rows to add more of the tomatoes. Last year, this area proved to be a great spot for them. Their little crop mixture of seeds and seedlings produced about eighty percent of growth furnished healthy and sweet tomatoes on the vines. So this year, they hope to double the output.

What perfect timing, two of his younger sons, Monroe and David Jr. were through with their normal barnyard chores. They could help with the planting. They were already familiar with the process after helping last year. That would free David Sr. to finish plowing the last three or so rows squeezing in as many as he could in that area.

They all headed for the area, with David walking and guiding Daisy the mule using leather reins. She was pulling a small designed hauling wagon specifically crafted for carrying small items to the fields. The little five by three foot two wheel wagon carried a barrel of water, four flats of seedlings, a bag of seeds, about two and a half dozen sturdy sized stakes, a couple of small shovels, and two small hoes for planting. The kids were cheerfully walking behind the wagon, asking questions as children do. His youngest, nine year old Peach ran after them, upon receiving the go ahead from his mama.

"Sambo, you watch out after those boys, you hear? Here comes Peach. He wants to go too," Sallie yelled as the group passed her porch on their way up to the field. She had given another small bucket of biscuits and bacon to Peach, asking him to give the container to Monroe to carry. "Um telling you, you all better look out for Peach up there," was Sallie's last instruction.

Monroe advised his little brother to, "Hurry up Peach. You gon' to have to keep up now, we got stuff to do."

Sambo smiled, he marveled at the little fellas who were more than willing to help their daddy. "You boys gonna work out fine. Just take your time and do it right, by making sure the seeds are planted just right, with the proper space needed between each spot. Monroe, you can mark the planting spots beforehand. How far apart should they be?"

Monroe demonstrated by holding his hands a little over twelve inches apart. "'Bout this far apart daddy."

"Good. Put that stake down in the ground, making sure it won't fall over and put dem seeds in the hole 'round it. Pack the dirt down real good and pour a little water 'round the stake. Yawl got that?"

"Yes suh," The boys answered with Peach following suit even though he was not sure and would have to be shown by his older brothers.

"Just like last year, huh daddy?" David Jr. asked.

"That's right boy, just like we did bout this time last year." Sambo answered.

There was not a day that went by, excluding Sundays that someone didn't stop in Sheriff Penelton office and ask how the Sampson murder investigation was going. The Sheriff's well liked personality and reputation was taking a hit on his handling of this incident. Most whites believed the entire Gravel Ridge community should be swept with all local whites joining in on a widespread manhunt.

For his part, he could predict the outcome of an armed mob of people looking for a Negro in a well-populated area. There would be moonshine, liquor, and hot tempers leading up to violence with the property being burned and innocent people killed. He was bound and determined this would not turn into another witch hunt similar to what happened in Elaine, Arkansas, a few years ago.

He was sitting in his office when old man Sampson, Bob, Clarke, and two other men he knew were Klan members walked in. Harvey Sampson took a seat in front of the desk while the rest of the men remained standing.

"Hi you today, Sheriff?" he asked.

"Why I'm OK, busy as ever but doing good. How is Petey doing?"

"Not so good. He just lies around in the bed feeling sorry for himself. I think he will be alright in time. We just got to give him time," he answered before pausing and asking. "You know, um

115

getting reports from people who've seen that Sammy boy some of everywhere."

"Me too Harvey; sometimes he been in two or three places at the same time. It turned out none of the reports have been right so far."

"That nigger must be round here somewhere," Bob added.

One look from Harvey and Bob shut his mouth and got back into place with the other two men. "I just want to see justice done for the murder of my Walt, not to think of what it's done to Petey. My wife is just sick about this, Sheriff."

"Well, I don't know if this will give you any peace but the last two solid leads I got said the boy hopped a freight train. He's probably up in Chicago or one of them northern cities."

One could see the faces of disappointment and anger on Bob, Clarke and the two men. Harvey summed up the general feeling for all. "Goddammit, I was afraid this was gonna happen. If you don't catch them right off, that's always gonna happen."

"The tips came in yesterday. So this morning, I sent a notice to the police departments in Chicago, Detroit, Los Angeles and Milwaukee. That's where a lot of our colored's go. They will arrest the boy and notify me to begin extradition."

"Damn, damn, damn, we got to be quicker next time. But um telling you Sheriff, just in case and you never know, just like I don't know who or where you got your information from, we gon' keep on the lookout for that boy. I came to tell you that we were givin' you a hand anyway. Some of our men are riding through those bottom farmlands looking for that nigger as we speak."

"All I got to say about that is if any of your men break the law, I will arrest them as I would any lawbreaker. I don't want any more shootings or hangings by mistake or otherwise, yawl boys hear me. I say, yawl hear me?"

"All right sheriff, calm down. We just want to give you and your deputies a hand. They know to bring him to you if there is anything left," Harvey, clearly agitated by the sheriffs slow response and or inability to act with force to find Sammy Parker felt he had said enough. He rose up slowly, steadying himself on the arms of the chair and finished by saying, "That's all I got to say. Yawl have a nice day now you hear?"

"Thanks for stopping by and I do appreciate the help as long as it within the bounds of the law. Would give my regards to your misses, Clara?" The sheriff said.

"Why I sho' will. Bye Sheriff." Old man Sampson said as he went out the door with the other men following him after shooting growling gazes at the sheriff.

About a half hour later, the sheriff advised his office clerk-deputy that he was going down to see Sam 'Skeeter' Purvis and would return shortly. He put on his hat, walked out of his office, and closed the outside building's door behind him. He would have to walk past McBain's General Store to get to Sam Purvis' store.

Approaching McBain's he noticed the two Klansmen, who were part of the Sampson visit to his office, were playing checkers at the makeshift table outside the store. Bob and Clarke were looking over their shoulder.

"Looking for Mr. Sampson?" asked Clarke.

"Naw." The sheriff responded while entering the store with Bob and Clarke walking behind him. A tall thin man in a deputy's uniform was coming out of a doorway, saw the sheriff, and quickly ducked back into the room out of view. He figured and hoped the sheriff didn't see him. He couldn't tell because of Penelton's' reflective sunglasses. Removing the sunglasses because of the dimly lit store, he walked to the end of the service counter. That's where he saw McBain talking to Sampson. Ever the lawman and suspicious of anybody behind him, he positioned himself against the wall at the service counter where he could see all in front, back and to his side. When you are among hostile men carrying weapons, you don't take chances.

The three men exchanged pleasantries if you could call it that. The sheriff tried to ease Mr. Sampson suspicions by telling them he was going to stop by this morning before Mr. Sampson visit. And that he was sorry for interrupting the two men's conversation. Mr. McBain seemed to accept his explanation. He continued by repeated the story of Parker's whereabouts tip along with his notification to the cities authorities, emphasizing they were still looking out for any local sign of the Negro wanted for questioning, not murder. He reminded Mr. McBain that he, the sheriff, was still in charge of the investigation and any official word or its status would come from him. There were a couple of non-relevant questions by McBain, which the sheriff answered, leaving the two old men just as exasperated as they were before he stopped in to report the development. He excused his brief visit, said his goodbye, and advised that he had to continue to make his rounds to inform a concerned public. The atmosphere was so tense inside that store between the two old men, Bob, Clark and the sheriff you could have sliced it with a butcher knife. There was no doubt about how Sampson, McBain and crew wanted this to end. They wanted to see a dead nigger, and it didn't much matter if it was Sammy Parker or not. Some nigger had to die for the death of Walt Sampson and Petey, who might as well be dead.

All Bob and Clarke needed was the green light from old man Sampson, and they would have shot Sheriff Penelton down where he stood, regardless of the two customers shopping at the time. All the men heard in the sheriff office and more of the same at McBain's was excuses and unacceptable foot-dragging. They saw Penelton as a nigger lover who needed to be stopped.

"One of these goddamn days, and soon, we gonna have to appoint a new sheriff. I got a feeling in my bones this man's gonna meet an untimely death," Harvey Sampson softly predicted to McBain as Sheriff Penelton exited the store.

The sheriff continued his updates by going in and out of the various storefronts reaching Ben Purvis' store almost at the end of the street. Skeeter's daughter was working the counter. She pointed out back at the sheriff's inquire as to the whereabouts of her father. They almost bumped into each other. He was going out as Skeeter was coming back in. They both went outside the front of the store, sat on the bench where the sheriff gave the latest update. He also told him about old man Sampson's attitude.

"You know that's always has been a terrible crowd in there especially when it comes to treatment of the coloreds. Now, I hear McBain's is the headquarters for the Klan in Banks."

"Yeah Skeeter, I know."

"You got to watch who you talking to these days. Those who ain't Klan got kinfolk who are. And most of the rest have the same feelings as the Klan. This . . . this Sampson boy shooting and stuff got people all on edge. The spark is there, all that's needed now is the gasoline."

"You right Skeeter, I know. There's one other thing, you know me, um just trying to keep the peace. But I saw one my deputies in McBain's a few minutes ago. He ducked back into a room trying not to be seen by me."

"Which one of 'em is it?"

"Charlie Oats. He works part time, but you have to assume he is with that crowd. I am not going to let on like I know. I just wanted you to know. Okay?"

"Damn. Alright, you watch yourself now, hear?"

"I have been at this a long time, maybe too long. But I am still a lawman and must represent the law 'til the end. Watch out for yourself, old man, we need folk like you 'round here."

"I got my kinfolk around, and we are on alert. Take care and thanks for stopping by."

"See you Skeeter," the sheriff said as he started to cross the other side of the street to catch another storefront office before returning to his office. He flagged down his deputy, Pierce Krause, who happened to be driving by at the time. He wanted to make sure him he understood what to say to Papa Warner.

"Ask him if they have seen Sammy Parker. Make sure he understands we are still looking for him. And if there is any Klan activity going on in the bottom lands I want to know about it pronto, right away, you hear? You tell him I said, somebody better get that boy into my office lickety-split, for his own good. Now go on."

"Okay Sheriff," Krause said, putting the auto in gear and heading out of town toward Papa Warner's store.

Colrolus stopped by the big house and waited while Monroe saddled Paint. It was the same horse that Sammy rode to get to the Hampton's. Word from the sheriff via Papa Warner had reached the Hampton's farm. Sallie was concerned, especially about Klan activity. She said she had not noticed anybody around here but would not put it passed them to come sneaking out of the woods, day or night.

"Yawl got an extra horse I can borrow for a while?" Colrolus asked.

"Yeah, we got Old Thunder. He's 'bout twenty years old. The horse was up in age when we bought him. What you need him for?"

"I think we better send Sammy's horse home. If you turn him loose, he will find his way back to the Parker farm. It's not safe for that horse to be 'round here."

Monroe came in to report that Paint had been saddled. His mother told him to unsaddle the horse. Colrolus told them both "hold on. I'll take Paint, saddle and all. I'll point him toward the Parker farm. Be back to get Old Thunder. No need for a saddle, I'll ride him bareback, and our boy can ride my horse."

"I guess you know best." Sallie agreed.

Getting on his horse and grabbing the reins of Paint, Colrolus told Sallie he would be back in about an hour or so. He took the horse down by the schoolhouse, riding past the Methodist church using the side trails. He knew that the sight of a black man riding a white horse leading a brown and white pinto would be easy for someone to remember. He stayed away from people and the main roads as much as possible. Finally reaching the main road leading to Banks, he crossed heading for the back trail bordered by trees. That would put Paint on familiar ground leading directly to the Parker place. As if the horse could understand him, and who knows it might since he was the animals' original trainer, he gave Paint instructions to go home. He reinforced his instructions by giving the horse a hard slap on its butt. Paint took off at a measured gallop down the mile and half back trail headed for home. Colrolus watched the animal stay on the trail until he disappeared into the bend of trees. It didn't matter because he could be reasonably sure enough that the horse, still carrying the saddle, would get home. He turned his horse, Batty, back toward the Hampton's place.

Thank God Old Thunder did not have a sway back. It would have made for a difficult bareback ride. Saddling the animal would have been difficult much less trying to ride a saddled swayback horse. Mounting him at the Hampton big house, Colrolus was able to ride bareback and lead his saddled horse up to the little house. Once he went inside, Sammy was glad to hear he was leaving the area. He was similarly sad for not being able to help John complete the repair work, or see his parents. John told him that Lemon, his father Sambo, and the youngsters were watering seedlings and newly seeded areas around the farm. Yes, he would thank his Daddy and Mama for Sammy. He would also pass on the fact that Colrolus and the Parkers had the Hampton's in their prayers, hoping that God would reward the family for helping a man in need. There was no time to waste, so the two riders mounted the horses, heading toward the direction of the schoolhouse and Methodist church.

"Horses are funny like that," Colrolus said, answering the question before it was asked. His horse, Batty, occasionally turned his head in his owners' direction to look at Colrolus riding another horse. Once clear of the Hampton's property, he gave Sammy details of the get-a-way plan. It was simple. The 3:25 p.m. Rock Island train would be running past the Strong's farm in little over an hour. He was to hop on that train, staying until it reached Hot Springs. Versia or James Boswell will be waiting outside the depot near the porter gate. Just in case they are not there, it's about a mile or so to the Arlington Hotel. You can go to the servant's entrance and ask somebody for Versia and James. She's a maid, and he is an assistant cook.

The two men now maneuvered their mounts into a gentle gallop in order to meet the train at the designated boarding spot. The route took the train in an area where it had to slow down to take a deep curve that led to a bridge crossing. It was the only time the train actually slowed down in this area and was deep enough into the woods for the men to inconspicuous.

"You got that, boy?"

"Yeah, I got it. But I thought I was going up North?"

"So did everyone else. Some think you there already. And, and by God, you still might go, just not today. Come on we gon' take this turnoff to the right."

After about a forty-five minute ride, they arrived at the boarding spot, dismounted, tied the horses to a tree, walked over to the other side of the track and took a seat on a tree branch that recently had broken and fallen off.

"Here is a few dollars yo' daddy sent you," Colrolus said while handing him a few rolled up bills. At that instance, they could hear the train coming miles from where they were sitting. The wait was no more than ten minutes before they could get a glimpse of the train in the distance down the tracks.

"Get ready, cause you might have to run a bit. Watch out for other hobos on the train. Get behind these trees until the engine and passenger part of the train passes," He advised.

It was all a little hazy for Sammy, feeling a little bit sad because he was leaving his home. He didn't say much, just nodding his head in agreement to Colrolus questions or instructions. The train was beginning to slow down as it approached the curve of the tracks.

"You will get to Hot Springs in about forty minutes so stay alert. Don't write, your family will be in touch. Versia will keep the communications open to let everybody know what's going on." They were so close to the train, they could see the blond hair, tinted with gray on a passenger's head. She was resting her head on a pillow while trying to catch a nap. The one compartment for passengers passed and was being followed by the trains boxcars and tankers heading into the curve of the tracks.

The last instructions Sammy heard from Colrolus was, "Git ready, set . . . and, go boy," He took off at a brisk run looking for something to grab onto and spotted a built-in ladder alongside one of the boxcars. Grabbing onto the bar he felt a sharp pain where the bullet entered and exited his shoulder, but managed to hold on. Quickly, he climbed up just enough to extend his left leg over to the open doorway, slinging his body through the doorway. Awkwardly landing on the floor of the boxcar caused a loud yet somewhat muted grunt. He grimaced, grabbing his shoulder as he sat up to check out his temporary riding car.

He heard a voice behind him ask "Are you all right son?"

The dark skinned black man staring at him was a burly man, not so much fat as muscular. He looked to be around thirty, unshaven, wearing blue coveralls, a checkered gray shirt, and sporting a derby hat on his head. He was seated leaning up against the far wall of the boxcar. Sammy could see the holes in the bottom of shoes from his seated angle. It looked as if something was put in one of his shoes to cover the hole. He couldn't tell what if anything was in the second shoe.

"Hey there fellow, you okay?" he asked again.

"Yeah I'm fine," Sammy replied as he stretched enough to let his left elbow feel for the four inch knife he had in his pocket. He sat up on the opposite sidewall from the guy next to the doorway, just in case, asking "Who are you? My name is Paul."

"Um Calvin Coolidge, Paul, do you have anything to eat?" The burly man asked. His dark skinned oval face lacked emotion, except to show that he was clearly annoyed with an unexpected drop-in to his private boxcar. His voice indicated he was looking for some kind of traveling fee if Sammy expected to ride in this car with him.

Once the train passed, Colrolus walked back to the other side of the tracks to retrieve the horses. He mounted his horse, grabbed the rein of Old Thunder and trotted to a spot he could see the train picking up speed as it crossed the bridge. Satisfied that Sammy was on the train without incident from his viewpoint he turned and headed for his house. It had been a long day. He was hungry and could not wait to get home to Lena and her kitchen. He would get the word of events to Clem Parker tomorrow.

The bride and groom to be, all kinds of in-laws from both sides were present and celebrating the pending marriage of John and Gracie. Frank and Harriett Hall along with Lena and Colrolus had just returned to the Hampton's big house. They all were given the grand tour of the little house. John and his brother Lemon had performed the tour guide honors. Gracie, who saw the house for the first time, was beside herself with giddiness. She could not stop smiling and feared if she did, those tears of joy she was holding back would burst loose like a flood.

David "Sambo" Hampton and Sallie were hosting Gracie and her mama and papa for the first time. It was the first time the mother and father-in-laws had time to enjoy each other's company. The fact this little affair was being held on a Saturday, just eight days before the May 4 wedding was memorable.

Sallie had prepared a spread. Each of the ladies, Lena, Gracie, and Harriett, brought their specialties. There was duck and dressing, field peas, turtle soup, fried chicken, bar-be-qued pork, pork chops, collard greens, boiled sweet potatoes, and corn bread, along with the usual vegetables, tomatoes, corn on the cob, onions, and so on. Of course, what would a get acquainted dinner be without peach and apple cobbler, a chocolate and a white icing cake? Obviously guest will take their favorite servings home to eat later or Sunday.

Add the Hampton boys, Lemon, Monroe, David Jr, and Peach and you have a guest list of twelve people who just now are sitting down to eat. They put out a small table for the youngsters. They also added a small three by four foot plank atop a couple of A-frame stands to make the kitchen table long enough to seat family and guest. The kitchen area was packed, but love and appreciation for kinfolk prevailed. Sambo began by asking all to hold hands while he expresses everyone's thanks to Jesus Christ.

"Dear God, we all want to thank you and please bless this gathering of your servants for celebrating, in advance lord, the marriage of our John and his bride to be, Miss Gracie Hall. We pray and hope you have a healthy and long life planned for them. We parents hope we have done our best to contribute to their start up needs. We also welcome our new in-laws and hope we can always show them the love and respect deserved. Thank you god for providing us with the tools and patience . . . ." That phase brought about more than a few amen and yes lords. Everybody around these tables knew you had to be patient for a plentiful harvest and love and affection for that matter.

"Oh God we say again, tools and patience to live." Sambo continued. "Thank you for all your blessings. In Jesus name, we pray."

"Amen," was said by all in unison.

"Let's eat and enjoy," a smiling Sallie added.

"Gracie, what do you think about the little house?" Sambo asked.

"Well . . . Mr. Hampton . . ."

"Honey, call me Sambo or David," Her future father-in-law asked.

". . . I just love it. It's a lot bigger that I thought. Yawl did a nice job, especially on the inside. It looks like a nice home with a lotta love put into it to make it that way, with all the new kitchen shelving, tables, and things."

"We gon' have to put in a water well 'round there somewhere. We just gotta get some information from the county seat before we start digging," Sambo added.

"Miss Gracie, you shoulda seen daddy come up outta our well when it was first dug. He had so much mud on him . . . , and his face; you couldn't see his eyes or nothing," David Jr offered from the children's table.

"Hush Junior, and stay outta grown folk's conversation. Honey-child, you don' have to worry about that kind of stuff, 'cause they gonna put in a fine well for you and John. Besides, Jr. talking about the time daddy had to reinforce our well. He had to go down in there to put the bricks around the sides to keep the mud out and the water fresh."

"Man, that's some dangerous work, 'cause I 'member a few years ago one of our people almost drowned reinforcing our well." Frank chimed in.

"Shoot! All I know is . . . until we get the new one dug, we gon' have to haul water from the big house well. Or go down to the little stream in the back of the house. Probably do a little of each if we don't get it in this summer," John added.

"Gracie, Sambo and John talked Papa Warner down to a good price on a Monarch iron cooking stove. Did you see the river board tank on the side for heating hot water? The one we had in there before wasn't fit to cook on. The top was rusted, it was just a mess," Sallie said.

"Yes ma'am, I saw it. It looks almost brand new, all nice and shiny."

"We think we fixed up everything in the little house to be cozy for the two of us. A new bed and mattress and everything, it should be enough room for a couple of kids just to start the family out right," A smiling John remarked.

David Jr. and his youngest brother, Peach, giggled at the thought of more babies on the farm. Still giggling, they looked at their older brother Monroe for some kind of sign that it was all right to laugh out loud. Instead, they got the eye from Sambo that they were teetering on dangerous grounds. The stare down from their mother was just as threatening. "Finish eating your food boys," Sallie instructed, just to be sure they got the full message.

"Oh, I think she and John are going to be truly happy in that little house. Just yawl waits and sees. It's just perfect for them," Harriett added.

"Kinda remind us of our house in the beginning, huh honey?" Frank asked of Harriett. She nodded her head in agreement while flashing a reminiscent smile.

It was a lunch serving fit for an after church Sunday afternoon meal. The food was hot and tasty with the conversations inviting. Although it centered on the wishes and concerns of Gracie and John, it also served as a get acquainted affair for the in-laws. The entire scene was reminiscent of a homecoming for family members who had not seen each other in a while.

They spoke among themselves comfortably, each participant feeling free to voice their agreement or disapproval of any subject brought up. John thought the after wedding celebration should be held at the new Hole in the Bushes. He asked Colrolus if the additions were finished. It was, but cash concerns, along with his bride, in-laws, and parents convinced him that any cash expenditure not benefiting the little house or its surrounding grounds would be a waste of money.

They talked about the need to have a smokehouse, a few chickens, a couple of pigs, a new hunting rifle, tools for planting, their own mule for plowing, essentially items that would feed a family expecting to have a few kids.

"We will always be here to help you son, but you need to have your own stuff to get by with," Sambo warned.

So they collectively decided that the wedding will be a small affair with one of their pastors performing the ceremony. The question became which pastor. Will it be Rev A.J. Payne from Gravel Ridge First Baptist church or the Hampton's Methodist Pastor, Reverend Morris Davis? They picked the bride-to-be pastor, Reverend Payne, because the newlyweds may attend the Oaklawn Methodist church on a regular basis. Although that has not been officially decided either. Keeping in mind the churches are only about a block apart. Harriett agreed to approach Reverend Payne tomorrow as they are running out of time. She will also ask if they can have an after service picnic to celebrate the wedding. Morning service is 10:30 a.m.; its regular time. The idea would be to have the marriage ceremony directly afterwards on Sunday, May fourth. The wedding reception and picnic would follow at around 1:00. Both pastors could make the announcement at tomorrow morning service. That would give the time and place of the picnic to those who wanted to attend from Oaklawn Methodist.

By now the younger's had finished the main course and dessert and wanted to be excuse so they could go outside and play. Sallie gave them permission to do so after they cleaned off their table. Monroe stayed behind to listen to the conversations. David Jr. and Peach took off walking fast out the front door. Before they disappeared, Sambo yelled after them not to go too far away.

"If you don't limit their travels right off, those boys might end up by Papa Warner's store." Sallie explained to the Halls.

Most of the family and guest had finished eating. A couple, like Frank and Colrolus, was finishing off dessert and showering compliments on the cooks. Harriett, after asking if she could help, pretty much ignored Sallie's answer of no. She, Lena and Gracie, began to collect the dirty dishes, separating them from the garbage almost making it unnecessary for the hostess to do anything at the moment.

Monroe took out the garbage, separated it from the bones, which if large enough, would become the dogs. He walked back to the house to find the men lounging on the porch.

"Hey John, I did hear you say you hunt too?" asked Frank.

"Yes suh."

"That boy loves hunting and fishing. If you can't find John, he is probably doing one or the other," Sambo offered.

"Boy do I have a huntin' dog for you. He is part bloodhound and part this, part that, just a good breed of mutt. One of the kids named him 'Oh No'. You see, all my other dogs could turn flips, but each time Oh No tried he fell on his butt. Some of the kids would say "Oh no" and clap their hands while laughing. After a while and a few more attempts, he'd quit trying. Ain't nothin' wrong with his hunting instincts, that's why I say he's a great hunter. Just don't ask him to turn flips. He's really a she, but we've called him he so long, it stuck. We wanted to call him Tomboy too, but the Oh No stuck. What you think boy?"

"I'll take it. For Gracie, it will be as she has a piece of home with her."

There was a enjoyable round of laughter from all around, especially at the dog's name.

"He will get to meet Spider, John's dog. I can just see them dogs running after a coon or treeing an opossum right now. Huh John? Monroe added. "Wait til' we get them dogs out there."

"Oh yeah, Monroe's the pure shooter in the family. He likes to hunt too." John said.

"Yeah, all my boys learned to take care of themselves and the rest of the family from a young age. I go away from time to time to work at a couple of white folk's houses over in Lee County. Mr. John Smith and his wife, Pearl, they got a big place over in Oak Forrest. Man, they pay decent money so I can't turn them down. It's how I make our day to day living money. Of course we live off the farm 'round here," Sambo told Frank in an almost whisper.

"I know what you mean, man. I have to work for a white man too. He's a pretty nice old man. His farm's next to Papa Warner's land. A man has got to make those ends meet and see that his family is fed."

"Then you sho'' know what um talkin' bout. That's it. Got to do what you got to do to get along," Sambo answered.

With the men outside, this gave the women time to talk. Sallie offered additional info that was not brought up during lunch.

"Our cousin, Lum Davis is going with John on Wednesday to post the $100 marriage bond," She said. "I didn't want to say anything in front of the men, but are you nervous, honey?"

Gracie could not remember the last time she felt so happy about something that was going to happen to her. It was impossible for her to put into words the different emotions running through her mind. She heard herself repeat something that she'd said previously, she has never been so happy. She told the ladies, who were intently listening to her every word, that what she heard and saw today validated her decision to marry John. She was thrilled to become a Hampton and looked forward to joining such a loving and caring family. The little house was perfect, "Just perfect," she told them. The plans John and her future in-laws had for the house and grounds around it were perfect. She felt that she would have input on those plans. She would feel at home enough to inject a few of her own plans to make a more comfortable home for her, her husband-to-be, and children who would follow as a result of the marriage. And finally, she said for the umpteenth time, "I am so happy, I feel dizzy."

Harriett, Sallie, and Lena had to wipe tears from their cheeks while looking and listening to Gracie. They were familiar with her feelings and held fond memories of days leading up to and the day of their own marriage.

At the end of the day, all involved could say it was a day of accomplishments. The families met, discovered they were comfortable with each other, confirmed that the couple-to-be were getting a great helping hand sendoff to the beginning of their marriage.

The Hamptons waved goodbye to the Hall and Strong family, they were pleased with themselves for putting out such a delicious spread and most proud of the hospitality they displayed to their future family members. One could feel and see by the hugs they received before their guests climbed onto the wagons, along with the smiles on their faces that they were impressed. On the days preceding this gathering, Sallie and Sambo felt as long as they were themselves, everything else would work out.

"Honey, that girl is going to be a strong woman for John. She gon' let him be the man but that family is gonna be in good hands with the both of them," Sallie told Sambo as she took a seat in her rocking chair on the front porch. They watched Frank and Harriett Hall, with Colrolus and Lena Strong right behind them; maneuver their horse team down the hill toward the main road.

"Yep! I wasn't sure at first, but John here picked himself a good one from a good family. Then, I'd heard they were good people a long time ago," Her husband added.

"Mama, daddy, um gon' take John down by the Hole in the Bushes place to listen to some music and stuff. We'll be back before it gets too late, Okay?" Lemon said.

"You 'all be careful down there now, and behave yourself, you hear?" Sallie cautioned.

"Yes sum, we will," Lemon answered.

"Can I go?" Monroe asked.

"No! That ain't no place for a kid, especially on a Saturday night," Sambo said.

"Yeah, go find them other two rascals and yawl gets your clothes ready for Sunday school tomorrow," Sallie ordered.

The momentous day had finally arrived. The future bride and groom, their in-laws and families along with the rest of the congregation listened intently to the words of Reverend A.J. Payne. He opened his sermon with words of encouragement and advises all to keep their faith in Jesus Christ. He briefly addressed the concerns of those who were being harassed by law enforcement authorities. He dammed the men who hid their faces behind pillow cases with holes in which to see. "They wear bed sheets to complete their uniform while riding through the night. They are simply trying to frightening you and your family. They are still looking for one of our own who was ambushed by three white men. The young man managed to fight them off and now they call him a murderer. We pray to God to keep the young man safe along with those in our community. Oh lord, keep our people out of harm's way, disregarding the wishes of an old man's revenge."

With the opening statements and acknowledgements out of the way, he announced, for those who did not know, the marriage of John Hampton and Gracie Hall would take place today with the festivities to follow. He spoke briefly about what a joyous and happy occasion marriage between to people in love can be. He went on by instructing the congregation to turn to Genesis 2:22-24.

He began reading by saying "Then the Lord God made a woman from the rib he had taken out of the man, and he brought her to the man." He asked the congregation to read aloud with him the next line.

"The man said, 'this is now bone of my bones and flesh of my flesh, she shall be called woman, for she was taken out of man."

Reverend Payne held his hand in a stop motion to the congregation and finished the passage, "For this reason a man will leave his father and mother and be united to his wife, and they will become one flesh."

He went on to expound on what this type of union means to those getting married, included their families. Finally, what this union means to the community in which they live and how it is the lords wish that they procreate. By raising their children as children of Christ, our savior will shower the family with the blessing of Jesus Christ.

He wrapped up his Sunday sermon by reading from Hebrews 13:4-7 that also was meant to serve the expectant bride and groom well. Reverend Payne said," Marriage should be honored by all, and the marriage bed kept pure, for God will judge the adulterer and all the sexually immoral. Keep your lives free from the love of money and be content with what you have, because God has said, 'never will I leave you; never will I forsake you.' So we say with confidence,"

Reverend Payne asked the congregation to read the next line by themselves, "The Lord is my helper. I will not be afraid. What can man do to me?" They complied almost in unison.

He read the remaining verse. "Remember your leaders, who spoke the word of God to you. Consider the outcome of their way of life and imitate their faith."

He ended by asking everyone to bow their heads and hold their neighbors hand while he said a simple closing prayer. "Oh Lord, bless those in attendance and those who wanted to be here but could not. Keep our little community and peoples safe in your arms throughout the next week. We shall all meet in our house of worship next Sunday to worship and seek your guidance. In the name of the almighty Jesus Christ, we pray . . . and everybody say, Amen."

"Amen," the church members said at the pastor's direction.

He announced a short recess. That would allow those from the Hampton family church to come from Oaklawn Methodist to Gravel Ridge Baptist to join in on the wedding ceremony.

One may wonder if the twenty-first century elaborate or traditional white gown, with all of its anointed accouterments, was worn by the bride. Or were the numerous bridesmaids, best man, and alternate, along with other representatives of the groom present? Then there are other celebratory and staged moments that we have become acquainted with in a modern wedding. Like the cute dressed children scattering about flower petals as they stroll down the aisle in front of the bride and the man who gives her away, large fountains, spewing colored water, champagne or whatever exotic beverage selected by the participants. There was no thought or talk of putting on a show at this wedding. Back in this day, the fact that two people were getting married and no slave master could separate them was enough for all.

Frank Hall escorted Gracie to her place in front of the preacher as Mrs. Payne, the pastor's wife, played "Here comes the bride" song on the church's small piano. The bride and groom wore their normal Sunday church attire with John in a black suit, white shirt and bow tie. Gracie wore a silk looking white long sleeve blouse that hung loosely below her waistline. The blouse hung perfectly over a black loose fitting skirt that cut off a few inches above her ankles. Viola Hall, sitting next to her daughter and husband looked on at her dressmaking handiwork with pride. The silk like material in the blouse was a special fabric she had found in the Sears Roebuck Catalog. Although wearing a normal horseshoe like barrette head band, the bride did not have a veil attached so one could see her smiling proudly at John. The best man was John's older brother, Lemon Davis. He sat in the front pew while holding the modest ring, a band without any stones until he was summoned. The family, friends and guest occupied the remaining pews.

Having expounded on the preliminaries in his sermon, Reverend Payne reminded all why they were gathered here today. He kept it simple as Baptist do, by asking, "Will you John Hampton, have Gracie Hall to be your wife? Will you love her, comfort and keep her, and forsaking all others, remain true to her as long as you both shall live?"

"I do," replied an obviously nervous John.

The reverend turned to Gracie and asked, "Will you Gracie Hall, take thee John Hampton to be your husband, and before God and these witnesses promise to be a faithful and true wife. Will you promise to love, honor and obey him for the rest of your life?"

"I do," Gracie answered.

The reverend asked for the ring which Lemon brought to John. He asked John to repeat after him while placing the ring on his future wife's finger. "With this ring I thee wed, and all my worldly goods I thee endow. In sickness, and in health, in poverty, or in wealth, 'til death do us part."

John repeated the words as instructed and placed the band on Gracie's finger. "I now pronounce you man and wife. You may kiss your bride." The reverend stated. After a brief kiss and hug, the happy couple stood waiting for more instruction from Reverend Payne. Not missing a beat, he asked them both to turn around. "Church, meet Mr. and Mrs. Hampton."

The couple started to walk toward the door but was surrounded by tearful eyed parents and friends. Men were patting John on the back. Both sexes were shaking their hands, men asking to kiss the bride. It was a display of love for all concern for a few minutes. That is until a church usher swung open the church doors and yelled over the chattering crowd, "Please, please everyone. Let's go outside to the picnic tables and continue wishing the couple happiness throughout all their days." The bride, groom, guest, and friends slowly made their way toward the door while continuing to accept well wishes.

Once the newlyweds reached the outside of the building, they were guided to a festive table reserved for them. People with congratulatory wishes quickly surrounded their table. Those in charge, Gravel Ridges Baptist Church ushers, directed the wedding couple's parents, siblings and special guest to a seat along each side of the couple or a table next to them. The remaining guest was asked to take seats at any of the other tables.

The action of the ushers was not happenstance. In their quest to ensure the happy couple receives their congratulations some people ignored the signs dictating where they should sit. The seating directions provided by the church's ushers enabled the celebration to be more orderly.

The food was served right after seating everybody. There was a time after the meal to present the couple with any gift, card or wish them well once more. That lasted for approximately another hour. Most people began to leave right after that, leaving a small core of family and close friends of the bride and groom. Some of which helped to load gifts and food baskets onto the couples wagon.

Finally, the newlyweds climbed aboard their wagon to leave the church area. They noticed the wagon was almost overloaded with gifts, food, and just about everything needed for a small house. Frank Hall pulled up beside them, yelled out to John, "Aren't you forgetting something son?

He didn't wait for John to guess. Edgar untied "Oh No", the Hall's dog that could not turn flips. He walked him over to the Hampton wagon; put him in the foot well between John and Gracie. For his part, Oh No took a sniff of Gracie, looked up as if to say, yeah I know you, started wagging her tail and barking. Gracie had to settle the dog down before they could drive off. She bent down and gave her father a tearful thank you and goodbye peck on his forehead. She waved to her mother and Viola with Edgar and Mae Ellen sitting in their wagon. She blew a kiss to her little friend, who had tears streaming down her face. Viola attempted to console her daughter but the little girl was hurt at the thought of not seeing Gracie every day.

Sambo and Sallie Hampton, with their sons, pulled their wagon onto the road heading for home. The newlyweds guided their wagon onto the road directly behind John's parents. "It has been a long but wonderfully blessed day, dear," Gracie said while gently placing her hand on her husbands.

John, guiding and holding on to his wagon teams reins, managed to hold Gracie's left hand too. He affirmatively nodded his head to agree with Gracie. He looked at her and smiled. She understood the expression on his face. Both realized they were now a married couple. They barely could wait until they were alone to begin enjoying the fruits of marriage.

CHAPTER 5

The Honeymoon & Shots Fired on the Road to Banks

Gracie climbed down from the wagon, never taking her eyes off the little house that was now their home. It was the home of the Hampton's, John and Gracie, her husband and her or was it her husband and I, she thought.

John climbed down and playfully asked, "Missy, is this the home of Mrs. Gracie Hampton?"

"Why it sho' is," she answered.

"Would you tell her we have a big delivery out here for her?"

"Why sho' I will, suh."

This little exchange had been amusedly observed by John's brother, Lemon. He only could take so much humor, because his feet were hurting from helping to load the wagon at the church. Now anticipating the unloading, he was anxious to get on with his afternoon Sunday rest. It was the one day; he could take it easy for a few hours.

"Come on chillen," He said. "The quicker we get this stuff unloaded, the faster I get outta here and take this wagon back down to the little house."

Gracie reached up and grabbed a folded quilt that was tied together by a string from the wagon, ran up to, opened, and through the door of the little house. She laid it on the bed and ran back out of the house to help with the other items.

She saw Lemon handing down a box of small pots, pans, and assorted kitchenware to John. She grabbed the box from his hands, stating that it was light enough for her to carry and again disappeared through the front door. On her way back out the door, she propped a stool against the door to hold it open. The door, too heavy for the stool, pushed the stool along the porch flooring. John, noticing this, pushed the door, and stood back against the wall, placed the two twenty-five bags of sugar he was carrying on the stool.

"That did it," he said, turning and almost running into Gracie carrying a box of cooked and prepared food through the open door into the kitchen. He ran back to the wagon to get something else to carry.

This went on until the only things left were a couple of heavier items like the rocking chair given by someone. It was old but in great shape. Whoever gave it to them had put a fresh coat of varnish on the wooden areas and provided nice comfortable pillows.

By now Lemon was laughing so hard at Gracie and John practically running back and forth from the house he woke up Oh No. The dog had been asleep in the foot well of the wagon all the time until he heard all of the commotion. The three of them stopped unloading to watch Johns dog, Spider run from the big house to see what dog had the nerve to be barking at his house.

Spider ran up to the side of the wagon which Oh No was barking and went crazy at the sight of the dog. With both dogs barking at each other, Lemon grabbed Oh No, who was wiggling and still barking, climbed down off the wagon and sat him down on the ground next to Spider. Both dogs stopped barking, sniffed each other and sort of stepped back as if to get a command from the humans. Spider looked at John, at Oh No and back to John like he was waiting for instructions.

"Now, be nice. This is you new brother." Spider rolled his eyes, let out a small bark, sniffed the new dog while being sniffed and led Oh No to somewhere around the back of the house.

"Them dogs is just getting to know each other," John continued, with all three people laughing at the entire dog scene.

The trio finished unloading the wagon and had carried everything inside that belonged inside, including the rocking chair. The couple waved goodbye to a smiling Lemon who drove the team back over to the big house barn.

John and Gracie turned to each other and smiled, realizing they were alone. They thought for a moment and called out each dog's name. There was no sound, bark or otherwise from around the back of the house. Nor did the animals re-appear.

"Oh hell, they'll be alright. Spider is showing Oh No the ropes out here." John told his bride.

She nodded her head in agreement. "They getting to know each other all right. You know that Oh No is actually a she dog?"

"I thought he . . . , why do they always call him a he?

"'Cause she acts like a boy dog. We wanted to name her Tomboy, but . . . oh never mind. Just so you know she is a female animal."

"Oh well, Spider will like it."

The both of them clasps hands and walked through the door. This time, they closed it behind them. It was still May 4, 1924 on a Sunday evening around four o'clock in the afternoon. Yes, they had gotten married earlier that day. They had a kitchen table full of cooked food. There was only one celebration left. After all, they are on their honeymoon.

There was no need for words. Human nature has its own way of guiding two inexperienced lovers in the ways of lovemaking. They both sat down on the same side of the bed.

It was a normal size country bed made for two. A wooden frame and legs with a nice, thick mattress filled with cotton and dried grass. This combination is used by the locals in pillows too, which gave it the proper firmness for sleeping and whatever else one might want to do on a mattress. The bedroom of the little two and a half room house was small but just cozy enough for young people. The far side of the bed was pushed up against the back wall with the head flush against the front wall of the bedroom.

"Are you hungry dear?"

"No, are you?"

"No," she answered in a low whisper. "I think I'll lay down a minute. Um tired and just wanna rest a while"

"Yeah, me too."

She began to take off her clothes and gently lay them on a chair beside the bed. John watched as she removed all of her outer garments leaving her wearing only a slip and underclothes. She motioned for John to stand up so that she could turn the covers down in order to get in the bed. He did while looking at her fully curvy body and big pretty legs. She pulled the covers over her womanly frame and laid her head back on the far side of the bed pillow. She turned her head toward John and asked if he was coming to bed too.

"Yeah," He replied.

He didn't want to seem nervous, but it was a tall order for him not to be awkward. After all, he had never been with a woman in this manner. One could count the times he'd kissed his wife on one hand. That would also include the kiss after the marriage vows today. Nevertheless, this was a time when a man had to step up and be a man because that is what a wife expected of her man, he thought.

The sight of him undressing was probably not as sexy for Gracie as the picture of her undressing was for him. It really didn't matter because once he finally got into bed; they lay next to each other, legs and arms touching causing their sexual temperatures to rise ever more. He turned on his side and placed his hand on her stomach. He felt the quivering motion of her stomach. She turned her head towards him, and he kissed her with a passion that was unfamiliar to him. His instincts began to take over as his left hand raised her slip so that he could have access to her naked body. He was not aware when she took her panties off, but there was no feel of panties on his bride.

After the foreplay, they made sweet love to consummate their marriage. Gracie, being the virgin that she was had to reassure John that he was not hurting her. Their initial try at love making was warm, loving and pleasing. It was also experimental because it was their first time. Feeling as though they now had raw experience, the second time was a lot more passionate. Spent and realizing that this part of the marriage was all that they had heard and more, they rested and talked for little over an hour. Fully rested, both of them confident in their personal knowledge of lovemaking, they started kissing again. Both felt ecstatic while feeling each other's body. Each enjoyed the reaction of their mate's body to the touch of their hand. It didn't take long before they were fully embraced in another round of making love. Only this time, it was more passionate than the last with the ending resulting in a release of raw passion and sounds that almost scared them both. They were so spent this time, they could hardly move. Finally, John rolled over on his back with Gracie once again curled up in his arms.

"That was special. I didn't know it could be so . . . good," She whispered into while kissed her husband's ear.

"Yeah, me too," He answered causing Gracie to giggle.

A few minutes later and awful hungry by now, Gracie got out of bed and fixed them both a midnight snack from the food given them at their picnic reception. All the nervousness between them was gone as evidenced by their laughter and conversation. It was as though they were made to be together, validating that fact by making love.

Their bodies filled with food, with a glow of happiness between themselves, they lay back down in the bed. Once again she curled up close and in his arms as he lay on his back. Only this time the outcome was different. The both of them were asleep inside of ten minutes.

They slept soundly and too long. John kept hearing a pounding on wood. He was thoroughly annoyed because he felt they would scare the rabbit he was trying to bag for supper. Quiet, he heard himself say. The pounding persisted and got louder. Suddenly, he realized it was someone at his front door.

"Hey Bro, don't make me come in there. Wake up and get your butt out here. It's going on eight o'clock in the morning. John! Get out here, now!" Lemon screamed.

"Alright, hold on, um coming," John yelled back. He looked over at Gracie who was still sleeping.

"Oh baby, I don't know how you can sleep through all this noise." He said aloud.

He pulled the bolt back on the front door, opened it to see Lemon standing there, shaking his head in frustration. Their little brothers, twelve year old David, and ten year old Peach were standing beside Lemon looking confused and exhausted.

Somewhat short of breath himself, Lemon began to scold his sleepy eye brother, "I hope this marriage thing not goin' to your head. How come you didn't open the door when these boys were knocking on it like crazy? They ran back and got me. Hell, I thought something was wrong over here. John, we got stuff to do this morning. Come on down to the big house barn. Daddy wants to talk to you about something. Tell Gracie, mama want to talk to her this morning too. You hear boy?"

"Dad-gummit Lemon, I hear you."

With that, the older brother and the little ones turned and ran back toward the big house.

John closed the door, turned around to see that his wife had waked up during that conversation. He didn't have to ask because she nodded her head as if to say, I heard and here I come. They took a quick wash up, got dressed and headed toward the big house which was only about a long city block away.

They slowly walked along, holding hands while talking about what a nice sunny morning it was and making love last night. Gracie remarked what a blessed sight the new crops in the fields were as they were responding to the water and care they were given by the family. She also told John what a lovely time she had last night. She felt things she had never felt before. And asked if John knew she truly loved him? John said he did and went on to tell her that he didn't realize how happy he could feel after marrying her and, of course making love last night. The conversation sort of went on like that until they reached the big house. Gracie told John she would see him soon, very soon, she stressed and disappeared inside the big house door.

Sambo was cleaning out the horse stalls when John walked through the barn doorway, calling for his father.

"Morning Daddy, you wanted to see me?"

His father placed the pitch fork on a hook, and motioned for his son to follow him. They saw David and Peach heading into the barn. The boys stopped in their tracks at the sight of their father.

"That's right boys; I started your chores for you. Yawl can go on and finish cleaning out the stalls and feed the animals. Yawls watch how you walk round them horses, hear? If you ain't careful, one of them might just kick the snots outta you."

"Okay daddy." They both answered continuing to the stalls.

The two men walked over to the other side of grounds where the groundwater pump stood, just on the other side of the farm's well. Sambo pumped fresh well drinkable water into a bucket. He and rubbed them with a piece of homemade soap on a rope. Then he rinsed, and wiped them dry with a rag he placed back on a bench next to the pump.

"Yeah boy, me and your mama, mostly your mama, 'cause the land came from her father, Oliver Davis, want to give you and Gracie some land. It's a pretty good piece that runs from the little house to beyond the stream in the back, bordered by the main road and runs clear back over to the tree line on the other side of the big house.

"Daddy, I thought that was for Lemon."

"He knows about this. He, like you, knew that we were saving the little house for whoever got married first. There is a good portion of land left to give all you boys. Your share is about forty acres. Tomorrow, your mama and me are going into town to have it registered in your name. Boy, we think you picked a special young lady. Work the land and it will feed you, yo' wife and our future grandchildren well."

They headed toward the big house to share the news with the women. There was no way to express how John Hampton felt after the marriage, picnic, last night, and now this. It was like God gave him all he needed in life at one time within the last two days. Walking along with his dad made him proud to be a son, husband, and man of means, especially after his parent's gift. It also made him realize this gift came with a lot more responsibility.

After their trip to town, where they completed the paperwork required for the land transfer, they all stopped at Papa Warner's. As usual, he was sitting on the porch in his rocking chair throne. Gracie, who went to Banks with John, Sambo, and his wife walked into the store. Sallie joined her while she was looking around.

The men spoke with Papa Warner. Specifically, they were looking for someone who could use a water witch, a diviner. Anyone who was familiar with the tools needed to locate a spot to dig a well by the little house. That was the method used to locate the well on Sambo's farm.

He didn't remember the fellow's name. He knew the guy was successful finding water. Utilizing the "water dowsing" method, he found the perfect spot to dig a well on many of the African-American farms and a couple of white farms a few years ago.

Papa Warner told them the man spent most of his time wandering through the southern states helping farmers and others find water. He warned that the man was not as successful lately as he was in the past. No one knew why, except it's just not a 100 percent accurate science.

As they continued talking, it dawned on them that the entire Hampton farm area was ripe with groundwater from rock, springs, ponds and the growth of plants and crops. That was probably how the guy was able to be so successful in this area.

"We got swamps and lakes all over this county. Shoot, there are lakes, waterways, tons of springs in neighboring counties too," Papa Warner said.

"Maybe we ought to try and find the water ourselves daddy. If we could get one of those willow tree forked sticks, I heard some people have found places next to their main well to put in a water pump. Come to find out they tapped into a new groundwater source that way," John offered.

"Well, I don't know. I heard some of them missed the waterline or it tapped out too," Sambo said.

"Look, you can wait for this guy to show up, whenever that will be. Or take a chance and try to locate the water yourself. Or you can go to a Hydrologist up in Warren. I betcha they'll find you water. If you got the money to pay 'em, they will find it."

"We ain't got no money, and we can't wait until God knows when," An annoyed Sambo stated.

"All right, I tell you what I'll do. We got one of those wire rods for finding water. We got the thing from the farmer's edition of a Sears and Roebuck catalog. Or maybe it was another farm catalog? Anyway, we got one and have found water with the thing. How 'bout I send my son, Joel, up there to help you find a digging spot? If you find water, you can pay for my son's services. If you don't find any water, you don't owe me nothing."

"I know Joel, daddy. We can work that out," John volunteered.

"How much is this going to cost in the end?"

"Dammit Sambo, I told you, nothing if you don't find water where he points you to dig. It will be one dollar or so if you find the water. I'll just put it on your tab. Keep in mind; Joel is not going to help you dig the well."

The two men shook hands to consummate the deal. Papa Warner called Joel over and he agreed to stop by in a couple of days. After which the Hamptons collected their wives and left returning to the farm.

Joel Warner stopped by the next day. He walked the ground in the general area John indicated he wanted the well. Lo and behold the rods crossed at a certain spot. To ensure, there were no false readings, he walked around once more, this time approaching the spot from different angles with the same result. Satisfied, John, and Sambo marked the spot and declared that was where they would dig.

A couple of months had passed and as expected August brought on the hot and humid days. The nights were not that much cooler. Yet the fact that the sun had gone down brought relief to man and animals alike.

The not so newlyweds got a surprise a few days ago. Gracie could not remember if it was her father or brother that kept telling the family that Oh No was a male. It really didn't matter now because the joke was on her husband.

All those times she tried to turn flips, ending up on her back. You would have thought someone would have noticed the small row of nipples on each side of the pups' belly, or the fact the dog didn't have a penis, but that didn't happen. Since she stopped trying to turn flips while growing older, no one actually paid attention to her sexual orientation, kept calling her a he, until a few weeks after Gracie and Johns wedding.

John needed to take a break from well digging. He and his brother, Monroe went fishing down by the spring behind the house. They were playing with Spider and Oh No on the way back. Oh No rolled over on her back for a moment exposing her nipples. Now they were quite visible within all that hair.

They walked the dogs down to the big house and showed the females nipples to Lemon who immediately stated Oh No might be pregnant. "I thought he, or she . . . , was a he? I just thought because yawl called her, him . . . I don't know what I thought now. One thing is for sure now; I think this dog is pregnant."

"Pregnant," John shouted looking at Spider who seemed fully aware of what was being discussed. Spider lay down on all fours putting one of his paws over his nose as if to hide his face, occasionally looking up at John with eyes that said, "I'm sorry?"

That brought about a long round of robust laughter from all three men. They started making all kind of jokes about just when did Oh No turn into a girl dog. Evidently Spider thought this discovery was not going to be a problem for him, even though he was the expectant father. He got up, started barking, and licking John's hand. John stopped laughing a minute and told his dog, "Um not the one. Wait 'til Gracie hears about this."

It was getting late in the evening and almost dark that day. Monroe took a spot by the barn and began to clean his catfish catch. John and the two dogs walked back up to the little house. He waved at Gracie, held up his catch of catfish and walked over to the shed to begin cleaning them.

Oh No, seemingly fatigued by the entire ordeal laid down in her favorite spot in the back of the shed and went to sleep. For his part, Spider, sitting on his hind legs was intently listening to John as he rambled on about how the pregnancy occurred.

"So that's what happened on our wedding night. You and your little girlfriend here ran off. Nobody saw you two for a couple of days. Shame on you, yawl had just met. Well, I can't say that I blame you much. But um telling you, how I feel and how Gracie feels might be another thing."

With that, Spider got down on all fours again and put one paw over his nose in his "I'm sorry" pose. John laughed, got up, and headed for the house carrying the cleaned fish in a bucket of water, fish guts wrapped in paper while giving Spider one last bit of advice.

"You better make yourself scarce for tonight."

Spider barked as if to say okay. He then went around back of the shed where the expectant mother of his pups was sleeping.

Over the next few weeks, Oh No nipples got bigger, and more noticeable as the hair around them began to shed. She went through the loss of appetite, weight gain, restlessness and finally irritability. It got to point she no longer wanted Spider around her. For John and Gracie, her pregnancy period was a sight to see, clear up until she had the litter some sixty-nine days later. Oh No produce five healthy mutt pups without anybody's assistance. Two was solid black with a streak between their shoulders at the base of their necks. They were the same color as Spider, including the birthmark. The other three was a dusty light brown just like On No. One was found dead which John buried. Looks like four males and one female.

So after almost three weeks, mother and pups are doing great. Spider is running around as if he wants to start another litter. Oh No is having none of that, so things have not quite returned to normal at the Hamptons. To top that, there is one other bit of relevant news that is about to be discovered by Gracie.

She was telling Sallie that they could have a couple of those pups if they wanted them. She planned on giving another two to her sister, Lena, and would be willing to part with one more if anybody wanted it.

The women were sitting on the porch of the big house sewing patches together to make a quilt. It should be ready just in time for the coming winter. For now, they were enjoying the slight breeze brought about with the disappearance of the sun over the horizon for the night.

The men, along with the younger boys were all taking part in digging the little house's well. They knew the fellows would if they haven't already, knock off for the day. No one wants to go down in that hole after dark. As of this morning, they were pretty close to hitting groundwater.

Gracie, who had not been feeling so well as late, brought this to Sallie's attention.

"I don't know what's the matter with me. My stomach feels funny most of time now-a-days, especially in the morning."

"Have you been throwing up?

"Yes sum."

"Ain't nothing wrong with you that won't be taken care of in about nine months."

"Yeah, but, it's gettin' on my nerves, I don't have time . . . Did you say nine months?

"Yep!"

"You think um pregnant?"

"Could be."

"Pregnant, you say?"

"Yes, it sounds like you're pregnant to me. You can go see Doctor Morgan Purvis in Banks. Or better yet, talk to my cousin, Bessie Davis. She is one of the mid-wives for these parts and most likely will deliver the baby when it's born."

Gracie stood up; put her part of the quilt in a bag with the other scraps of material, immediately excused herself, ran down the porch steps and hollered back at Sallie, "Goodnight, I'll be back tomorrow. I got to see John."

"Girl, you better be careful with that running. You might fall and hurt something."

"I will. See you in the morning."

She ran past Sambo, Lemon, and the boys on her way to meet John at the little house.

"Girl, what you running for?" Sambo hollered after her while looking around to see if someone or something's chasing her.

Running up that slight incline caused her to slow down while trying to catch her breath. Just because she had slowed down did not contain her excitement. She finally got to the doorway of the little house and stopped. She gathered herself, paused to slow her heart rate down, and catch up to herself.

147

Doing all the commotion, and especially seeing somebody running up to the door, Spider started barking and running towards her. She yelled for him to go away. He recognizes her voice and stopped barking but stood his ground until she got to the front door.

John opened the door and saw his wife standing there trying to compose herself. She blurted out before he asked what was wrong, "Um pregnant."

He hugged and kissed her at the news and then asked, "How do you know?"

"Your mother told me. I got all the symptoms. Um pregnant dear."

"Is it a boy or girl Can you tell?"

"No, silly willie, I just know we are going to have a baby."

After all the excitement subsided, Gracie warmed up leftovers from the day before. They ate and went to bed. It was confirmed the next morning with Gracie waking up, once again with morning sickness.

She heard the door slam as John went out. Gracie was still lying down trying to settle her stomach. She decided to at least get out of bed. She sat at the kitchen table to drink a cup a herb tea or something. Yesterday evening, in her excitement, she forgot to ask Mama Sallie the best remedy for morning sickness. "That woman has had five boys, and looks strong enough to have five more kids, so she should know something," Gracie thought. She got up and looked out the window down by the digging area. "Yep, seems like the gangs all here for another day of well digging. I'll be glad when they finish. Toting water from the stream or the big house is getting old. Even though, once a day, they put water in a couple of big barrels and drop them off, Lord knows we use a lot of water every day." With John working on the well, she was once again alone with her thoughts.

Sambo began to wonder if this was the right spot for digging the well. He knew that Papa Warner was a hard bargainer, but he was also a man of his word. He wouldn't put us through this

148

for nothing, he thought to himself. Still, it was taking a long time to reach water.

They started digging a hole. It had to be wide enough for two men to work at the same time. They used pick forks, shovels and a man-made hoist that lowers a bucket to haul up dirt.

They had already dug about sixty feet down looking for what book-learned folks call the "water table". That is where groundwater is found seeping between our earth's rocks. Its part of the precipitation that trickles down through the soil until it reaches those rocks. The water is stored between the spaces of the rocks. Then it gradually moves underground, normally downward and eventually trickling out of an opening in the ground, say like on a hillside. Flowing from an opening that works like a man made pipe protruding out from the hillside, with water dropping or flowing to the next flatland surface. It starts like a drip but over time, maybe even years, nature takes its course and the opening can turn into something as large as a waterfall. The water continually flows downward to eventually find a temporary resting in a stream, lake or even an ocean. This is not unlike the source of the stream, although not even remotely resembling a waterfall, that's located a couple hundred feet behind the Johns little house.

The Hampton's are taking shifts digging the well. There are still other matters that must be tended to on the farm. Today, John and Monroe are the diggers with Sambo working the hoist.

Around one in the afternoon, they hollered up to Sambo that they are finding moisture around the bottom which is a positive sign. They probably have dug another two and a half feet deep to the wells bottom. The moisture sighting was the best news they've had so far. They have to continue to dig until the water raises high enough to threaten the safety of the diggers. They will still have to line the wall of the well with bricks and a concrete curve to prevent the collapse of the walls. But that comes later, for now, it's more digging.

The next day, they finally reached a level of water that was flowing into the hole fast enough, whereas they could consider the well deep enough to start reinforcing the walls. They were approximately seventy-five feet below the ground. In the end, they didn't have time to erect another hoist; they just lowered another bucket down by hand to double the removal of what was clay, now turning to mud. By that afternoon, they had started lining the well. Tomorrow, they will finish the real work of lining the well. The guesswork is over, Gracie and John will now have a well on their property.

It is September of 1924, the year in which the Bradley County Chamber of Commerce was founded. Today, the entity website boasts, among other things, of promoting community economic development, increasing the level of prosperity and an enhanced quality of life for all the citizens of Bradley County. One can't help wondering did that apply to anyone and was it practiced in the county. There are signs that say it didn't, not for all the people in the county.

Yet, there were accomplishments by African-American business that served other black folk. An example in this story is the Hole in the Bushes. The proprietors, Henry Strong, Jr. and his wife Carrie had managed to turn what started out as bar-b-que, fried fish stand in the woods into a business that offered a restaurant style eatery and a well-managed social place that housed entertainment for its guest.

On a whim, knowing that Versia and her husband, James worked in a first class hotel in Hot Springs, they wrote them a letter. Besides the regular update, they invited them to stop by and see the addition and improvements, on their next trip to visit their parents. The Strong's, who knew their place was not as upscale as a hotel, wanted to assure themselves that their business was not labeled as another juke joint. Carrie told Henry the happy news the other day after receiving a reply from Versia. The Boswells would be in this area on the first weekend in September. She asked her not to tell her mother and father because they wanted this to be a surprise visit. They promised to arrive about midmorning this Saturday. The only other people who knew of their trip were her sisters, Gracie and Lena.

Lena and Gracie had not seen the improvements themselves or had time to talk in the last few weeks. They had a lot of news to catch up on agreed to meet at the Hole in the Bushes themselves. Colrolus had brought a truck. Of course, Gracie was pregnant, Oh No had a litter of pups, and there was all kind of news to pass on between them. After which, the sisters would let Versia and her husband visit Frank and Harriett Hall by themselves, which would allow for a more personal visit with her parents.

Colrolus and Lena arrived first in their new 1921 dark blue refurbished Model TL truck. The "Tin Lizzie" was impressive even though it was three years old. He bought it a few weeks ago from a white guy (Fred Downy) in Warren, Arkansas, the county seat.

The little city of Warren was filling up with Fords. The automaker had sixty percent of the new car sales in 1921 while its competitor; Chevrolet was only able to sell one car to every thirteen Fords sold. With a sale price at $370 each, Fords goal was to have everybody own a car. Fred Downy was taking in all the old Ford Model T's he could find. He repaired whatever needed repairing and resold them as used vehicles. Mr. Downy realized that in this year of 1924, Fords competitors were following the same principle as Ford; an assembly line producing a large quantity of cheap and reliable vehicles. Used cars, at an even cheaper price, was a growing business market that brought about even quicker sales.

Henry, Carrie, Lena and Colrolus sat in the patio restaurant part of their place. They could see the truck from their table. Colrolus who had done his homework on Fords told Henry that eventually he, too, was going to need a truck for his business. They all knew how slow a horse drawn wagon could be. The Model T, with its four-cylinder motor, or twenty horsepower engine, if you will, can reach a top speed of forty-five miles per hour.

"Why Ford all by themselves have put out a lot of different models. There's the landaulet, town car, runabout, coupe, and touring car. I think there's some new one's I forgot. But this is the way to get around now-a-days," Colrolus explain.

"Does your truck have a crank?" asked Henry

"Heck naw boy. I picked this one because it has a starter. They said a body can almost break their arm trying to start a Tin Lizzie using a crank."

"It's a bumpy ride over these back roads but fun and fast." Lena added.

"Yeah, I have to be careful with it 'round my horses cause it scares the mess out of them. But this guy Fred is the man you want to see. He got a pretty large lot with different kinds on it. Papa Warner bought one a week before me. He was the one who told me about Mr. Downy. If um not mistaking I think that's where Clem Parker got his car."

"I know one thing. It sure would help our business 'cause people could ride down here over the new part of the road smoothed out just to get to our place. Maybe people want be so scared the "The Thing" is going to jump out and get them on the way home late at night." Henry stated.

"The Thing", "Ha! "People don't know if that's real or not. Could just be an old wives tale, as they say. Nobody ain't never seen it. It just makes noise in the woods and scares the bejesus out of people," Carrie said with a disgusted expression. "Talking about a nice car, here come Versia and James now."

The Boswell's still had their 1923 Ford Tourer which James drove over the wooden bridge and parked their car next to Colrolus truck. They got out and were immediately struck by the new additions to the old eatery. The entire grounds area now looked like a resort hideaway neatly tucked in and surrounded by woods. Workers had cut down a lot of trees around the old place. The wooded lines were far enough away from the structure to ward off any of the native bears, wolves or coyotes looking for food. For added protection from wildlife, they set animal traps in varied patterns to capture unwanted guest. Precautions and security was tight because this facility also served as the owner's home and a few staff members living quarters. Versia noticed the armed security with dogs, approaching road improvements as they neared the wooden bridge. The enclosed patio restaurant section was a neat touch. And that was just the outside changes.

Henry and Carrie smiled while noticing Versia and James facial expression as they got out of their automobile.

"Ooooo-we girl, you and Henry have been busy. Look at this place James," Versia remarked as she and her husband walked through the gate leading to the patio area.

The couples greeted and hugged each other with almost everybody talking at one time. All Versia could say was "wheew!" as she surveyed the tables and seating areas within the patio. She had a reference in her mind as she'd envisioned the place before the improvements were made. Her husband had no such reference. Even though this was his first time, one could tell he was impressed.

"We were going to wait until Gracie and John got here, but we might as well show you the other changes. Come on yawl, follow me," Henry J said.

Henry and Carrie began the full tour for their guest. There were add-ons that even Colrolus had not seen. The kitchen area had been enlarged with another grill like stove, and one more cooking and baking stove added to the two that were already there. A new medium sized plus two small sized windows were added for ventilation purposes. The planting of local shrubbery around the structure, accents to the halls, they added outhouses leading from the patio area. The other significant change, besides the enclosed patio, was the entertainment room. There was the tabled seating area, shaped in a horseshoe fashion around what was obviously a dance area. At the head of the room was a small stage that looked like it could hold a band with instruments of about six people.

After seeing all the changes and estimating the Strong's financial limitations, Versia asked if they had struck it rich or something. Henry J intimated he had help from his father and Papa Warner. One of the new stoves was donating by the Gravel Ridge community, who longed for a venue where they could be entertained. A lot of people volunteered their time and services in order to see a dream come true. Even with the investment of Henry Strong and Papa Warner Johnson all the services and other progress could not have happened without involving the community.

"We are blessed to be part of such a supportive group of people in this community," Carrie added. "So what do you really think? Do you see anything out of place or around that we have left out or need something else to make this a better place for our guest?"

"Naw baby, this place would stand up to any place I've ever seen. It's clean and proper from my view. How about you honey?"

"Well," James Boswell began, "Indoor city plumbing would top it off. Since that is not possible around here, you've made the best possible alternatives. I see you are using generators for some of the lighting. Like I say, you have worked miracles, given the location of your restaurant," He concluded directing his critique to Henry and Carrie.

"Coming from the maid and assistant cook at the famous Arlington Hotel in our famous Hot Springs, um glad you like it. We put a lot of thought into how we wanted to represent ourselves." Henry J said.

"Really Henry J, I can see some white folk that would be jealous of what you managed to make out of this place," James added.

"Let's all go back out to the patio. It's a little after twelve, your sister and new brother-in-law should be here any minute now," Carrie advised.

By the time they got back to their table, they saw John and Gracie Hampton coming through the gate. They came the old fashion way via a horse drawn wagon. In their excitement of seeing each other, Versia and Lena ran toward Gracie with her arms held wide for acceptance. They met in the center of the patio floor, hugged, kissed each other, and squealed like teenagers.

"Look at Mrs. Hampton," Versia said in a teasing manner. "And let's not forget Mrs. Strong."

"And you are?" Gracie and Lena said in unison.

"Why, I'm just little old Mrs. Boswell," Versia replied. "Wait a minute, hold your horses. Gracie . . . , is that a tummy bump or did you swallow a small cantaloupe this morning?"

"Yes it is . . . , and I'll tell Mama and Daddy. Don't you say a thing, you hear?"

"Didn't you know this when I seen you at church Sunday before last? Why did you say something then?"

"I wanted to be sure. And it is still early so just hold on a minute. I am so happy to see my big sister from Hot Springs and my little sister from no springs," Gracie teased. "Oh yeah, Oh No is really a girl dog and had 5 little puppies last month."

"Girl dog? Gracie, we all knew that. We were just fooling around with you and Lena," replied Versia laughing out loud.

"Girls, Girls," Carrie called out trying to cut in on the sisters conversation without success.

"John, long times no see." Henry J said holding out his hand to shake young Mr. Hamptons. "Ladies, Ladies will you all join us at this table so that we can continue to visit.

Finally, everybody was seated at the table, having greeted the late comers and congratulated the expectant mother who was now four months pregnant. John had made the same observation as the other men had about the grounds and additions to the place. Just like James Boswell, this was her first time seeing the famous Hole in the Bushes place. Even at that, some changes were evident from what had been described to her.

Since it was lunch time, they decided to eat before actually taking a second grand tour to show Gracie and John the place. They had a light lunch of freshly cut vegetables, sliced ham, cheese and cool buttermilk or ice tea, depending upon your preference. They all enjoyed one of Carrie's baking specialties, blueberry cobbler for dessert.

There is nothing like fresh conversation between friends and, even more so, between family. As normal among any group of people, around desert time, the conversation turns to serious matters. Within this group, it was a question from Colrolus directed at Versia and James.

"I never did hear anything back from Sammy Parker. Did he get in touch with you two when he got to Hot Springs?"

"Yes he did." Versia started.

"Yeah, that's right. We didn't put it in a letter of anything, in case it might get opened by the wrong people. You know what I mean," James chimed in.

"Yeah, he had some beefy black negro with him. He says he met him on the train. He called him CC, talking 'bout it was short for Calvin Coolidge," Versia continued. "Imagine that, another black man named after a US president. That big negro made me nervous."

155

"They stayed with us a couple of days and found a place of their own about a week later," James added. "We see them from time to time, especially around the hotel. It looks like Sammy has grown up. He is hanging around the white gangster cliental at the Arlington. From what I hear, they have taken a liken to him and that big CC fella."

"That's right. I think hustling, and who knows whatever else, is their thing these days," Versia said. "I think both of them boys are up to no good, with their stylish clothes and running around with loose chicks and carrying on. Do you know if he got in touch with his folks?"

"Has anybody heard if that's so? 'Cause I hadn't heard a thing up 'til now," Henry Jr added.

Everyone around the table agreed that this was the first news they'd heard about Sammy since he left this area. For John, the fact that Sammy may have fallen in with the local gangsters or whoever seemed about right considering how he left here. After all, he was a black man on the run. It wasn't like he had a lot of options.

"At least it sounds like he is taking care of himself. I imagine his mama and daddy will be glad to hear that. I'll stop over there next week and make sure they get the latest news," John volunteered with Colrolus nodding his head in agreement.

"Oh thank you brother-in-law," Versia said grabbing hold of Johns hand in a playful gesture. "For real, we thought he had let his folks know how he was doing and all."

"He might have. Um just going to make sure they get this bit of news. I'll clean it up the best I can. Cause I ain't going to tell them he is running with gangsters," John said.

"Baby we're going to have to take off if we want to spend time with your folks," James advised.

It was about two o'clock in the afternoon and time was getting away from them all. James and Versia said their goodbyes to each individual member of the lunch party. Versia saved her longest goodbye for her sisters, promising to see them as soon as she got a few days off. They agreed to write more in order to keep in touch, especially since they were no longer living with their parents. She told them she would tell their papa and mama that she had lunch with them at the Hole in the Bushes place, and all was good. No, she would not tell them of Gracie's hot news leaving that for her to do. They complimented Henry and Carrie once again on a putting together a beautiful place for black folks to come and enjoy themselves. The left headed for Frank and Harriett Hall's house.

Meanwhile, Henry and Carrie were more than glad to give the tour to Gracie and John since they missed it earlier. Colrolus and Lena went along for the second time. This time when they reached the entertainment room, there was a local boy turned singer fiddling around with his guitar and singing a couple of notes. He recognized John as he entered the room. He smiled, nodded his head and kept on practicing.

William 'June-bug' Davis, Jr, is a cousin of Johns. They played baseball together as kids and attended school together. He is about three years older than John. He ended up sitting in John's group because the teacher told him he could not handle his age groups assignments. It wasn't the first time he was pushed back by the teacher. He was one of those kids that seemed like he did not belong there, had a hard time keeping his mind in the room with everyone else.

His father had left his mother before they got married, which is how he ended up with his mother's last name. Gossip says he has never seen his father, even though he knows his name. His mother stays with her father on his farm. Consequently, the grandfather tried to get June-bug acclimated to farm work, which didn't work either. For a while, they thought he would be slow all of his life and a hopeless case depended upon others to earn his keep.

The story goes, shortly after turning twenty years of age, his mom Flossie, took him with her on a trip to Warren. She went to visit a friend of hers; Romo The guy kind of liked Flossie but was not a farmer and hated the country areas. He was an older guy than Flossie, forty-six to her thirty-five years of age, and he used to be a traveling musician. He could play a couple instruments, like the piano, guitar, and drums. He noticed June-bug's interest in the sound of the guitar right away. He found out that if he taught him a couple of notes and gave him a chance to play on his own that would keep him busy for a long time. Then Flossie and Romo could really visit in private. It went on like that for about six or seven months. Every weekend Flossie would visit Romo, taking June-bug with her because her grandfather refused to watch a grown man.

After a while, Romo and Flossie realized that June-bug was able to interpret the instructions, remember, and apply them as requested while learning how to play the guitar. Sometimes with Romo's help, other times on his own, he was developing his own style.

Once they found out that June-bug had found his calling, Romo, Flossie, and his grandfather pooled their funds and found him a 1918 Gibson L-1 brand acoustic guitar for Christmas.

A year later, here he sat, a twenty-one year old self-made musical prodigy that was now beginning to study the origins of the blues.

That brings us to this point. Some have moved on, yet there are still a lot of folks around these parts that use to tease June-bug to no end. They called him stupid, a walking dummy, you name it. Now, many of the same people pay their money to see him perform on Friday and Saturday night at the Hole in the Bushes.

"Who could have guessed how he would turn out? I tell you, I don't think I have ever been so happy to see a guy making a living at doing something he loves, than I feel for June-bug here. Right now, he is just about the best guitar player around these parts. And he sings," Henry J said,

"Yeah, we got a women's trio coming down to give him a breather between sets too," Carrie added.

"I been hearing good things about my man over the last few months." John said.

Meanwhile, June bug was providing a melodic riff sample for the owners and their guest. He seemed to be in excellent spirits even while playing the Memphis blues. After about a half hour, he finished the set. He packed up his guitar and came over to greet his small audience.

They all sat for a short while talking about old, current, and times to come. He was really grateful that Henry J and

Carrie provided him a venue to show off talents. He told them would never forget it. He knew Gracie and also knew that she was the love of John's life. The fact they are married was not a surprise to him. Colrolus and Lena's marriage was a surprise, probably because he did not know Colrolus before today. He and John agreed to catch-up on old times whenever time, gigs, and chores gave them some free time. Meanwhile, Gracie gave him an open end super or Sunday meal invitation. He accepted, excused himself and said he wanted to take a nap before tonight's show. The others were all left with the impression that the wall flower had bloomed. The turtle had come out of his shell and, yes, it is possible for a blues singer to be content, at least when he is not singing the blues.

Sheriff Penelton was not feeling as much heat from the regular white folk as time passed. He'd done his best to defuse a potential race riot by getting the story of his investigation out to townspeople and those in the surrounding areas.

He had to work fast and get to the right people to head off old man Sampson's people and their Klan backers. He knew most white folk didn't care about what went on in the Negro community as long as it didn't affect them. They also knew the Sampson was part of the local KKK.

The key component to getting the truth of what actually happened on the day the Sampson boys were shot was the white community's knowledge of the boys. If ever there were people who were considered white trash, Walt and Pete Sampson fit the bill. People were aware of their underhanded dealings before they joined the Klan. Added to the believability factor was that the boys didn't care who they wronged, black or white folk. They had a reputation and were not to be trusted among decent folk.

Therefore, most folk accepted Sheriff Penelton interpretation of what happened that day. The primary fact was Sammy Parker and his former cousin, Elmo, was defending themselves from the Sampson boys and their friends. It was they who were ambushed, not the other way around.

The Parker boy was still wanted for questioning as the sheriff had yet to take a one on one statement from him. Although the authorities feel he is in one the northern cities, the sheriff stops by the Parker farm every now and then to remind his folks he still needed to officially clear him.

He was waiting in his office for his deputy, Pierce Krause, to return from his morning rounds. After which they'd drive out to the Parkers, stopping at Papa Warner's, and a few other places to let people know they were still looking for Sammy. It was routine but might take most of the day.

Deputy Krause returned around ten o'clock. Sheriff Penelton didn't waste any more time, He was anxious to get back to town early this afternoon. Before leaving he put Deputy Charlie Oats in charge.

The stop at Papa Warner's and the Jennings' farm went rather well. A little conversation, providing an update on the Parker and other legal matters, how's the family, were their crops successful, and there you have it. Goodbye and be seeing you. The next one was critical and must be handled with tact. He didn't want to stop, but the Sampson Farm was next in line.

Deputy Krause pulled the police marked Model T Roadster pickup off the road and turned right going through the opened entrance gate. About fifty yards further up the road were another gate. It was closed and manned by two security men with rifles. This was new, thought Sheriff Penelton. Even though the guards saw the police markings, they used walkie talkies to alert the main house the sheriff was coming up the road. It was only about another fifty of so yards before one reached the main house.

Old man Sampson was sitting in a chair on the porch. His son Petey, sitting in a wheelchair besides his father, looked uncomfortable and agitated. They both glared at the law officers getting out of their vehicle.

"Morning Harvey, Petey. Hi yawl doing this morning?" The Sheriff asked, stopping at the first step of the porch, propping his right leg on the second step and leaning against the bottom post of the railing.

"We doing all right Sheriff. What brings you and young Pierce out this way?"

"I hope they brought some good news and saying they caught that Parker nigger. 'Cause we are tired of waiting for you to do . . ."

Petey was literally interrupted by his mother Clara, who had returned to the porch with a big picture of lemonade for her husband and son.

"Hi you Sheriff, would you and your deputy like a glass of lemonade?" Clara Sampson asked.

"That sho' would hit the spot. It's kind of hot for the middle of September.

"I'll just get some more glasses." Clara said before returning to the porch with two more in hand.

Sheriff Penelton gave the Sampson family the same update he gave Papa Warner and the Jennings family. The lemonade was so refreshing, and welcomed on this humid day that he lingered a little bit longer. He talked about this, and about that, purposely avoiding the topic in which they would be most interested. He gave them the latest about the Parker investigation initially but didn't expand on it. He finished his conversation with the word that authorities are still on the lookout for Sammy in Chicago, Milwaukee, Detroit, and other north and eastern cities like New York. There were also pictures and feelers out for him in California.

"And you still haven't heard nothing 'bout him showing up anywhere?" old man Harvey Sampson asked.

"Naw. But we still looking and one day, he'll turn up," Sheriff Penelton concluded.

"I hope . . ."

"We're hoping you find him soon Sheriff," Clara said, interrupting Petey once again.

"Thanks for the lemonade Mrs. Sampson. Yawl folks have a fine day. I'll be back to see you soon or sooner if I hear any news," The Sheriff stated.

Deputy Krause turned the vehicle toward the road leading to the main highway, leaving the Sampson's sitting on the porch. He drove past the same guards and reached the front gate which was still opened and turned right headed toward the Parker Farm.

John Hampton was sitting on the Parker Family porch. He rode "Old Thunder" over the back road to relay the information about their son. Clem and his wife Cora were grateful to hear the news about their boy. John left out the part about him possible running with gangsters. He did tell them Sammy met a friend on the train. Everyone thought they gotten a place together and was doing odd jobs to earn money.

He lied and told them their son had sent his love and that he would try to keep in touch with them. John lied because he knew Sammy didn't know the Boswells were driving up to see Versia parents. Otherwise, he would have sent such a message to his own parents. At least this little bit was welcomed news for the Parkers.

Clem asked John how married life was treating him. His response was predictable. It was wonderful. He couldn't be happier. Clem asked why he decided to stay in this community to raise a family. This was a question being tossed around by blacks in numerous households in the entire south since the First World War, no doubt because some black folk had land, stock, and machinery to work the land. A small number managed to eke out a pretty good standard of living despite the laws of Jim Crow and some white folk attitudes in Gravel Ridge.

"We are one of the few who can say, we make out okay," Clem said. "But then take this mess about Sammy and the reaction of old Harvey Sampson and others like him. His land is next to mine. Look at the increased KKK activity 'round here. Suppose they decided to attack and burned us out in the middle of the night? Where would we be?"

"In trouble, that's where we would be," Cora said out loud before she realized it. "We are a KKK raid away from being poor and not having a pot to pee in ourselves.

"That's why I ask you the question. Tell Sambo and Sallie, um not trying to run you away from here. But then a lot of older folks, much less than young folks are gettin' up outta here. They are moving east, west or north to have a better life for their families." Clem said, pretty much in summary of what is happening on a weekly basis within the Gravel Ridge community.

"I thought about it. I haven't talked to Gracie, so I don't know how she feels about it. I, we have friends, relatives we went to school with that moved to one of those northern cities. For me, I want to farm the land. I love it here. I don't know if I could live anywhere else," John replied.

"Besides that, it is extremely hard to leave the ground your people are buried in. Our ancestors are from here. I don't care what the white man says; we earned a right to be here with our blood and the sweat off our backs," Cora said with eyes misting from the thought of her statement.

They heard the sound of the car before they actually saw it. Old Thunder was getting excited and milling around trying to break free. They could see the dust the auto was kicking up as it approaches the Parker house. Finally, Deputy Krause pulled up to the porch area and turned off the motor. At least that calmed Old Thunder down. Both men got out of the car and walked toward the steps of the porch.

"Afternoon, Sheriff Penelton. How yawl doing today?" Clem hollered out to the sheriff.

"Doing fine Clem, just fine. How you folks coping with this humidity?" he countered.

As the sheriff and deputy Krause got to the porch, they walked up the steps looking at the two empty seats. The sheriff sat down like he had just completed eight hours of backbreaking work. The deputy took the other seat, took his hat off, wiped his forehead with a big handkerchief, and stared briefly at the sun as if to say, don't you ever stop shining.

"So hi you doing today, Cora?"

"Fair to middling, Sheriff, fair to middling, want some cold water, tea or something?" Cora asked.

"Some water will do fine. Give me some good news. Tell me your boy is here so I can get that statement from him."

"Naw Sheriff. Sorry, but we haven't seen or heard from him." Clem answered.

Always in the police officer mode, Sheriff Penelton could not shake the idea that he knew John. Occasionally looking at John's face while trying to remember, he finally recognized him. "Say, is your mother named Sallie Hampton? He asked.

"Yes suh."

"I thought I recognized you. Your daddy's named Sambo, at least that's what they call him. You're David Hamptons' boy."

Yes suh."

Cora brought two glasses of water back, and the officers drank them practically before she could step away. She put the empty glasses on the little tray she used to serve. Refreshed, the sheriff began to give them the same update as he had provided the others. It was a short and to the point. With no questions from his audience during the update, he wrapped it up pretty quick. He knew Sammy Parker was in the wind and wasn't coming back. Why should he. God only knows what would happen if he showed up around here again. To some, the legality situation wouldn't matter. By all accounts, he would not be charged for defending himself. Yet, his life would not be worth a plug nickel. Harvey Sampson or his people would see to that. The Sheriff knew that, his folks knew it and one had to figure, Sammy knew it too.

The officers thank the Parkers for the water while standing up to leave. "Remember now, if you hear from him, tell him he got to give me an official statement. That's the only reason I need to see him. Yawls take care now, you hear. Boy, tell Sambo and your mama I said hi."

"Yes suh."

"Okay Sheriff. You stop by anytime, we'll see you next time." Clem said as he waved goodbye.

They walked down the steps to get in the police vehicle. "You get in the other side Pierce; I'll drive back to town."

Shortly after they watched the sheriff's vehicle head back toward the main highway, John got up to leave. He told them he'd let them know if he heard anything else about their son. For now, he had to get back because Wednesday was still a work day. There was a few hours left before sundown.

They waved goodbye as he untied Old Thunder and jumped up on the bareback horse. At least he had a bridle with bits and split reins to guide the animal. John headed for the back roads shortcut to his place. He gently slapped the horse behind with his baseball cap yelling "Git up now." The horse responded by getting into a gentle gallop fully understanding the rider wanted to get home.

Meanwhile, the Sheriff and Deputy Krause pulled onto the main highway headed back to town. They passed the Sampson and Jennings Farms to their left and the driver's side of the vehicle. They saw Papa Warner sitting on his stores porch on the passenger's side of the vehicle, and blew the horn. He waved as they drove by. Even at about thirty miles per hour, the vehicle was leaving a trail of dust on this hot and humid afternoon. It wouldn't be long before they are back in Banks.

The sheriff didn't hear the first shot it happened so fast. Deputy Krause head was jolted backward from the bullets impact followed by his body slumping, falling forward and coming to a rest in a lifeless heap with only the vehicle's floor holding him upright.

He wasn't sure what happened until he heard the second and third shot, not seconds later, tearing through the tarp like top of the T Roadster shattering the windshield. One of the shots tore through his right shoulder causing him to feel a pain that may be akin to childbirth if he had that as a reference. He uncontrollably yelled out while trying to maintain his composure.

He lost control of the vehicle, which jerked right, then left rolling over on its side, sliding down the short embankment, and coming to a rest. He wasn't sure of exactly how many shots were fired. But the first shot, the one he didn't hear until the bullet went through his deputy's head, came from the passenger's side of the vehicle. His policemen's mind, trained over the years to interpret what happens at a crime scene, realized just before he lost consciousness. He figured somebody was really shooting at the passenger in the vehicle. Since that is where he normally sat, he correctly deduced they were trying to kill him.

They say a person's life passes before their eyes just before they are about to die. Sheriff Dan Penelton wasn't sure if he was dying or what. He thought the bullet went through his shoulder area. He wondered if that shot could have or if it killed him. Could it have been another bullet that entered his body that finished him off? He just wasn't sure.

An ardent student of the civil war, he was an admirer of President Abraham Lincoln. He was born within two miles of Banks. Southern born and bred except he was a maverick in his beliefs. Unlike all of his family members, he sided with the North when it came down to why the Civil War was fought. You wouldn't call him an abolitionist or Negro lover. He simply did not believe one man should own another. That was where he drew the line when it came to his southern roots. Nor did he believe in the superiority of the white people over blacks. After all, he knew some smart black people and dumb white people.

Selected as Sheriff, solely on the strength of his strong family ties in this area, at twenty-one years of age, he wanted to serve his community. Danny Boy, as his family called him, took a leave of absence from the sheriff office at thirty-three years of age to join the Marines in 1914. He wanted to do his part for his country in World War 1.

This was who he was a servant to his community and country. His reputation as a fair man to one and all could not be reproached. And there lies the problem he had with the Klan and people like old man Sampson. He knew his deputy was dead from a shot meant for him.

By now, he could hear, or was he imagining being pulled from the overturned vehicle. Somebody said this one's alive. The other one is dead. He felt pain coming from his shoulder as someone was placing him in an ambulance truck. He must be the live one, he reasoned. "You're gonna be alright Sheriff", he heard another person say. Then he felt the vehicle moving down the road. Yet why couldn't he talk and why was he still unconscious?

God-dam it, he thought. Deputy Pierce Krause was dead. He was not only his best deputy, someone he could count on, but he also considered him a friend. Who would tell his widow and children? He wanted to be the one to do it but wasn't sure if he could get there before someone else. They had to be told. He had such a nice family. He felt himself falling into a deeper coma. Somebody must have given him a shot or something. Subsequently, he lost all thoughts and awareness.

The ambulance almost hit the maximum speed of forty-five miles per hour while heading into Banks. The driver had to honk his horn more than a couple of times, having to come to a complete stop one time. After all, this is the country, and if a farmer's herd of stray sheep has to cross the highway at that specific time, what can you do, except stop the vehicle and let the ten or more animals go across. Other than that there were no more incidents for the ambulance which pulled up to Dr. Morgan Purvis clinic.

Dr. Purvis, anxious about his friend's health, was waiting outside for the ambulance to arrive. The vehicles driver and the doctor hurriedly carried the stretcher with the sheriff still unconscious into the clinic. The doctor's nurse, Ms. Doyle, who went with the driver to pick up the sheriff walked briskly behind them.

The town had already been alerted to the Sheriff's shooting before the ambulance returned to Banks. They also knew the Deputy was dead. It turned out there was another vehicle about a quarter of a mile behind the Sheriff's police vehicle at the time of the shooting. It was a local farmer, his wife, two children, and brother, who heard the shots, and saw the tail end of vehicle as it rolled into the short embankment. They, along with a black couple and their grandson, coming from the opposite way were the first people on the scene. The shooting occurred two miles outside of Banks. Clemy Collins volunteered to turn around and return to town to alert the authorities. He took his wife, Alice, and grandson, Barris, with him. They also heard the shots and saw the vehicle roll into the embankment.

Part-time Deputy Charlie Oats had been standing outside the clinics doorway for almost an hour trying to calm the crowd and cut down on rumors, or was he. It was ironic the very man Sheriff Penelton suspected of being involved with the Klan and at least a loyal friend of Klansman McBain, the store owner, was now in charge of entire Sheriff's office.

Shortly thereafter, Doctor Purvis came out to give everyone the good news. His father, Skeeter Purvis had joined the crowd of about twenty people. He walked down from his store to see about his friend. Doctor Purvis, fully aware of how any incident can take on racial overtones, ensured the deputy and everyone that Sheriff Penelton was going to be alright. He told the crowd that he sent a man out to inform the Sheriff's parents. He told them Sheriff Penelton had a shoulder wound but would fully recover. The wound has been cleaned, dressed, and the patient had fallen back to sleep. Besides a few scrapes and bruises, he expected the Sheriff to be back on the job shortly.

No such good news for Deputy Pierce Krause. His family has also been informed that he was dead, killed by an unknown assassin's bullet. We assume it was the same person or persons that shot the Sheriff. Before he fell back asleep, he told me he was going to bring in an experienced officer from another county to take his place until he physically could return to the office. Meanwhile, Deputy Oates will handle the load until further notice.

Most in the crowd welcomed the good news and sadly accepted the bad. A couple people, as in most crises, absorbed the update with no emotion or comment. The Deputy was asked by Doctor Purvis to inform the mayor and advise him that the Sheriff would be available for a visit tomorrow. The doctor smiled and acknowledges his father in the crowd before going back in the clinic.

He then instructed his nurse, Rebecca Doyle, to keep an eye on his patient. Make sure he is notified soon as he wakes up. She smiled, nodded her head in agreement and returned to her desk.

After the clinic door had closed, a stranger from the crowd received personal instructions from Deputy Oates. He took off, walked down to and disappeared into McBain's store. Skeeter took note of the stranger and deputy's actions. Meanwhile, the deputy walked towards the Mayor's office.

The opened ended question was who was going to do the investigation of the shooting today if anybody. Looks like nobody. Although the sheriff is unable, he would be the first to say someone needs to examine the scene of the crime. Where did those shots come from? Can they locate where the shooters were standing? What kind of weapon was used? Are there any bullets lodged in the vehicle. Did anybody get the names of any potential witnesses? What did they see or hear? Are they available for follow up questions? For now all questions, will be asked later and not sooner as they should be.

Papa Warner had just come from the outhouse when he got the news. The Collins family drove up in their truck and was fit to be tied. Clemy got out, ran up to Papa as he settled into his rocking chair and blurted out, "Sheriff Penelton been shot. His deputy, Krause I think that's his name, is dead."

"What'd you say?"

"The Sheriffs been shot, and the deputy is dead. We saw it happen, coming down the road."

"I'll be dammed. What happened? Where is the sheriff now?"

"He's at Doc Purvis' Clinic. He will be all right, but his deputy died on the spot."

There were a few other patrons, along with Joel Warner. They all came out of the store when they heard Clemy talking. They were shocked to hear the news. By that time, Alice Collins and her grandson, Barris got out of automobile.

"Did any of yawl see the shooters?" Joel Warner asked.

"No, but I heard them shots and seen their truck roll over into the ditch," Clemy answered. "I drove back into town to let his office know. I told that part time deputy of his. Then as I came out of the sheriff office, I saw Doc Purvis and told him. He's the one that sent the ambulance out there. The Sheriff was out like a light when we pulled him out of that vehicle. But he was breathing."

"They wasn't shooting at you were they?" Papa Warner asked.

"Nobody could be that bad of a shot. Our vehicle wasn't even close to the sheriff's. No, they were shooting at the sheriff," Clemy concluded. "We got to get on home; I just wanted to let you know so you can spread the word."

The Collins got back into their vehicle and drove off toward their home. He passed other people pulling into the store's parking area. Over the next couple days, Papa Warner gave everybody who came by the news.

This little country store continues to act as the unelected, but designated community shopping and meeting place in lieu of going to town. It's a place to get the latest news, gossip and crop information. Patrons can also get the latest copy of Sears & Roebuck and other sales catalogs, Arkansas major newspapers, the Democrat and Gazette, Negro publications, and community interested correspondence brochures' or pamphlets. All of the reading material made available indicated a major change from years past. It provided evidence that a substantial amount of black people in the Gravel Ridge Community had the ability to read, comprehend, own property, and conduct business in a way that was profitable to themselves and their enterprises.

Visitors and shoppers this particular Saturday included Lemon Davis, Sallie Hampton's son, and their cousins, Dempsy and Mansfield Davis. They drove their wagon team up to get a few supplies for the Hampton and Davis farms. The fall was here, and winter was approaching, so they needed items like tobacco for rolling cigarettes and Sambo's pipe, a few containers of Papa Warner's famous syrup, flour, sugar, rice, rubbing alcohol and lamp oil. They were to pick up a couple pair of winter boots they had repaired. There would be a few more trips, but they were beginning to stock up today.

People were picking up or dropping off their own repair items, completing their shopping, and hanging around in the parking area to talk. They exchanging ideas and concepts as folk do wherever they congregate.

All the talk was still about the shooting. No one had been caught, and no one had been blamed. A couple of people brought word back that the Sheriff was up and about, although his right arm was in a sling. They say he returned to his office to work two days after being shot. Words out that he is looking for a new deputy to take Pierce Krause's place. Gossip was that Doctor Purvis' nurse, Rebecca Doyle, is a regular visitor to the sheriff's office. They are trying to keep it hush-hush, but it looks like a budding romance from an outside perspective.

In the background to all of this talk was the not so secretive planning for next year's June 13th wedding of Papa Warner's oldest son and second in charge of his operations. Joel Johnson and his fiancé, Ms. Viola Ross has been in love for quite a while. The boss, Papa Warner, wouldn't let on, because it always seemed necessary to him to project this gruff side of his personality in order to function in business and personal relationships. Yet, he is excited and approves of his sons choice.

170

Even though Joel is second in command, Warner and his wife, Dora has two older children. Carlee is his oldest child and daughter while Edna is his second oldest child and daughter. Both are still as much involved in the workings of this mini-conglomerate as any of the other children. All members of this family are involved in the many services and goods offered at his store or farm. It's a testament to the family structure and an example of how to run a family business.

No one child is more important in this family than the other. It's just that one's position might seem like it's more important than another's. Let no one doubt that within the family ranks, each member fully understands their importance to the business structure and more importantly, their standing as a member of the Warner and Dora Johnson family. There is only one boss, and that is Papa Warner.

Just like the inner workings of his family is kept close to the vest, so are their current or even potential relationships with those outside of the family. So it was a bit unusual to hear of this pending marriage so far in advance of the actual date. You don't need this much advance notice to plan. The answer and the other popular news came out by accident.

There were to be back to back weddings of two Johnson children. They probably were not planning to release this information today or this month. The future groom let the cat out of the bag.

A man, who could have passed for white, drove up to the store. He was well dressed and didn't look like your local farmer. This is why he caught the attention of almost everybody. He acted as though he had been there before and had a purpose for being there now. He sat on the porch while talking with Papa Warner. The two men shook hands. Then the mulatto man headed for his vehicle.

He turned back toward Papa and yelled out, "Oh yeah, I am so sorry. Thanks for giving me permission to marry your daughter. We're gonna make you proud."

With that said he drove his auto off the lot and across the road through the Johnson's front gate headed for the main house. Most of the people who saw and heard this exchange were surprised and well . . . , surprised. They started putting two and two together and waited. It did not take long.

Papa Warner spoke briefly to Joel. Shortly afterwards, the word started getting around the store and parking area. Mr. Edward Childs has asked for and received permission to marry our sister, Edna Johnson. The wedding will be next year sometime in July to avoid conflict with our June wedding.

(Authors Note: The union between Edward and Edna is notable because the daughter of these two will bear this Author.)

Dempsey began to maneuver his wagon team toward the main highway headed back home. He, Mansfield, and Lemon got more news that they expected today. They had all the supplies they wanted for the day. They all laughed at the thought of the ladies being thrilled with news of both marriages. It was a social bonanza at Papa Warner's today. The boys hardly could wait to spread the news.

"Come on now, git up there horse," Dempsey called out as both animals woke up to improve their trot speed while looking for their chief nemesis on the road, the horseless carriage.

Sheriff Penelton was in his office going over local applications for his vacant deputy position. He recognized a couple names like, Bob and Clarke as pure Klan and staunch supporters of old man Sampson. One more name was unfamiliar, with another he knew to be local. The problem with that one was the absence of information about the young man's politics. He had no clue, but would find out by checking out his associates and family background.

It was a couple of weeks after the shooting, and the urgency was to get a full time deputy in place before the winter sets in. He decided to read the full application of the unknown person, one William J. Stovall. It looked pretty convincing. He had all the qualifications required, currently holding down a deputy position with the Hot Springs' Sheriff Office. He was twenty-seven years old with five years of experience. The candidate was married with a three year old son, with good references. There was even a letter from his Aunt Gladys Purvis.

"Purvis? I wonder if . . ." he thought out loud. At that instant, Skeeter walked in the door.

"Morning Sheriff. I see you still got your sling on. How's the shoulder?" He asked, taking a seat on the other side of the assistant's desk.

"Hey Skeeter, I was just going over these applications and . . ."

"Gettin' at it early huh? Have you had your breakfast yet? Maybe we can go over to the diner this morning. Come on Dan, you need to eat. That is if you are not expecting Ms. Doyle to bring your breakfast," He interrupted.

The mention of Rebecca Doyle took his mind off everything. The mere mention of her name caused him to think about her. Yeah he was smitten all right. That woman knew she had got to him. And the way it's looking, he has returned the favor. He could tell when he kissed her after their second so called date. He wondered if she was going to bring him breakfast this morning. Then just as suddenly remembered she told him he would be on his own today. She needed to catch up on her housework. After all, she had almost been his private nurse for the last two weeks. Today, she was going to take care of Rebecca.

"What'd you say, Skeeter?"

"Come on Dan. We're going to breakfast. It's seven-thirty in the morning. Bachelors need their morning coffee and eggs. I need to eat before the Saturday morning crowd gets in. It's probably going to be a long day. Let's go."

The sheriff grabbed his hat and joined his friend putting a sign on the front door that read back in thirty minutes. The diner was practically next door, in actuality four doors down from the sheriff's office. They took their seat and ordered the usual, two eggs over easy, country sausage, biscuit, and coffee. The cook wasted no time in filling their order nor did the waitress in serving it.

The two men chit-chatted about nothing, finally with Skeeter asking, "Did you see my nephew's application in with your others for the deputy position?"

"I don't think so. What's his name?"

"Josh Stovall."

"Naw, I didn't . . . , wait a minute, are you talking about William J. Stovall from Hot Springs? Your nephew, he must be . . ."

"He is my sister-in-law's son. He wants to move out of Hot Springs and figured he might as well move closer to his Aunt Gladys and me. He's a good kid with his head on straight. I can tell you, he is not Klan material."

"Then he is perfect from where I stand. He has the experience, and I need to fill the position fast."

"Good because he and his family are driving up today. They should be pulling in here around one o'clock. Can you see him sometime after that?"

"Make it two o'clock."

"Got any idea who shot you and killed Deputy Krause?"

"Not yet. I went back out to the crime scene and didn't find anything except a couple of shell casing where I figured they were standing while shooting. I also found an empty moonshine pint bottle. I sent the evidence up to the Little Rock Police Department Crime Lab. I hope to get a report back by next week, no later than Monday after next."

"Yeah, I think you are right when you said they were shooting at you. A buck says that old man Sampson or McBain knows something about it."

"I would not take that bet because I'd probably lose. My money is on Harvey Sampson. It could have been Bob or Clarke, maybe both. It's a hangover from his son, Walt, getting killed and the other one paralyzed. We will build our case and get out man sooner or later."

"What about Deputy Charlie Oats?"

"I know he is a McBain favorite and a card carrying member of the Klan. I keep him on a part time basis to keep him near me. You never know when I might have to send a message."

"Well my friend you always know what you are doing. So I will leave you to it. I got to get back down to the store. See you later, Sheriff. Watch yourself. Josh will be good for you if you hire him."

Skeeter, leaving a half-eaten plate of food, left the entire cost of both meals, plus tip on the table, hurried out the diner's door on his way to his store. His daughter, Beverly Purvis was holding things down until he returned.

The sheriff, always the optimist, felt happy about having a potentially great deputy fall into his lap. He will have to read that letter of recommendation written by Gladys Purvis when he returns to the office. On another issue, he had not even noticed himself using his right hand to grip a fork and eating with it. Hopefully he will be able to discard the sling in the near future. For now, he's just appreciative to have friends like Skeeter and Rebecca.

CHAPTER 6

John and Gracie Hampton's First-Born

Gracie was snug as a bug in a rug and sleeping soundly until she heard a familiar sound. Hazily waking up, she couldn't be absolutely sure if it was the same rooster or not. Finally fully awake, gathering her senses she realized the rooster crowing now could hardly be the same one from her father's house. There was no way that Red was now their property too. No, that's the Hampton's Farm rooster. She thought they just call him Rooster. However, he must be a family member of Red because he sure does sound like him and is just as loud.

She heard her husband's feet hit the floor and head outside to take care of his morning ritual. Knowing he would return in about a half an hour, she got up, started the fire in the stove, and put the coffee pot on the burner. She grabbed a shawl, wrapped it around her shoulders, and retrieved the night bucket they used as a bedpan, taking it outside to empty. She ran back onto the porch, placing the night bucket right outside the door. She would rinse it out with lye soap and water later this morning for tonight's use.

It was colder this morning, as opposed to yesterday. They had yet to get their first snow of the winter, even though it was the middle of November. She'd heard they were expecting that to change next week or maybe in a couple of days.

Now, she is into her sixth month of pregnancy. That baby is kicking up a storm inside her. It must be a boy 'cause he turns and kicks like he is impatient and want to see the world right now, meaning today. It's funny as hell to her husband but not as humorous to her. She will remember this one, probably because it's the first one. The baby is getting bigger and so is she. She has not seen Lena or Versia in a while, although she did receive a letter from Versia.

She tries to take it as easy as she can these days. She is still going to church, but the bumpy wagon ride is getting harder to take. Consequently, this might one of the last few Sundays this month until she's had her child. If it is snowing next Sunday, they won't attend church. Besides, her parents are coming over for Thanksgiving, weather permitting.

John comes back inside, smiling, and looking for a hot cup of coffee. He sat down at the table while Gracie poured them both a cup.

"I forgot to tell you that your folks are coming over for dinner this Sunday."

"I thought they were coming for Thanksgiving."

"The way this weather is, it might be snowing a week before, or on Thanksgiving Day. You know how these dirt roads can get in crummy weather," He offered. "They're coming now while the roads are clear. Yep! We would be able to go to church either. So they want to see you while they can."

"Guess who think they're pregnant too?"

"Who Lena?"

"Naw, your mama. She told me yesterday, she feels the signs."

"You talking 'bout my mama? Not my mama," He asked, looking as surprised as if it was his baby.

"Yes John, your mama, Sallie Hampton. She don't want us to say anything to the boys or Sambo just yet, but she is pretty sure she is pregnant."

"Woo-wee, I got to get something together to cook for Mama and Daddy. They didn't say they were bringing anybody with them did they? Woooo! What can I cook?" Gracie asked herself out loud.

"Did you ask me a question, baby?"

"Oh never mind, I need to go see your mama today."

Gracie gave her husband a piece of leftover chicken from yesterday for breakfast to go with his biscuit, Papa Warner's syrup, and coffee. She ate the last piece of chicken and biscuit. Chewing on her biscuit, she remarked out loud how better this batch turned out. They were light, and you barely could taste the baking powder.

For John, to hear that his mama is pregnant was a shocker and, then again it was not. After all, mama and daddy aren't that old. This time he hopes to get a sister. After five boys, it's about time mama had a girl. Whichever she has will be a blessing from God and accepted into the family with love. He was sure his mama felt the same. He looked forward to the day she made an official announcement.

The Halls went to Sunday school but did not stay for the pastor's service. They were just that anxious to see their daughter. They wanted to visit with Sallie and Sambo at the big house, too, except that the Hamptons were not yet back from their Oaklawn Methodist Church service. So they proceeded to drive their wagon team to the little house, arriving around noontime this bright Sunday day.

Surprise, surprise from an old friend. Oh No, the two puppies left that were not given away, and Spider put on a show for the Halls as they drove up. Frank and Harriett recognized Oh No right away. They were aware she had a five puppy living litter. What was a surprise was they all acted like their mother when company came by for a visit. Here was Oh No, a little bit heavier, who also recognizing her former owner's, came running from behind the house barking. Her two puppies were right beside her. And she was still, yes still trying to turn a flip. It didn't matter because her offspring had mastered the trick. They were flipping over their backside and side while barking as if they were reading from a script. Spider, who the Halls knew as John's dog, was taking it all in.

The scene was so funny and warmly felt by the Halls, it caused Frank to comment to his wife, "I don't think the father dog know what the heck is going on."

It was the first belly laugh that Frank had in some time. Harriett was laughing and crying. Gracie and John walking out to the porch in the middle of the dog's performance thought it was funny too, especially since they had not done this to anyone before. The couple warmly greeted her parents.

Oh No let Frank and Harriett know that she remembered them by licking their hand as they petted her and the other pups. Dog tails were wagging in friendship all around.

John helped Frank tie down the team on the side of the little house. "It looks like you've restarted a tradition from our little place," Frank told John. They laughed and joked about the Halls reception while returning to the little house to join the ladies.

They felt like intruders interrupting Harriett and Gracie's conversation about her expectant child. The ladies spoke quickly in a nonchalant way as they tried to make up for the lost contact between them. One would not believe they just saw each other at church last Sunday.

"Oh, um sorry daddy, you want some coffee or something before we have dinner?"

"Yes, I would. Hi you been girl?" Frank responded.

"Fine, I been good."

"Baby, I'll get the coffee. Do you want some Mrs. Hall?" John asked.

"Yes dear, I'll have some too. Gracie, who is going to be your midwife, does she live close, somewhere around here?"

"I don't know mama. I suppose I can talk to Mama Sallie about that. She must know somebody close. I just hadn't thought about it yet."

"Well child, you ain't got as much time as might think. The little tike could come early or surely come in little over a couple of months.

"We've been takin' care of her and her condition, so you don't have to worry about that. But you right about the midwife. Mama always uses Ms Belin to tend to her. And there is a couple more, like my cousin, Ms Lula Davis, Dempsey's mama." John offered.

"That's good son," Harriett replied.

They all talked for a while longer, going over everything they felt important enough to mention. Gracie and her mother compared letters and comments from Versia. They talked about Lena and Colrolus being happy down there across the railroad track. Oh No and her pups were a topic of conversation once again. They could not get over, nor could the Hamptons, the reception. Both parties spoke of their successful crops year. Neither family would be getting a truck or any type of vehicle anytime soon because money was tight.

Gracie had cooked cabbage, sweet potatoes, hot water cornbread, a rabbit in gravy and another fried, served with some tea cakes she was experimented with. The meal was well received. They ate until they could not eat no more.

The Hampton's didn't see Viola and Edgar at church last Sunday so they wondered where they were. Viola had caught a miserable cold that Friday and had it through the weekend. That kept her home.

Harriett told Gracie, "Viola and Edgar wanted to come but couldn't and sends their love to the both of you. Instead, they went to Warren to see their folks for the weekend."

"Yeah, they were supposed to go that weekend she got sick." Frank said.

"For this weekend, just like us, they are trying to beat the snowfall," Harriett said

By then it was time to start back home for the Halls. They went outside and got a good send off from Oh No and family. Not much barking or turning flips this time. Frank drove the wagon down the short distance to the big house. The ladies and John walked, with Spider going along to keep them company.

They visited for a short while, finally pulling the team onto the main road turning right headed for the little side road that would lead them to their place. It was an enjoyable visit for Frank and Harriett Hall. They could see their daughter was happy and in capable hands. What more could they have wished for?

Sheriff Penelton had gotten the evidence report back from the Little Rock Police Department. The shooting happened the previous month. Here it was the middle of January in a new year, and he was no closer to arresting anyone for the murder of Deputy Pierce Krause than he was in locating Sammy Parker.

He really didn't expect to hear from Sammy again, but he did expect to catch the shooter that killed his deputy and wounded him. The report revealed two clear fingerprints on the moonshine pint bottle identifying Clarke Peterson. Little Rock had access to Army records, which had Clarke's full set of prints. All that confirmed was that Harvey Sampson's lapdog dropped a bottle at what looked like the area where the shots were fired. When, and how the bottle got there, could not be proved.

The shell casings came from a normal local hunting rifle carried by more than a few hunters in and around Banks. There were no notable identifying marks on the casings, nothing that would further link them to Clarke. If someone had been able to get to the suspected shooting area sooner they may have found additional evidence. Without additional staff, with the sheriff recovering from his wound, that didn't happen.

The sheriff was keeping this knowledge to himself. At least he knew that one of, his guess, two shooters was Klan and worked for old man Sampson. He remembered seeing Clarke at the Sampson Farm gate with Bob on that morning visit before the afternoon shooting. Both men were guarding the entrance to the farm and carried the kind of rifles that could eject the ammo casings he found. He also remembered Sampson's warning that someone was going to die for the death of his son Walt and paralyzing of his other son, Petey. He was almost positive Clarke meant to kill him. All in all, this would take a significant revelation or unknown clue at this time to bring anyone to justice.

There was excellent news. His new deputy, Josh Stovall was working out perfectly. He brought new ideas to the job he learned firsthand in Hot Springs. He did not harbor any malice toward anyone. That made him a fair man. All one had to do was notice how he and still part-time deputy Charlie Oats interacted with each other. That would tell a person all they needed to know about that relationship. Deputy Oats was also angry at the sheriff for not hiring him as his full time deputy. Sheriff Penelton told him he lacked the experience Josh had and never gave it a second thought. He considered himself lucky to have Deputy Stovall.

The little town of Banks was covered with snow which had been falling on and off for about a week. All in all, there was probably six to seven inches of snow packed in areas that had not been shoveled. The dirt roads in the surrounding rural area were taking a beating. Since the weather was not quite freezing, the snow tended to melt pretty quickly turning the dirt roads into a quagmire in some spots. This caused the residents to be limited in their ability to travel to the next farm much less than to town. This was especially true if they were using what still was a crucial mode of transportation in the area, a horse and wagon.

The main highways were usable for automobiles and trucks. However, there still was a lot of mud that could even cause a Model T to get stuck. Therefore, the main street of Banks was somewhat deserted for a Friday afternoon. Deputy Stovall had made his morning rounds, limited it to within the town. He returned the office and found the sheriff looking at paperwork with a puzzling expression.

"Morning Sheriff Penelton," he said, dusting the little bit of snow off his hat, hanging his coat on the coat rack along with the hat

"Hey Josh, how's it going?"

"Slow and quiet, this is just the way I like it," he added while making his way over to the potbellied office heater to warm his hands.

The sheriff laughed and replied. "This ain't nothing like Hot Springs. I hear tell there are some real characters down there."

"Yep, to tell the truth, the gangsters that visit for the hot baths and get away from those northern cities are pretty tame while they are in town. They are coming down there to relax and enjoy themselves. The parties might get a little loud, but the bosses keep their entourage in check most of the time."

"They can't stay in the bathhouses forever so what else do they do?"

Josh made his way over to the deputy desk after warming his hands, sat down to begin taking in the heat of the outer-office administration room.

"Oh, they do a lot of gambling," he began. "The town council is even trying to promote more gambling in order to draw more people to the town. Single girls are flocking to the town. This coming summer promises to be even bigger than last, when it comes to new money coming into town."

"You know, I never did ask why you didn't want to stay on the force down there. Certainly promotions and more money would entice anybody to stay."

"Well sheriff, I just didn't know who I was working for down there, my boss or one of the mobs. And from the looks of it, a lot of influential people wouldn't mind turning their heads if it came down to a choice between an officer and a gambler. Like I said before, it became uncomfortable for my family and me in such an environment."

"Well, their loss is my gain. How you like the slow grind of my town so far?"

"Fits me and mine perfectly, I got folks in this town. My mother left Hot Springs and ran off with some guy from Chicago that worked for Al Capone."

Just at that moment, Rebecca Doyle walked in the office. Her coat was sprinkled with white snowflakes. You could see her reddish brown hair shinning under the sheer head scarf, which also had its share of wet snowflakes. She made her way to the potbellied office heater after entering. She was on a lunch break from Doctor Purvis clinic and wanted to go to lunch with the sheriff. It was official; although no announcement had been made that these two were a couple. Everybody in and around town knew it and by now so did the couple in question. Josh volunteered to man the office while they walked down to the diner. Funny, Josh thought, he had not realized it before, but it's true what everyone else is saying. Rebecca and Dan Penelton don't seem to notice other people or hear them for that matter when they are around each other. Neither one of them responded to him when he told them to have a pleasant lunch. For Josh, his three years old marriage was still new so he can relate to that kind of love.

There were places in the shed that John could let Spider, Oh No and the pups get out of the cold weather. They closed the open end up for the winters and placed rags and old quilting on the floor for the dogs. There was a twelve by twelve trap door section covered with a thick piece of leather, which allowed them access to the outside. Believe it or not, the dogs knew not to mess up their little area. They managed to go in and out and keep themselves fairly warm. John kept fresh food and water in there.

The horses and mules find shelter from the weather in the barn next to the big house except during the day when they mull around in the corral or on mild days are let out to pasture. Then, of course, it's a lot of dirty work keeping the barn clean.

The chickens and roosters have the hen house to get away from the elements. But make no mistake, there are times when it can get so cold, any animal, horse, mule, cow, pig, chicken, whether wild or domesticated can freeze in continuous cold elements. This goes for a man too if caught out in the elements for an extended time. You can usually tell how cold it is outside by how populated your front yard or other areas of the farm is experiencing.

Up to this point this area of Arkansas has experienced a mild to occasional cold winter. The good news is that the cold weather has not lasted over long periods of time.

A young woman going through the last trimester of her first pregnancy becomes concerned about the weather when she has to depend on someone else to help deliver her child. It doesn't matter if the midwife lives close by. The inclement weather decides if a road is useable or not. When a woman's body wants to produce the baby, normally nine months after the fetus has developed the child is born. Or at least it goes through the act of extracting itself from its mother.

Gracie Hampton was worried. She is due to have her baby the first week in February. It's Saturday, January 31, 1925. Tomorrow begins the first week in February. It's snowing outside on already shaky roads.

Her husband is worried about his wife and unborn child. He says Gracie has never looked so beautiful, even with her fat stomach. He is worried about losing her or the baby, or God forgive, them both.

Consequently he spoke to his mama and daddy. They both agreed that Cousin Oliph's wife, Lula Davis should be summoned today. John would have to take their horse, Old Thunder over there. The Davis family had their own horses so she could ride one back to the little house. There was certainly no need to try and convince Mama Sallie of the need. She remembers how she felt when she had her first, Lemon Davis. Now she was pregnant again with an expectant delivery sometime in July.

John told his wife of the decision and walked her down to the big house. He got back with Lula that afternoon. They put the horses in the barn with her paying a short visit with Sallie. Gracie, Lula, and John all walked up to the little house for the night. Lula, who had birthed eight children of her own and assisted in several more acting as a midwife, was a calming force to Gracie.

John fixed a pallet for himself on the kitchen floor. Although Gracie wasn't crazy about it, he insisted that Lula sleep with his wife. The wife wanted her husband to in bed with her. Instead, Lula took a quilt and got comfortable in a rocking chair next to the bed. With everybody finally satisfied, they all settle down for the night.

By the next morning, the snow falling had stopped. It was cold but not freezing. John got up early, as always to see to the animals and take care of his before breakfast chores around the little house.

Lula, who woke up shortly after John left the house, let Gracie sleep for another hour or so. She prepared a fresh pot of coffee, emptied the bed buckets and brought in some wood for the stove.

The Hampton farm's rooster was not so kind to Gracie. He woke her up with his morning call as he does every day. She stirred around in bed for a moment trying to get her bearings on the day of the week among other things. She had gotten so big from the pregnancy it was awkward for her to hop right out of bed. She could see that Lula was getting ready to prepare a breakfast.

Finally she got up, using her coat as a robe; she sat down at the kitchen table.

"Hi you feel this morning child?" Lula asked.

"Oh, I feel big but um okay."

"Do yawl always have a big breakfast in the morning?"

"No, ma'am, we just have coffee and whatever meat we had for supper and bread."

"Well, you got to keep your strength up, so how about a slice of ham to go with your biscuit. I brought a big piece of ham with me along with a few other things."

"Ms Lula, you don't have to do that. We got some leftover chicken from last night."

"Baby, we can have that for lunch. Believe me; I got enough for all us to eat. You just sit there; I'll take care of everthin'."

John came in just about the time the ham was pan fried. He gave her four eggs he found in the hen and chicken house, which Cousin Lula quickly scrambled. By putting them in a covered pan sitting over a pot of boiling water, she steamed six of the day old biscuits until they were hot. Gracie watched the older woman move around the kitchen like her mother, Harriett, used to do for her kids. Added to this well rounded breakfast was some homemade butter for the biscuits, topped with Papa Warner's syrup. They all sat down, said a morning prayer, and began to eat.

Ms. Lula turned the morning conversation toward God and what a glorious blessing a pregnancy is for newlyweds. With today being Sunday, it was kind of appropriate that she reminded Gracie and her husband that the deliverance of their child was actually in God's hand. She assured them that not only were she the mother of eight healthy children, but she took schooling in midwifery from her mother. Her mother helped bring black and white babies into this world. Yet, most importantly, it is God who chooses and works the hands of the midwife to help bring one of the Almighty's children into this world, for all babies are a child of God.

"John dear, I don't know if your mama told you, but I was the midwife that helped brought you and your brother, Monroe, into this world."

"I didn't know that Cousin Lula. I guess I never thought about it or asked."

"Well, I would'a tended to your mama and help bring her younger ones to this world, but I was pregnant myself and could not be there for their birthing."

Throughout the day as they talked, sometimes the two women talking among themselves, John felt having Cousin Lula there before the birth was good for Gracie. He noticed that Gracie has now gained complete confidence in the midwife. It was a load off both of their minds.

The night was uneventful except for false pains. Gracie was becoming more uncomfortable sitting up, sometime just lying down was a struggle. She was beginning to toss and turn in her sleep. Lula attributed some of it to nerves. Monday came and went as if it was truly passing through. Tuesday morning arrived with a bang.

The Hampton farm rooster started it off with his three o'clock wake-up call at the crack of dawn. The weather had gotten a little colder but not freezing. So the roosters call was loud and clear for all to hear. The big house Hampton farm rooster was a full grown eleven pound bird that took his responsibility to ward off any and all attackers seriously. His aim was also to announce he was the top cop on this farm.

This particular morning was the coming out of the little house rooster. He was hardly full grown. No one knew why he picked this particular morning to follow its instinct and try this crowing thing. John, waking up to the second and different crowing, reasoned his rooster finally figured out what roosters do. His call didn't sound as commanding, but it served its purpose.

John got up, folded up his pallet and stored it in the corner. There was a curtain hanging over his bedroom door to give his wife and Cousin Lula a little privacy. He heard a soft moan, which he knew belonged to his wife. While putting on his boots, the second sound came. This was a piercing half scream from a person in pain. He rushed to just outside the curtained doorway. Immediately he heard his cousin ask.

"You okay now honey?"

"Wooooo-weeeee, I felt this pain right at the top of my stomach all the way round to the middle of my back. This baby feel like it's a twisting and turning inside me."

"Uh-huh, well it may be that he or she wants to see the world today. Just lie back honey, I'll be right back."

Lula almost knocked John down coming out of the little room. "Oh, there you are. Honey get some more firewood and bring in some buckets or water from the well. I think yawls baby is ready to come out. Take your time but hurry, you hear?"

John almost turned around in circles trying to decide which to do first, following instructions or wanting to see that his wife was doing okay. He quickly remembered this was Cousin Lula's domain and ran outside to fetch the wood first.

Lula, as she did the last few days, grabbed her coat before going outside to empty the bedrooms night bucket. She rinsed it out with a little of the well water left in the wells bucket, quickly returning to the house.

Checking on Gracie, she asked her if she felt another sharp pain like the first one.

"No, ma'am." She answered looking wide eyed and alert.

After putting more wood on the stoves fire, placing the coffee pot on a burner, Lula returned to Gracie's bedside. She told the obviously nervous expectant mother that this was probably the first stages of delivery. She rubbed the young woman's stomach, legs, and calves with what she called her special new mother's oil. All the while telling her what a wonderful mother she will be to the little one.

"That child's gonna be lucky to have you as its mother. Sallie told me so much about you and the kind of family you come from. You a church goin' woman and sho' do love your husband. He loves you too. I can see that just from the few days I been here."

Gracie was enjoying Cousin Lula personal touch until she felt the second pain which was a little more intensified than the first one. She cried out but not as loudly as before. She looked at Lula for more encouragement; the midwife was rubbing her arms and smiling.

"Okay child, time to comb and braid your hair."

It was the first time that Gracie felt doubt about any help Cousin Lula could give her. "What the heck is she combing my hair for, are we going somewhere? I wish my mother was here 'cause this ain't going well at all," She thought.

"Now you don't want the baby to see its mother looking like a witch or something. It might scare the little thing to death,

God forbid. You want to look pretty the first time you meet your child," Lula continued while she combed out the tangles in Gracie's hair.

Just as quickly as she had doubts, her confidence returned. "Somehow that makes sense," she thought.

Her husband couldn't help himself, so he pulled the curtain back, poked his head in, saw that his wife was okay and smiled. She returned his smiled letting him know that everything was all right. Satisfied, he let the curtain fall back into place and returned to his morning chores. He didn't mind staying busy; otherwise he would worry himself sick about what is going on in their bedroom.

He checked on the dogs, chickens, and the half-grown rooster that crowed for the first time this morning. The young bird looked at him kind of funny as if to say; "I told you this was going to be a special day." John smiled while heading for the well to get another bucket of water.

Later on, he would go down to the big house to let everybody know what was going on. For now, he better stick close, he reasoned. He returned to the house just in time to hear his wife's reaction to the third pain. It was a muffled scream but a scream never the less.

The pain was so intense this time, she had to scream. She tried to cover her mouth, not wanting to worry her husband. The pain itself lasted almost a full minute. The baby was no longer twisting and turning, which was a good thing. She told Lula as much.

"That's good, honey. That means the baby has found, what doctors call the birth canal," She replied rubbing Gracie's stomach, this time without the oil.

"Oh Cousin Lula, I ain't never felt this kinda pain before. I heard women talk about it but, woooo-weeee; I guess you have to feel it for yourself to know how it feels.

The pains were coming quicker now and after a few more, Lula asked Gracie to lie back down on her back, position both soles of her feet flat onto the bed by bending her knees and spread her legs wide. She wanted to take a look and see if the baby was coming.

Lula couldn't see the head, so she stuck two fingers into Gracie's vagina. She could feel the baby's head, which had worked itself into position.

"It won't be long now," she told Gracie. "Just stay in that position right there."

Lula poured a little cold water into the hot bucket of water she had by her chair to cool the water down. Sticking her hand in the bucket water to test the temperature, she poured a little more cold water. Satisfied, she turned to a sweating Gracie whose pains were every two minutes or less. You could look into her eyes and tell she was trying to be brave, but the pain, oh the pain she was feeling.

"Let me take another look honey," Lula told her.

All Grace could do now was follow any directions given and hope this ordeal would be over soon. She was bound and determined not to mess this up. She was also anxious to meet and see her baby. But this pain, she screamed once more.

"I see it, honey. Here comes the head. Now push, baby, push. Wait for a couple seconds, let out a good breath of air like I told you and push again."

All kind of thoughts was flashing through Gracie's mind. Would the baby have two arms, legs? Is it a girl or boy? Who will it look like? Can I take the time with it that my baby is going to need? Can I protect my baby from anybody? Her thoughts were interrupted by the pain and then Lula's voice.

"Come on, honey, it's almost over. Push, I said, push and take another breath and push again. That's it, honey, push hard, harder . . ."

All of a sudden, Gracie felt a jolt of relief and then just a numbing like pain. She almost passed out but remained conscious enough to hear.

"It's a boy, honey, a little old boy. That's what was giving you all that pain, this here boy," Lula announced.

She cut the cord with a sharp pair of scissors she'd boiled in the water on the stove. She did this before placing them in a small pan of warm water resting on a kitchen chair by the bed. Meticulously washing the new birth off the little boy and wrapping him in a half sheet, she presented him to his mother who was simply exhausted.

While mother and baby became acquainted, she cleaned up her patient's body delivery area and placed a clean towel under her buttocks to provide additional comfort.

Grabbing the small pan and pouring its contents into another bucket of lukewarm water, she left the room carrying the bucket to go outside. Again, she almost bumped into John who was standing directly outside of the curtain.

"You can go on in now, baby. Yo new son is waitin' to meet his daddy."

She turned to look over her shoulder just as she was going out the door and saw John still standing at the curtain looking at her.

"Everything's all right. Go on in now and see 'bout your wife and child," She said before closing the door behind her as she exited the house.

Disposing of the contents in the bucket into a small garbage can, she rinsed the bucket out with well water and refilled it. She washed her hands using the homemade soap and water bucket they kept by the well. Lula stopped for a moment. She wiped her face with her apron, not knowing why, because she was not sweating, it was just habit.

It must be about six o'clock now, she thought. The sunshine and rays were peeping through the snow clouds. It also seemed to be warmer than she originally thought the day was going to turn out to be.

Lula raised her hands to God, thanking him for a smooth delivery and good health of the baby boy. Feeling the chill, she realized she did not have on her coat. She ran back into the house.

The father was sitting in the bedside chair rocking his newborn son. His little eyes were closed yet he was still waving his little arms around.

John looked up at Cousin Lula and told her, "Thank you. We can work out the payment later?"

"You're family, John and Gracie. You two are family, no payment needed. What yawl gon' call this here boy, John Jr.?"

"It is way too many Johns in this here world. Naw . . ." John answered.

"We are naming him Codis," Gracie said. "Codis Hampton. I got that name from a history book in school. I think its Roman or Greek. Can't remember which one, I just know I liked the names of Codis and Cassius."

"How do you say that again? C Odis?" Lula asked.

Gracie managed a weak smile through the pain she still felt and replied, "Naw, Cousin Lula, you say it like Co-dis, not C Odis."

"Well there is some papers me and yawl will have to fill out and send them off to the County Seat but you can mark this down. Codis Hampton, a Negro male was born on February 3, 1925 in Bradley County, Banks, Arkansas to Gracie and John Hampton. Hi you feeling girl?"

"Cousin Lula, I could not be better. Oh, I feel tired and sore, but um glad that it is over. I don't know what I would have done without you. Thank you, thank you so much for being here with me, with us."

Lula smiled. "I'll rustle yawl up some food because you going to need your energy. That baby is starting to cry like he is hungry right now. You better get him used to feeding off your breast. Just get him in position and stick that nipple in his mouth. He'll take it from there."

John felt embarrassed, then privileged to witness his son's first feeding. While his wife did that, it was time for him to let the big house know that a new little Hampton was born. He kissed his wife and waved to little Codis, leaving Lula trying to cook something or the other.

He practically ran down the hill to tell his mama and daddy. "His older brothers have been expecting this to happen," he thought. "It's going to take some doing to explain this to his youngest brother Peach. But then again, his mother is pregnant and due in July; she can explain it to him."

He burst into the big house yelling, it's a boy, it's a boy! Sallie, Sambo and Lemon were sitting at the table eating and drinking coffee. They smiled at the thought of having a new addition to the Hamptons.

192

"All these knuckle head boys, I guess it's up to me to have the first girl. How is Gracie son?" Sallie commented and asked.

"She's fine, mama. She's feeding little Codis right now."

"Little who?" Sambo asked.

"Codis, his name is Codis."

"That's a funny name. It's not a girl's name is it?" Sambo said, asking for clarification.

"It's not, and he is a he, daddy." John proudly stated.

"Lula's gonna want to get home this morning to see about her family. Somebody should ride back with her." Sallie thought out loud.

"Monroe." Sambo called out.

"Yes suh daddy," Monroe answered as he came out of the boy's bedroom.

"Help Lemon here, saddle Lula's horse and Old thunder. Afterwards, you gonna ride back to her place with her. You can visit for a short time, but you better git your butt on back here so yo' mama won't be worried." Sambo instructed.

"Yes suh."

"For now, sit down and eat you some breakfast before yawl saddle the horses." His mother said.

John excused himself, telling his parents he would let Cousin Lula know of plans for her to return home. Now that he has informed his folks on the birth of his son he returned up the hill to his immediate family's little house, wife and newborn son.

As soon as Frank and Harriett heard the news of the arrival of their second grandchild, they were pleased he was alive and well. Their first grandchild came from their son Edwards's marriage to Ruth King. They had a little daughter naming her Missy. Some time ago, he and his family left the King family farm in Lawrence County, moving north looking for jobs and a better life.

Lately, Edward Hall seems to always be on the move to somewhere in search of a better life for his family. The last letter to his parents came a month ago from Cleveland, Ohio. Even though they had seen their granddaughter a few times while they were in Arkansas, they had not seen Edward or his family since they moved north.

In the last few months, they have seen little Codis three times more than they ever saw Missy. They've only seen him five times. That has been enough for them to notice the little baby's expressive personality.

"That little boy can't stay still for one minute. Look at him wiggling and carrying on. What yawl feeding that child besides breast milk?" Viola Hall asked.

They were all sitting outside in Gravel Ridge First Baptist Church yard enjoying another after service dinner. Frank, Harriett, Viola, Edgar, Lena and Colrolus were watching people come over to see baby Codis sleeping, yet twisting and trying to turn even in Gracie's arm. Mae Ellen was splitting her time between playing with the other kids and running back and forth to check on the baby in her friend Gracie's arm.

"Yep, he is a little frisky, been that way all his life." John said.

"Yeah, almost six months old and it seems like a long time too. Every now and then I stick something soft like a bit of mashed sweet potato pie in his mouth but otherwise he is still breastfeeding." Gracie answered.

"Sho' he is. Did you think he was going to be eating fried chicken?" Harriett asked.

"No, ma'am, I was just teasing. Still, he is a busy little boy." Viola replied.

This was the first time that Gracie and John had brought their baby to church. Reverend Payne blessed him right after the service. A lot of people stopped by the table to welcome Gracie back and to see her son.

They ate from picnic baskets, talked about the sunny weather, crops, people who were still moving north, west and those who were staying. They compared their news from Versia and James in Hot Springs. All was well with them. She did tell them that Sammy Parker and his friend CC were still hanging with the local small time hoods. They were just as tight with their northern gangster friends. Please don't tell his mother and father about this, Versia pleaded.

John was asked about his mother's pregnancy and happily announced she'd had another boy. She was fit to be tied after having six boys with no girl in sight. They named the July 9th born boy, Calvin, Calvin Hampton.

"It's funny because my just over two week old brother, Calvin, is now my almost six month old son's uncle," John offered.

The conversation elaborated on the fact that Sallie Hampton had six boys and no girl. Some gave their opinion of which one is easier to raise, an age old question. As always, there was no consensus for boys or girls. All agreed that it depended upon the child. That is, some children need more encouragement because they are shy and others you have to tell to "be quiet" because they talk all the time. This particular trait is not exclusive of a girl or a boy.

Then there was the discussion of which gender is more nosy or inquisitive. Instinctually they want to know everything about anything. Again, there was no clear winner of which sex was more "curious" than the other. They all agreed that can be a dangerous trait for a black person, especially in the south.

"Girl, when can we expect a playmate for Mae Ellen? How 'bout another little Viola or Edgar Junior?" Gracie asked.

"We are trying, it just hasn't happened yet," Viola said.

"Nope, I can tell you. It's not from us not trying," Edgar said to a round of muted laughter.

"Probably not as hard as um working on it," Colrolus added to more laughter.

"So . . . , you doing it by yourself, are you?" Lena playfully added to another round of laughter.

"That's all right yawl. Your little bundles of joy will be coming round soon enough, you'll see," An experienced Harriett counseled.

"Yeah, then you might not be able to turn off the spigot," Frank said, with the men laughing louder than women, who seemed somewhat embarrassed by this kind of talk.

"You hush Frank," Harriett scolded while noticing Mae Ellen running back to check on the baby.

"Well, my sisters and me are thankful you live close to mama and daddy. At least we don't feel so bad about getting married and leaving them alone," Lena said, speaking of the younger Halls'.

"One thing 'bout it, we get to see each other right here on Sundays." Colrolus added.

"Yeah, that is a good thing. Come to think of it, I ain't ever been to Gracie's house, and she ain't been to mine either," Lena said with a smile while teasing her sister.

"I know, huh. Time is moving so fast, and we always have so much work to do," Gracie said while gently rocking her sleeping baby in her arms.

"Ms. Harriett, I just wanted you and Frank to know that next Sunday we probably going to go up the road to my folks' church. We need to show them church folk our little baby too," John said.

"Sho' honey, we understand. Little Codis need to be shown off. He's so cute sleeping like that," replied Harriett.

Just then, Reverend Payne and his wife, Hattie stopped at their table to wish everyone a safe week ahead, and goodbye if he doesn't get to say it before they leave. Harriett congratulated the pastor on another excellent sermon. The couple exchanged greetings and well wishes with everyone seated around the table and excused themselves so they could move on to parishioners at the next table.

All agreed, it was time to go as little Codis was beginning to stir, awaken by all of the handshaking initiated by the Pastor. The families hugged, sometime tearfully, saying their goodbyes and returned to their respective modes of transportation. Colrolus drove his truck; everyone else came by wagon team. Viola, Edgar and Mae Ellen rode with Frank and Harriett.

John and Gracie had to pick up his brothers, Lemon, Monroe, David Jr, and Van D (Peach) up the road at Reverend Davis' Oaklawn Methodist Church. Sambo had stayed home with his wife to see after Calvin, their newborn.

Waving goodbye as they peeled off to go in different directions, it was a enjoyable visit by all. It is always gratifying to see and talk with family. By now, little Codis were wide awake and hungry. Gracie obliged by breast feeding him with a little towel over his face and most of her breast. The baby had to get used to the roll of the wagon as he kept losing his nipple. Gracie laughed as he finally got the hang of breast feeding on a moving wagon.

"This boy is hanging on for dear life." She remarked as they approached the Oaklawn Methodist Church.

The boys climbed onto the wagon and sat down to enjoy the ride back to the Hampton Farm. Gracie advised the youngest, Peach to sit down before he fell out of the wagon. She correctly figured out he was trying to peek at the baby breast feeding. The ride was not that far, about a mile and half up a low hill.

John drove up to the little house, not before Monroe, David Jr. and Peach was let off at the big house. Lemon stayed in the wagon so that he can drive it back to the big house barn and unhook the team.

Spider, Oh No and their two pups were happy to see John and Gracie. They performed their now normal welcome home show of barking and wagging tails with the two pups turning flips.

Finally, back at home, John went back out the door to feed the chickens and dogs. Gracie laid her son down for a nap while she started her Sunday house work. At this very moment, Gracie Hampton was a happy woman. She really enjoyed visiting, but like they say, there is no place like home.

CHAPTER 7

The Significance of Four Years prior to The Crash

The rest of America, especially in major cities, was in a period of sustained economic prosperity. So much so, they called it the Roaring Twenties. Automobiles were the personal choice of transportation. Twenty million autos were on the road by 1925. Citizens had use of the telephone, indoor plumbing and electricity. They could listen to Jazz music, which was increasing in popularity, and other forms of music on the radio. The little box, plugged into an electrical outlet, offered political speeches, news, drama, and comedy shows to an ever-growing audience. Or, one could take his family or date to a motion picture show at the local theater. 1925 saw a whopping forty million people go to the movies each week.

Women were rebelling against what was considered proper and acceptable behavior. White and black women bobbed their hair, wore excessive makeup, and short skirts. The media or someone called them flappers, a term associated with a young bird flapping its wings while learning to fly. They drank, smoked cigarettes, and had their own ideas about sex. Each woman would decide who they was going to give it to, whether to wait for marriage, or not, and they wanted to enjoy the act just as much as their lover.

In a lot of cases, the shy reserved girl was replaced by the initiator of conversation, impatient with slow men, anxious to chart a different destiny from their parents' wishes. In many respects, girls just wanted to have fun too.

To put economics in perspective, one dollar in 1925 had the same buying power as thirteen dollars and twenty-seven cents does in this year of 2013. The dollar comparison for 1926 is twelve dollars and eighty-three cents, 1927, twelve dollars and ninety-seven cents, and 1928, back to thirteen dollars and twenty-seven cents.

In New York, chicken was selling for 39 cents a pound, milk 28 cents a half gallon, bread 10 cents a pound and eggs were 55 cents a dozen in 1926. A pound of coffee would cost you about 47 cents, a Harley-Davidson motorcycle was $235 in 1927.

Yet, the southern rural areas of this country were not privilege to have all those modern city trappings. Indoor plumbing was still mostly limited to larger cities rather than smaller towns or rural areas. Electricity was available to capitals and some of the largest cities in the southern states. Automobiles, trucks other mobile units were increasing their presence in the southern States and, somewhat surprisingly, on a lot of rural farms. If you saw a flapper in the south, they probably were just passing through.

The events of 1925 through 1928 would see a series of events that would affect the community of Gravel Ridge, town of Banks, Warren, and Hot Springs.

The most costly and destructive act of God in Arkansas history occurred in 1927. According to records, and as noted in the Encyclopedia of Arkansas History & Culture, the Mississippi River Flood of 1927 covered about 6600 square miles flooding some thirty-six out of seventy-five counties across Arkansas.

It goes on to say, the effects of the floodwaters (thirty feet deep in some places) on farmland (over two millions acres), people (over 350,000), deaths (over 100 people), families receiving Red Cross relief (some 41,243 people), was devastating. The monetary loss alone was upwards of $1 million dollars to a growing economy.

Before the flood, man-made levees were built to prevent the overflow of rivers which tended to rise to overcapacity after heavy rains. This particular spring brought a record amount of rainfall throughout Arkansas, so much so that the grounds were saturated. All bodies of water, i.e. lakes and rivers were full.

Added to the problem, was the fact that the warm spring caused the snow to melt early in Canada filling the upper Mississippi to its capacity. As the river, already filled, flowed toward their normal destination, the Gulf of Mexico, its gushing waters met the enormous rains the South was experiencing, precipitating more overflow in the local bodies of water and levies, which eventually could not hold all of the water, contributed to the flooding itself. The enormous amount of water simply had nowhere to go except to spill out onto the land, farms, and homes of the area.

A lot of areas within Arkansas remained under water from the spring up into September of 1927. You can't farm or do much else if your land is underwater. In fact, you can imagine man and animal health issues that are a direct result of standing water that has been there for a long period of time.

One can also imagine the confrontations resulting in the resistance met by outside Red Cross Relief workers and others in trying to assist those in need, regardless of race color, or creed. To a large majority of people in the areas, as has been continually mentioned, there is a certain pecking order in this part of the county that does not change in any circumstance. In fact, many will unapologetic stress in particularly clear terms, their kind need all the help they can get and black people are welcomed to whatever a white person don't need.

The fact that the federal response under President Calvin Coolidge was muted to all locals aid requirements, contributed to the problems of the poor, black and white. His policy was to deny any federal dollars in direct aid to flood victims of the south. Therefore, who would get serviced first, last, or if at all, was left to the discretion of the various area local officials.

The Plantation system was to be protected at all cost. Black and white sharecroppers saw their movement rights restricted. The planters feared they may not return to the fields after staying in warmth and comfort of the Red Cross camps. The planters became their spokesperson under a local mandate. The Encyclopedia of Arkansas History & Culture reported in particularly "African Americans needed a pass to enter or leave the Red Cross camps."

Even at that, several benefits were realized from this tragedy. Besides the obvious rebuilding and building of new infrastructure throughout the affected area, there was talk among the federally and local government on how to handle these types of occurrences in the future.

There was evidence on the power of this new media, radio. It showed the impact of how fast and far the facts of any newsworthy items could reach the United States' public. It reminded Americans that tragedy can strike suddenly, causing them to look inward and ask themselves how they would have handled it. It allowed people to hear about the southern treatment of sharecroppers, the plantation system still in place, the fact the Mississippi River's flood stage lasted a record 153 days.

As a direct result to the Republican Party's non-response to the need of black people in particular, a demographic shift to the Democratic Party ensued. These people had stuck with the Republicans; Abraham Lincoln's party, through thick and thin, all through the civil war, up until this flood. To this day, most African-Americans are democrats.

Authors Note/comment: I remember as a kid, my father telling me never to vote Republican. They don't have the best interest of black people in mind, nor do they care anything about our race of people. Writing this book, I couldn't tell you how old I was or approximately when he said it. He said it more than once. It had to be back in the sixties. Those warnings have become ironic as I look and listen to the Republican party of today.

It reminds me of a joke I heard Whoopi Goldberg tell on one of her last one-woman television specials. She said every time this pet store parrot saw this lady customer come in his owners place, he would look at the lady, burst out laughing and say "You sho' is ugly." After this happened during a couple more visits, the woman had enough. She scolded the store owner, told him how embarrassed she was and told him to keep that bird quiet. She told him if his parrot repeated those words to her one more time, she would not be responsible for the consequences. The owner assured her that it would not happen again.

The next time the lady visited the store, her eyes glared at the parrot, he said nothing. She walked around the store and selected her purchase and went to the counter to pay. The bird, which was located next to the cash register, looked at her and didn't say a word.

She paid for her purchase, took one last look at the parrot, turned, and walked toward the front door. As she reached for the door knob, she heard the parrot kind of whisper under his breath, "Ain't nothing changed."

So today, for the Republican Party, if my father could see your decisions of today, he would roll over in his grave, stick his finger in the air, and say without a doubt, "Ain't nothing changed."

End, Authors Note/comment.

It should also be noted, all the people listed in this story so far, survived the Flood of 1927. I can't say there was no loss of property, but overall, these people, revealing how tough they were and by the Grace of God, still survived.

There would be more births, such as this author's father, Codis Hampton. It is funny how the simple pronunciation of Codis' name would be different. As he grew, many would call him C Odis with the emphasis on the C and O. However, it is essential to remember the fact the correct pronunciation of Codis is Co-dis. Some family member and friends said that C Odis was the country pronunciation. Co-dis were thought of as the city folk pronunciation.

The birth of Codis' Uncle, Calvin Hampton, the last child from the union of Sambo and Sallie Hampton, was significant as these two people would be close as brothers for life. David (Sambo) Hampton Sr., whose first marriage was to Lou, bore a girl named Wadie. That name would come up again in Gracie and John's household. Sambo would also have another girl name Verna, by Lizzie Falls. Sallie Davis, whose first son Lemon Davis, father was Buck Davis. He was born before her marriage to Sambo.

1926 started off with an event that would concern baby Codis, who was almost 1 year old. January 29th would play a significant role in his life. Papa Warner Johnson and Dora's daughter Edna Johnson married a mulatto man named Edward Childs on July 8, 1925. To this union a girl, Doreatha Childs was born on January 29, 1926. The little baby girl would grow up to become Codis Hampton's wife and this author's mother. Later on, approximately forty years, her mother would confess to Doreatha that her real father was Harvey Momon. Never-the-less, one more child was born to the union of Edna and Edward. She was born on June 13, 1927 and named Gertie Mae (Nookie) Childs.

Papa Warner and Dora saw another one of their children get married a month before Edna. Their oldest son, Joel married Viola Ross in June of 1925. To this union was born Georgia Mae, Virgie, and her brother JO.

Georgia Mae and her sister Virgie played and hung around with their first cousins, Doreatha and Gertie Mae (Nookie) through puberty, on through their teenage years. Virgie and Georgia Mae's brother, JO would be around but mostly hung with the boys, like the Hampton and Davis boys.

Many of Papa Warner's grandchildren followed in their parent's footsteps by working on his farm in some capacity or another. That would also include the backbreaking work of picking cotton since that was a cash generating commodity their grandfather chose to grow.

Gracie and John would welcome their second child on March 13, 1926. A girl they named Lacirene Hampton. Needless to say, Sallie was fit to be tied. Her daughter-in-law got a girl on her second-go-round. After that Sallie accepted her faith. She was not going to birth any girls or, more boys for that matter, within her lifetime, which was Gods will. At least that was her wish. She'd just have to be satisfied with all her knuckle headed boys.

The union of Gracie and John experienced their first loss of a child. A girl was born in January of 1928 but did not last but a few days. It was a difficult birth. During which time, the midwife had to help the baby turn in the right direction for deliverance by inserting her hands into the birth canal. Gracie lost a lot of blood but managed to survive the ordeal. The child was delivered alive and named Vasemae Hampton. Unfortunately, she died within days from the traumatic birth experience. It was a wonderment felt by all that she lasted as long as she did. She had difficulty breathing the entire time she was alive.

John took the extra time to console his wife, just like the rest of the family. Gracie was shook to the core and not sure if she wanted any more children. A long conversation with her mother-in-law Sallie convinced her that life sometimes takes these twist and turns. Only God knew what was best in these type situations. Sallie told her that God always knows what is best for all of his children. That would also include if they should be born, how long they should live, if at all. She confirmed that everything happens for a reason in God's plan. Gracie felt better and agreed with Sallie that ours is not to wonder the why of things. That did not stop the family from grieving for baby Vasemae, only gave them hope that the next child, if there were to be a next child, would be born healthy, and the mother would go on to see all her children grown up to be adults.

Meanwhile during this three year span, the Hole in the Bushes place was becoming a fantastic fun and dance get-a-way, along with acting as the Gravel Ridge and surrounding community's cultural center for black people. One could experience exquisite dining while showing their customers they could find black sophistication right here in the boondocks too.

The blues were still being practiced, sung with style enhanced by William 'June-bug' Davis, right here every Friday and Saturday night. The young boy just had a knack for writing lyrics, sometime while playing a set in front of an audience. The guitar tricks he'd picked up from his mother's boyfriend was paying dividends. June-bug was making a name for himself as an innovator, composer and singer right before his audience eyes.

The style itself was still a work in progress. This allowed a talented individual to test different sounds, or a new way of playing instruments as long as the core of the blues was untouched.

There is a W. C. Handy's story written in his autobiography. He says, around 1903 while sleeping on a train traveling through

Tutwiler, Mississippi he was jolted awake by this strange music being played on a guitar by "a lean, loose-jointed Negro beside me." He said his clothes were rags, and he had holes in his shoes so much so "his feet peeped out of his shoes." "His face had on it some of the sadness of the ages. As he played, he pressed a knife on the strings in a manner popularized by Hawaiian guitarist who used steel bars." He went on to say, "The effect was unforgettable. His song, too, struck me instantly. The singer repeated the line ("Goin' where the Southern Cross' the Dog") three times, accompanying himself on the guitar with the weirdest music I had ever heard."

Mr. Handy used that very line when he wrote, "Yellow Dog Rag" in 1914. After the term 'blues' was recognized by the masses, he retitled the song to "Yellow Dog Blues." His form of blues was more like ragtime with a taste of blues and jazz to augment your senses and soul.

June-bug plays what he calls our down home blues. He is familiar with Ma Rainey, had heard a version of Mamie Smiths' "Crazy Blues" release in 1920, yet considered their styles as written and performed from a women's perspective. He liked to refer to regional and local issues without getting political. He strictly concentrated on a man's love life and troubles around his southern roots and home life. That is what his audience responds to and contributes to his popularity.

Through this same time span the town of Banks, its residents and officials survived. There is no doubt that the overall economic loss, availability of goods for sale, was felt here. Some of the roads were under water or in need of repair around here too. Yet these little Bradley County towns, as do throughout the entire state counties, have a way of going on with life.

During the summer of 1928, Sheriff Penelton still had not found his shooter or shooters in the death of his deputy. Sammy Parker never came in. Ms. Rebecca Doyle announced their June 17th of next year wedding date. His deputy, Josh Stovall was still employed, and second in charge to Deputy Charlie Oates chagrin.

Skeeter Purvis' entire family was still intact, son the doctor, daughter helping out at the store, with his oldest son continually trying to farm. Business was slow for Skeeter and McBain's general store.

The fact that all survived and was going on with their lives is attributable to mankind willingness to take things in stride. They would be tested again for the resolve they all came up with this time.

CHAPTER 8

Ill Economic Winds Bring Harder Times & Personal Grief

The Hampton's farm survived with average damage despite experiencing saturated planting areas from the heavy rainfall in the spring of 1927. With the land sitting atop a little hill, it proved to be beneficial to the farm and house grounds. The spring behind the little house overflowed with water flowing downhill to settle around the area of the Oaklawn Methodist Church, schoolhouse, Gravel Ridge First Baptist Church and the surrounding valley areas. Yet, even with the rain and modest overflow from area waterways, most of the Gravel Ridge community did not suffer the standing water devastation realized by so many other Arkansans. As Reverend A.J. Payne of the First Baptist said in a sermon during the time, "God is good, we are humbled and thankful."

Codis was four and Lacirene three years old by now. The sad experience of losing Vasemae a few days after birth was still in Gracie mind, but she was pregnant again and looking forward to having a healthy child. It was as though God rewarded them for their faith in him. Gracie and John were more than happy to add another boy to their growing family. Baby Curtis Hampton arrived on January 24, 1929. He wasn't as frisky as his older brother and certainly not as serious looking as his sister. He was a cute baby that had the makings of a lady charmer, or so Gracie thought.

So far the winter months had caused a bit of a hardship, not because of the weather. The problem was their crops were not as fruitful as prior to the flood. The residual water from overflow and rain kept the soil too moist for seeds or seedlings. A lot of farmers planted what they thought would grow anyway, resulting in weak plants. They received much smaller yields for their efforts. Therefore, the normal food storage for the winter was down by about fifty percent. This year, families learned to expect the bare minimum for meals as the head of the households were stretching their food supply to last through the winter.

There were small to substantial accomplishments going on around the world and throughout the United States. There were also veil warnings of things to come. Commercial and military airplanes were here to stay. The length of flights was growing with flights between Europe, North, South America, Asia and Australia. For example, Charles Lindberg began a 3500 mile flight from Detroit to Cape Horn.

The US saw the first appearance of the car radio. While the world of technology, travel, personal comfort, and leisure time saw steady improvement, there were events that made a splash in the news. There were others that hardly made a ripple but were just as important or a preview to what's to come. February would bring two significant incidents that would cause concern both here and abroad.

A national incident that brought about a lot of attention on the US underworld occurred on February 14, 1929. Some say Hot Springs vacationer and Chicago resident, Al Capone initiated one of the most violent murders of a rival gangster in history. It was known as the St. Valentine's Day Massacre. Four men, two dressed as policemen, with the other two in hats, suits, and overcoats were seen leaving a garage on Chicago's North side. It looked as though the police had arrested the two men and took them off to jail. A roomer, from across the street, was sent by his suspicious landlady to see why a dog was howling and barking. The animal was actually tied to a truck inside the garage. After entering the building, the roomer saw seven gun riddled bodies lying at the base of a wall. The sight was so sickening that he immediately ran back out of the garage.

It was the aftermath of an attempt to lure Bugs Moran, Capone's chief rival, and his gang to the garage for slaughtering. Bugs Moran was not there because the killers probably thought one of his men was Moran himself. Frank Gusenberg, a Moran enforcer, was shot fourteen times. He was not dead when the real police arrived. Asked who shot him, he replied, "Nobody shot me." Three hours later he was dead.

For his part, Capone made sure he was out of town, staying at his Palm Island estate in Biscayne Bay, located on the outskirts of Miami, Florida. Investigators concluded it was the work of the Capone gang and went about investigating the clues and close ties to the mob of individuals who were identified from those clues. It also put the country on notice to the ruthlessness of the mob, causing new tactics, formation, and added responsibilities for crime fighting organizations.

Another major incident happened that would cause the world problems before and during World War II. Adolf Hitler, Germany's founder and leader of the Nazi Party, approved the Lateran Treaty between Vatican and Mussolini's fascist government. This would further establish Mussolini's Italy and Germany as allies.

Hitler was quoted in the Völkischer Beobachter as saying, "the fact that the Curia is now making its peace with Fascism shows that the Vatican trusts the new political realities far more than did the former liberal democracy with which it could not come to terms . . . . The fact that the Catholic Church has come to an agreement with Fascist Italy . . . proves beyond doubt that the Fascist world of ideas is closer to Christianity than those of Jewish liberalism or even atheistic Marxism, to which the so-called Catholic Center Party sees itself so closely bound, to the detriment of Christianity today and our German people."

Hitler also had words for the Germany's Catholic Center Party. At the time, they still supported democracy. He added, "By trying to preach that democracy is still in the best interests of German Catholics, the Center Party . . . is placing itself in stark contradiction to the spirit of the treaty signed today by the Holy See."

The organizations support eroded over the next few years. The Reichstag delegates of that same Catholic Center Party ensured passage of the Enabling Act, officially ending Germany democracy in favour of a dictatorship under Adolf Hitler.

Unaware as to how Hitler would affect all Americans, a Gravel Ridge community was happy to hear that one of their own had gotten the news they waited for almost ten years to hear. Edgar and Viola Hall were married in 1919. They often kidded among family members and friends of their attempt to have their second child. They were almost convinced that Mae Ellen, now going on 14 years old, born four years before they were married, would be an only child. Their announcement of Viola's pregnancy was met with congratulations at last Sunday's after service picnic. The happy couple and their daughter were beaming with pride and expectation.

A week later, just as they've done every Saturday since Gracie Hampton got married, they walked up to Frank and Harriett Hall's house to have supper on a Saturday evening. With the Halls getting on in age, their family, mainly Versia, Lena and Gracie asked their cousin Edgar to look in on their parents occasionally to ensure they were getting along on a daily basis.

Sometimes human nature or pride prevents some older individuals from asking for help although they need it. The girls were trying to avoid that scenario with their parents. Harriett and Frank weren't aware of any extra attention; they just saw the younger Halls' visits by family. The Saturday meal ritual was just family, who lived not a half of a city block from each other, getting together to share a meal.

The one difference in today was that Viola was finally expecting another child. May Ellen was just as happy as her parents. It was the topic a, b, and c until the conversation turned to a letter received from Versia in Hot Springs.

"Child, I got a letter from Versia yesterday. She said that Sammy Parker boy has turned gangster all the way. She says the boy and his friend, CC is running and selling moonshine from some still or 'nother for a white man down there. She don't see him with any job, even tho' he dresses in suits and drives a new car." Harriett reported.

"Oh my God, that boy is gonna git himself killed, carrying on that way," Viola said.

"Yeah, I imagine he thinks he the big cock on the walk down there now. Struttin' around with all them important white gangsters from back east." Frank added.

"I'm with Viola on this. He sho' can't expect to have any kinda life like that.' Cause the moment the law catch up to him; it gon' be all over," Edgar said as he reached for another piece of corn bread.

"That's right," Frank continued. "I betcha' when that happens he will find out how fast his friends gonna act like they don't even know him. He gon' turned into just another spook, far as they concerned."

"Well, she say, a lot of the local colored gals are swarming around him like bees these days," Harriett added. "Course, he was always a nice lookin' boy anyhow."

"Mamma Harriett, when is Versia gonna get pregnant?" Viola asked. "Do her and James still want chillen?"

"Child I don't know. She don't talk about it in her letters. I know at one time they were waiting until they could buy a house or some land. They still haven't bought either one. I got to ask her the next time I see her."

"Well, Gracie is sho' spittin' 'em out almost every year since her and John got married," Viola said causing loud and long laughter from around the table.

"Yeah, John keeps planting his seed with a new crop popping up in nine months." Edgar said almost choking on his food. He had to take a drink of water to get his food down.

"They sho ain't lettin' no grass grow between their toes. Naw, they lettin' it rip while the ripping is good," an almost hysterical Frank added. "That's my girl Gracie. She ain't never waited around for nothing."

They laughed about that for a little while. They talked a while with Edgar who told Frank and Harriett, they were not going to church with them in the morning. They were going to drive their horse team wagon to Warren to see their folks. He said they would be back on that Monday afternoon. They asked if Harriett or Frank needed anything from Banks or Warren, no need to drive over twenty miles roundtrip, and not pick up something you need.

Frank asked if they could bring his some tobacco. Harriett needed a package of sewing needles; otherwise that's all that was needed. The sun had set when they left to walk back down to their own house. Little did these couples realize, this was their last meal together, nor would they all ever see each again.

The next morning, Edgar hooked the horses to the wagon. He wanted to get an early start in order to spend time with their folks, yet start to return early enough to get home before dark. These days it was a little scary driving a horse team on the highway. The locals had acquired more and more automobiles over the last decade, there were more cars on the roads. Some drivers were a little rude as they drove around the wagon, especially youngsters who had been drinking or in their words just having fun. Passing, they would deliberately swerve close enough to the horses trying to spook them. At least, these two animals were used to autos so it would not be a new experience to have them pass them on the road.

Edgar figured traffic would be very low on a Sunday morning because most residents would be in church. It was sparse as compared to a spring day Saturday, when people were traveling to and from Banks, Warren or wherever taking care of their weekend business.

He, his wife, and daughter drove off toward Banks en route to Warren Arkansas. As he turned onto the road, one could see clear as far as the eye could see. His horses' rolled along at about four miles per hour walking, to about eight miles per hour trotting, hoping to reach Warren in an hour and a half.

The horses were in a gentle trot over the dirt road as they passed the road to Clem and Cora Parkers farm. The county still had not put blacktop on this part of the road to Banks. They could see the front of the house from the road that sat atop a slight hill. The next farm on their left belonged to Harvey Sampson. You could not see any buildings from the road because of the trees that lined the fence along his property line. They could see the turnoff road leading to the gate a few yards from the highway.

They also saw the two men guarding the gate. They quickly turned their eyes back to the road to avoid any thought from the two that they were being stared at by the family.

They'd gone about forty or fifty yards passed the Sampson road turnoff when they noticed a truck carrying two white men approaching them from the opposite direction. They could not identify them, but the driver was Bob with Clarke sitting in on the passenger's side. They were probably heading for their boss, Harvey Sampson's farm.

Edgar slowed the horses to a walk as the auto was clearly on the wrong side of the road heading directly for the Hall's wagon. Finally, Edgar stopped the horses in their tracks so as not to startle them. Just like they could see the fast approaching vehicle, so could the horses. They began to shuffle their hoofs in anticipation of danger while Edgar braced to control the reins as the oncoming vehicle was headed in direct line for them.

The vehicle finally swerves to its right, trying to pass the wagon. Unfortunately, it came too close to the horses. The animal directly to the left of Bob the driver had reared up turning to its left, with both his front hoofs coming down into the bed of the truck. The force of its hoofs being jerked as they hit the trucks wooden back tailgate caused the horses body to uncontrollably turn in the direction the vehicle was traveling. Simultaneously, the other horse frightened by the truck, the sudden force of its mate turning, was also pulled to its left. It was as if the entire wagon carrying the family was jerked in an opposite direction, causing the wagon to begin tipping over into the ditch.

Mae Ellen, sitting in the wagon's bed, was the first to be thrown out and the farthest. She landed on top of a small patch of ground shrubbery braking her fall though knocking her unconscious. Almost simultaneously, Viola and Edgar followed, being thrown from the now overturned wagon. Viola's body hit the embankments far wall before she lifelessly slumped from the impact and slid down into the ditch beside the road. Edgars head and neck hit the embankment, instantly killing him too, before sliding down into the ditch.

The wagon had tipped over with its back part smashing onto the embankment and partially breaking up with its parts ending up in the ditch too. The front part of the wagon mostly left intact lay straddled across the ditch.

The horse, which got his legs caught in the truck bed and broke, lay on the road writhing in pain. The other horse somehow managed to break away. It was now running up the road toward the Jennings' place dragging the rest of the harness with it.

Bob was able to stop the truck, which had significant damage to the wooden bed and back end of the truck. He and Clarke, not wanting to be seen, turned up into the Sampson turnoff, disappearing behind the gate and trees.

There was no one else on the road. No automobiles or wagon teams in either direction. No witnesses to what could be considered an act of vehicle homicide; no one except an old black man and his grandson, who was walking to Papa Warner's store. They were not on the road. They were walking alongside the road and saw the entire incident.

The man, in his fifties, was a member of the Tatum family. He was doing as he promised his eleven year old grandson, taking him to get a candy cane and soda pop at the Papa Warner's store.

He and his grandson ran toward the scene of the overturned wagon. After surveying the scene, he sent his grandson running up to Papa Warner's store to bring help. Not before he told him not to tell anyone what they saw. Don't say anything about the white men in the car or where it went.

"We found these folks just like this. The accident had already happen', you hear me boy? This ain't no joke. Do you hear me?" the old man instructed.

"Yes suh."

"You gon' tell anybody what we saw? Say, like your mama or papa?"

"No suh."

"All right then, gon' on ups to the store and git somebody down here."

With that, the boy took off running. About forty minutes later, he returned with Joel Warner, in an auto and a couple of men on horseback. They took one look at the Halls' bodies and shook their heads in denial.

By now, Mae Ellen had regained consciousness and was crying uncontrollably after realizing her parents were dead. Sitting on the back of Clem Parker short bed wagon, she was being attended to by his wife Cora. The conclusion was no limbs or ribs were broken. She was just trying to deal with the reality of her loss.

"Wasn't Viola pregnant?" Joel asked.

"Yes she was," answered Clem Parker, who'd got to the scene about twenty minutes after Rand Tatum's grandson ran to Papa Warner's. "My god, I don't think she was over eight weeks with child."

"Sherriff Penelton is on his way down from Banks. We shouldn't move the bodies." Joel said.

Finally, there was a single shot that startled all the people standing in and around the wreckage. The horse gave one last squeal, gasped and lay silent as an unknown white man carrying a hunting rifle in his truck simply said, "Somebody had to do it, and after all, that animal had been suffering for too long."

He put his rifle back in his vehicle, got in and shouted at the crowd before he drove away, "Tell Sheriff Penelton to come see Len Jennings. My name is Jennings, and I got a place right up the road on the left." Most of the onlookers and others watched as old man Jennings turned into the little turnoff and headed for his house.

It took almost fifteen more minutes for the Sheriff and Deputy Stovall to arrive at the wreckage scene. Both men got out of the police vehicle, walked over to the ditch, and immediately shook their head in disbelief.

"Did anybody else see what happened here?" Deputy Stovall asked as he began to walk from small groups to one of two people standing side by side. All he got was a few shrugs and one hundred percent agreement that no one saw anything. This was preliminary beginning to his offices investigation. He knew he had an eyewitness to the incident from a victim in Mae Ellen Hall.

Banks part-time coroner arrived shortly after the Sheriff and his deputy. He was examining the bodies while the Sheriff joined his deputy in canvassing the crown for an eye witness or anybody that heard anything and the time they heard it.

The Sheriff, an old hand at this sort of investigation walked around looking in the eyes of those standing around. Most old black people, having learned from their parents never to look in the eyes of a white man tended to look down, saying such things as the lawman went by them, "I ain't seen nuttin', Sheriff." "I just got here, Sheriff." "Naw, Sheriff, I didn't see nothing."

Deputy Stovall filled him in on how everybody got notified and pointed out the old man and his grandson as the first people on the scene. The Sheriff told him to make sure they didn't leave. He finished his questions, thanked all for their cooperation, and asked the non-essential people to leave the area. He told them he would get in touch if he needed anyone who was there. His last words were a reminder that if anyone thought of anything, please let Deputy Stovall or him know. The only people left at the scene besides Mae Ellen, Clem and Cora Parker, were the part-time coroner, Deputy Stovall, himself along with the old man and his grandson.

He went over to the Parker wagon got a brief description of what happened from thirteen-year-old Mae Ellen. She didn't recognize either of the two white men in the automobile. They hit the horse on the side of the wagon, causing the wagon to tip over and the next thing she knew, she was waking up while lying on the ground. Since the girl was not hurt, she was allowed to leave with the Parkers who stated they would get in touch with Frank and Harriett Hall, as well as the girls grandparents living in Warren. Before they left, Sheriff Penelton told them he too would inform Frank and Harriett in an official capacity since they were the next of kin in the immediate area. He also asked Clem to advise him when and where Mae Ellen would be moving.

Afterwards, he walked toward the other witness. Recognizing the old man, he looked, slapped his leg while laughing and yelled out, "You old dog! Damn! I did know that was you, Rand Tatum." I ain't seen you in these parts in years. I thought you moved north."

Old man Tatum couldn't help but smile. He and the sheriff knew other from way back in the day. Rand once worked for the Sheriff's folks. He left moving up North looking for greener pastures and found a better standard of living. Yet now he was getting older and longed for his family. Thus, he moved back South after he retired.

"That is all well and good Sheriff, but I still ain't seen nothing to help you with this matter." Rand said.

"Oh, I know if you had seen anything you would tell me. I am doggone sure of that, Rand, 'cause you good people. What were you and your grandson doing out here?"

"I was takin' Peanut here up to Papa Warner's store for a candy cane and soda pop."

"Peanut? Now what in the world is a peanut, and what is your real name son?"

"Peanut is what they call me. My real name is Rand Tatum III suh."

"That's a long moniker. I think Peanut will do just fine. Go over there and tell the Deputy to get that candy cane out of my little bag and give it to you, 'cause you and me are gonna be friends just like me and your grandpa is. Go on now . . . ," he urged.

Peanut, ever so grateful somebody remembered what this trip was about, thanked the sheriff and ran over to where his deputy was waving goodbye to the part-time coroner. He happily relayed the news, walking and skipping with the deputy to the police vehicle. The boy grabbed the candy cane like it was lost treasure and began to enjoy the red stripped flavored treat.

While Sheriff Dan Penelton and Rand reminisced about the grand old days, how things have changes yet stayed the same, the deputy and Peanut was carrying on a private conversation.

"Tell me something, Peanut, where did that car go? You know the one that ran those nice folks off the road. Did you see which direction it was going?"

"Sho', it went up in that little road over there." It took him a few seconds, realizing what he'd said; he stopped licking the candy cane. He looked at his hand still pointing to the road the deputy knew as the turnoff to Harvey Sampson's farm. Dropping the candy in the dirt, he ran back to his grandpa's side and grabbed his hand. There was no need to tell his grandfather what happen, the old man knew the cat was out of the bag.

Deputy Stovall picked up the candy cane. Taking a canteen from his vehicle, he poured a little water over it to remove the dirt and dried it with his clean handkerchief. He then joined the two men and the boy standing where the two bodies once lay before being removed by the part-time coroner.

The three man clean-up crew was working quickly to clean up the debris. They had already hoisted the dead horse onto their wagon team to clear the road. Now they were picking up the last bit of the shattered wagon.

The Sheriff also felt that these two individuals, a man he had grown up respecting and who he reminded of that fact now, and his grandson had additional information that may lead them to who committed this act of murder on the road. He stared at Rand, who returned his gaze with a guilty expression.

"What did the little girl tell you happened?" Rand asked.

Sheriff Penelton smiled slightly, and started at Rand without answering.

Rand looked at Peanut who looked to him for acceptance and guidance more so ever right now. "It's alright Pea. We have a duty to the two people who lost their life here today. It just wouldn't be right not to tell what we saw."

Rand went on to provide in detail all that he witnessed, including when the auto began to speed up after spotting Viola and Edgar in the wagon. Then, driving straight toward the couple, and at the last minute, trying to swerve around them, causing the wagon to overturn, etc. etc. Finally, just as Peanut had told the deputy, the car, being driven by a white man whose description fit Bob, with another white man in the passenger seat, that was either Clarke's twin or Clarke himself. Rand concluded by adding, despite the horse damaging the back of the vehicle, the driver managed to get control driving off and turning right onto the Sampson road.

Resolved to reviewing pictures of Bob and Clarke for an exact identification, Rand and Peanut joined the sheriff and deputy on their ride to the office. Peanut felt relieved that he could talk about this, especially to his parents. He had also been reacquainted with the candy cane. Rand Tatum felt a sense of relief too. He didn't realize the burden he was putting on himself and his grandson. What kind of role model was he projecting if he withheld pertinent information about a potential homicide of two of his own people?

All in all, he was doing the best for the individuals who were killed, for his grandson and this community. Regardless of what may or may not happen to him had no bearing on if he should tell what he saw. He understood why he hesitated. Had it been any other white man other than Sheriff Dan Penelton, he may have been forced to abandon his moral obligations because after all, only a white person could be considered a credible witness in a crime. In this case, causing a black family to be thrown off a wagon, resulting in the death of two may not be considered a crime committed by a white person. They may just consider this a terrible accident. However it turns out, at least now, justice had a chance of being blind with the sheriff in charge of the investigation. In the end, they needed to get those fools off the road before they repeat their careless act on some other unsuspecting person.

After reaching the sheriff's office, Rand and Peanut picked out Bob as the driver from among several pictures. Rand also picked out Clarke as the passenger. Rand signed his statement, was thanked by the sheriff, and asked to keep this to himself until further notice. It had been a long eventful day for Rand Tatum and his grandson.

Although the sun was going down, Deputy Stovall dropped the man and his grandson off at their home. He also stopped by Frank and Harriett's, informing them of what happened and where the surviving Mae Ellen could be found. He left the Hall's visibly shaken by the news of the tragedy.

Two days later, Colrolus and Lena had driven up to see Frank and Harriett. The drive was precipitated by the absence of Lena's parents in church this past Sunday. They arrived to see Harriett sick in bed. She, nor her husband, knew what exactly ailed her. Frank thought it may have been the sudden shock of Edgar and Viola's death or maybe something she ate, although Frank ate the same foods and wasn't sick. Her illness was going into the second day.

After making her comfortable, the three of them sat down at the kitchen table for coffee and a light lunch. It was then that Frank relayed the details of Viola and Edgar's death as told to him by the deputy. Colrolus and Lena originally found out from one of Papa Warner's people who dropped off supplies at their farm on Monday.

"When they didn't come back on Sunday evening, I had this feeling in my gut something was wrong," he said. "Then the deputy came by with the news. I couldn't get away because Harriett took sick."

"Well, a couple of Harvey Sampson's Klansmen were arrested by the sheriff the next day. They say the sheriff and his deputy had to draw their weapons in order to get the men away from old man Sampson. After their arrest, Bob and Clarke swore up and down they were innocent and never left the farm all morning." Colrolus reported.

"Yeah, but the law caught 'em in a lie right away. The Sherriff took pictures of the damaged truck found behind the Sampson barn. A couple of folks 'membered seeing 'em in Banks a half an hour before the killing happened. One of 'em identified the truck they were in while leaving town. After being caught in that lie, they didn't say anything more." Lena added.

The couple went on to report, besides Mae Ellen, there was a witness to the whole mess. They heard it was old man Tatum and his grandson. It was all hush-hush providing the witnesses some cover until the actual indictment and trial. The only way the Strong's knew the witness by name was because Rand Tatum also told them what happened.

Frank told his daughter and son-in-law. One of the best things for his wife would be to see and talk to Mae Ellen. Harriett was asleep the entire time they were there. Colrolus finally left, leaving Lena behind to help care for her mother. He had to leave to feed his hogs and let the horses out for grazing. He also had to pick up his cousin to stay at his place until he and the wife returned.

He told Frank and Lena, he would drive over to the Parker's place in the morning and bring Mae Ellen back with him. No one knew if Viola and Edger parents in Warren had been told, although they suspected that the Sheriff's office had taken care of that responsibility. If there was no overnight progress in Harriett's condition, then they should drive her to Dr. Purvis' clinic in Banks. They all agreed with the plan. Lena kissed her husband goodbye while giving him other instructions on matters of their place. As he drove off, she waved and went back into her parents' home.

Sheriff Penelton felt he had not had such high profiled suspects in his jail in a long time. By that he meant such notable criminal Klansmen as Bob Longley and Clarke Riley suspected of vehicle manslaughter.

He knew he had to move these men for the sake of keeping the peace and preventing a possible attempted breakout. He wasn't sure but could not take a chance that Harvey Sampson wouldn't try something. Tomorrow morning, he would have the men transported to Warren for housing in the county seat's jail. For now, he was waiting on the final paperwork from the judge that would include the updated arrest warrant and transportation papers.

He did not question the two men on the evidence report he had for the killing of Deputy Paul Krause. Occasionally the shoulder where he was shot during that ambush felt uncomfortable. As time went on, he was sure these two men were involved in the shooting. Yet he had no real evidence to prove which one pulled the trigger or was even responsible enough to bring them up on charges. All he had was Bob's prints on a broken moonshine bottle and a few common rifle shells found at the suspected shooting spot.

Meanwhile, old man Sampson and his minions were already at work stirring up the townspeople and locals with the insinuation that this was a tragic accident and not a double manslaughter. Their spin was to say the black couple or anybody should not be on the road with horse drawn teams in this automotive day and age. It's dangerous to horse and man. They summed up their version of events by reminding listeners that there was no further evidence then what happened when a vehicle got close to the Halls' wagon.

Their theory "the victim was somewhat the aggressor and just as much at fault" with the revelation that after all, "it was a black couple handling the horses." Although some white locals were agreeing, officials knew they could prove that banning horse teams on the roads were not practical in this rural area. At this time, to limit the roads to automotive travel only was impossible, no matter who it was directed toward.

Today was the day. Bob and Clarke were placed into a Warren County Seat's Paddy Wagon with two county deputized men acting in their capacity as driver and guard. They left the Banks' sheriff office jail, carrying the appropriate paperwork and headed down the ten mile trip about seven this morning.

Shortly afterward, they sent a wire to Sheriff Penelton informing him that the prisoners were delivered without incident and checked into the jail waiting for a bail hearing and a trial date. The charge and bail hearing would be Monday morning on March 18th, at 9:00am.

The sheriff was relieved to see the words 'without incident' on the wire. He reasoned that the Sampson bunch lawyer must feel they have a chance to free these men at the bail hearing and a possibility of not guilty verdict if there were a jury trial. The fact is he could not disagree with that scenario, for he had seen these kinds of social verdicts before, especially where the victims were colored folks. He would continue to collect any evidence in this case to forward to the county prosecutor's office that still had to make a determination if they wanted to go forward with the case.

Around noontime on Wednesday, John rode Old Thunder over the back road to Clem Parker's place. The trip was to pick up some extra vegetable seed in exchange for a few blocks of homemade soap Sallie made this spring. They had talked about this exchange at church last Sunday.

He was met with the news of Viola and Edgar's death. Cora told him that he just missed Mae Ellen who was picked up earlier by Colrolus Strong and taken to his mother and father-in-laws place. She also told him to tell Gracie her mother is sick. Clem also told him, he heard Bob and Clarke was supposed to be sent to the county seat's jail this morning, where they would be officially charged if the county prosecutor had enough evidence for a trial. Yes, there was another witness. It was Rand Tatum because he and his grandson were the ones that alerted everybody to the location of the overturned wagon and bodies. Normally, John would have stayed a few more minutes, maybe for a bit of lunch, but after hearing that sad news, he started to leave for home to inform his family. Clem told him that he and Cora had heard from their son, Sammy. He told them he was working for a white man and was doing well. He and his wife also wrote a return letter, sending it to the post office this morning. Clem figured their son had been gone long enough so that no one would be checking their incoming and outgoing mail. They wrote him the whole story on Viola's and Edgar's death.

Upon his return, he put the horse out to graze in back of the big house, passed the news on to his father, and ran up the hill to his house to break the news to Gracie. He walked into the house, where little four year old Codis and his three year old sister, Lacirene was eating apples at the kitchen table. Gracie was breast feeding baby Curtis, their newborn. She smiled as she saw John walk in.

He didn't waste time, after pouring himself a cup of water, acknowledging his two toddlers, he gave Gracie the distressing news. Gracie was totally shocked and upset when she was told of Viola and Edgar deaths. The news that Mae Ellen survived was at least some good news. She told John of the premonition she had of them being killed on the road to Banks. The exact scene in her mind was not as it happened, but she did see them both lying in a ditch with a sign on the road that read Banks, 3 miles. She confessed she didn't want to tell anybody because she felt it could have been a dream.

"I just didn't want to scare anybody. Who knows when these things are going to happen if ever," she said with eyes tearing up from the thought of her cousins and friends dead. She will never again be able to talk to Viola or Edgar. The tears began to run down her cheeks.

Now it was John's turn to be visible shaken. He'd heard his wife talk about her premonitions before, but never as accurate as this one. "Did you see their killers get punish?" He asked.

223

"No, nuthin' else. Just the both of them in that ditch and the Banks sign."

With baby Curtis finished and asleep, she gently laid him down in the crib. Turning back to John, all she could do was shake her head from side to side and say almost in a whispered fashion, "Why, Lord, why?"

John stood, quickly embracing his sobbing wife. While their two toddlers looked on in wonderment, the both of them stood in the middle of the room comforting each other.

They heard a knock on the door. John steered his wife back to her seat at the table. She was wiping her with eyes with John's handkerchief from a steady stream of tears when her husband asked the person at the door to come on in. It was Colrolus. The expression on his face warned of further grim news.

Colrolus took a seat at the table, unable to hide his grief and apparently not quite knowing how to say whatever was on his mind. He began by looking at the residual effect on Gracie's face and said as a matter of factually. "I guess yawl heard about Viola and Edgar."

Both John and Gracie nodded their heads in agreement with his statement. Both braced themselves for whatever else he was about to say.

"I just don' know how else to tell you this . . . but . . . Gracie, it's your mother. She just up and passed away in the middle of last night."

John was stunned to say the least. He had not had the chance to tell her that Cora Parker told him her mother was sick. He moved over to put his arms around his wife who, was almost in a comatose state with her eyes locked on Colrolus, with a lifeless stare. Her mouth suddenly dry, she managed to ask him to repeat what he'd said because she just could not believe she actually heard him correctly. "What did you say?" She asked.

"Baby, your mama died last night. Lena and your daddy were there, but they say, she just stopped breathing. They not sure what happen," he answered and continued in order to get it all out. "She'd been sick since Sunday. Couldn't keep no food down, throwing up, and shortness of breath. They said, in the end, she acted like she couldn't breathe, and just . . . up and died."

"Oh my God, they say these things happin' in threes. Does that mean three people like my mama, Viola and Edgar? I just can't believe it, my mama . . . ," she cried out before completely breaking down and crying uncontrollably.

By now Gracie was using a dry towel brought to her by John. He tried while attempting to control his personal grief, to comfort his wife. He was standing behind her now with his hands on her shoulders. Gracie, her left arm draped across her chest, grabbed his right hand with her left, rocking her body back and forth.

Little Codis and Lacirene sensing all of the sadness in the room began to cry themselves. Of course, they were not fully aware of what is going on, but they knew whatever it was made their mama cry.

"How's daddy doing?" Gracie asked.

"About as well as . . . , he's not takin' it well a'tall, Lena and Mae Ellen is with him, and both of them are upset too." Colrolus confessed. "I can take you over to the house."

"Oh Gawd, and that child Mae Ellen just losing her mama and papa too," she said in an almost whisper with grief. "Yeah, I better go and see what's going on. Honey can you . . ."

"I'll walk Codis and Lacireen down to Mama's. They can stay with my mama until we back. My little brothers will help her out with these little ones. You can get Curtis ready to go with us. I'll meet yawl down by the big house?" John ended by asking.

"All right," a grateful Gracie answered.

Gracie, holding baby Curtis and John were driven by Colrolus and arrived at the Halls' place around two in the afternoon. A few well-wishers were outside on the porch. They met Gracie as she entered the house, passing on their condolence. Mae Ellen ran up to Gracie, as tears rolled down her cheeks, she hugged her friend and cousin while saying "Um so sorry. Mama Harriett is gone." "Aww baby, um so sorry about your mama and papa too, but it's all gonna be all right. We both gonna be all right, don't you worry 'bout a thing." Gracie replied. Once inside the sister's eyes met with both Gracie and Lena breaking down to cry.

John took the baby from Gracie, allowing her and Lena to embrace and share a sisterly moment of grief. After a couple of minutes, they moved toward their father who was still sitting at his wife's bedside. The girls had never seen the type of expression they were currently witnessing on their fathers face. In a striking contrast, their mother never looked more at peace.

They had lit a few candles and place them around the room with the coal oil lamp giving off a sort of surreal scene. Although there was grief, some saw death as a celebration of life's journey coming to an end. There was not too much conversation between the father or daughters, just a final realization the fifty-eight year old mother who brought five children into the world and married Frank Hall on the 24th of October, 1894 was dead.

For Gracie and Lena, life would simply have to go on. There were arrangements to be made for her burial. Versia and James would have to be notified. They wondered if they could get in touch with their brother, Edward Hall. He was supposed to be in Cleveland somewhere.

Frank finally got up from the chair and went out the door, walking off the porch and going down by the well, taking a seat on a bench, and looking back at his house and across their few acres of land. Lena and Gracie followed him, concerned about the state of his mind. They managed to get a few words from their father.

Gathered from an emotional conversation between the three of them, one thing was clear, the sudden death of Harriett Hall left her widowed husband distraught and fed up with life in Arkansas. With his wife gone, kids out of the house, friends and relatives Viola and Edgar dead, he no longer wanted to stay in this area. The sooner he left, the better he would feel. The faster he put this unforgiving land, unholy white folk, backwards thinking colored folk behind him, the quicker his healing could begin.

It was something the family would have to deal with in the aftermath of Harriett's funeral. The girls did not even want to think along those lines right now. That issue would have to wait until another day.

Versia and James Boswell had driven up to the Halls' place from Hot Springs for her mother's funeral, scheduled for Sunday. The family wanted to bury Harriett as soon as possible. They actually had the wake in the Halls' house Saturday. To save on money, they prepared the body for burial in the Oaklawn Cemetery. The Reverend A.J. Payne performed the ritual at the cemetery.

They never got a response from Edward Hall, who didn't attend the funeral. The only boy from the Frank and Harriett union continued to be the elusive one who no family member has heard from in quite a while. Afterwards, a lot of those who were present returned to the Halls house for refreshments.

All three sisters decided after an informal but decisive meeting with their husbands and the subject herself. Mae Ellen would move in with Gracie Hampton and her family until further notice. Both set of grandparents, who still lived in Warren, did not attend the funeral because of travel issues. They would be notified of the girl's wishes along with Gracie and John's consent of her help with their growing family. Just as importantly, she could continue to attend the local school. In a couple of years, she could even move with one of them if they or she wanted to attend high school. They would assure the grandparents that Mae Ellen would be free to visit and stay overnight with them anytime.

The cause of Harriett's death was topic one among attendees. Family members revealed she had incremental asthma. That was a diagnosis from Dr. Purvis a few years ago when she became ill for a couple of days. It's brought on by the pollen in the spring air. The last two years, she had allergy issues in the spring, nothing so serious that would make her bedridden. She became more susceptible to asthma attacks the older she got. It was the collective opinion here, in consultation with Dr. Purvis; she had a severe asthma attack and lacked the medication in the house to treat the problem. There was no doubt the tragic death of Viola and Edgar contributed to the severity of the attack.

For Gracie, Lena, and Versia, there were no words that would provide them comfort in losing their beloved mother. They were aware that the well-wishers were sincere in their condolences. None of the ladies wandered very far from their spouse with all taking the time to continually console Mae Ellen. The ladies wanted and got that support when needed to get through this personal ordeal. That support from their husbands and each other helped them get through the family and friends get-together following the funeral.

There was no change of heart for Frank Hall. He was leaving in a week and a half for Cooter, Missouri. Since he couldn't find Edward, he located a cousin in Pemiscot County's little town of Cooter. When asked why he was leaving by his girls, he answered by saying he was an awful tired 56 year-old widowed ex-farmer who suddenly had his fill of the South. Besides that, he just could not see himself living in this house with memories of Harriett in every corner. He let any and everybody know in the most polite way possible his decision was not up for discussion. In the end, most people understood and would honor his wishes.

Monday morning arrived, so did the bail hearing for Bob Longley and Clarke Riley. Their lawyers and the judge made quick work of the entire procedure. The charges, including leaving the scene after causing fatalities by a vehicle were read by the judge. Each suspect was asked how they plead, both entered an innocent plea.

The judge set bail at $1000 per man which would be the equivalent of $10,723 in 2013 dollars. It was a low bail for individuals who were suspected of being responsible for two fatalities and leaving the scene. It didn't take Harvey Sampson long to post the percentage amount required for the bail. The two men were out in time for lunch.

Almost just as quickly, the community of Gravel Ridge, beginning at the Sheriff's office in Banks, Papa Warner's store, and the surrounding areas were aware of the 'released on bail' status of Bob and Clarke. They were seen walking around in Banks, in front of McBain's store looking like 'chess cats' as the country folk say. The black community understood the bail system. Still, they were not pleased. That was an understatement.

There was the feeling that sooner or later, these two white men were going to get away with murder. Either the county prosecutor, who had a habit of favoring the white person's viewpoint in all racial issues, would find a reason not to go forward with the prosecution. The witness would be intimidated or, worse, killed. Or, if the case went before a white jury, they would be found innocent of all charges. There was not a lot of trust in the Bradley County justice system for African-Americans.

Somebody took the matter into their own hands. By Friday, the bodies of Bob Longley and Clarke Riley were found lying in the same ditch embankment as Viola and Edgar. They were not at the same location, but it was on the road right outside Banks. Both men were shot in the head behind the right ear. It was similar to a Chicago gang styled execution, where a small caliber handgun was more than likely the murder weapon. Somebody was trying to send a message. That was the conclusion reached by Sheriff Penelton.

It was a white couple who finally reported the bodies. They just happened to look down while driving by and saw the men. They turned around, went back to make sure of what they saw before reporting it to the sheriff's office. They also said they don't know why other people couldn't see those bodies as they passed by the location.

"I'm sure other people could see those bodies from their vehicles or wagons. I wonder why they wouldn't say anything." Deputy Stovall remarked to the sheriff while observing the position of the bodies in the ditch.

"Assuming some of those who saw them were colored, would you report it?"

"No, I see what you mean." he replied.

The Banks Coroner was also at the crime scene and going about his business. He was a man who always offered his opinion whether asked or not. Naturally he had thoughts about this shooting too.

"These two were involved in some of everything including the Klan. Um sure I ain't telling you nothing you don't already know, Sheriff. You don't think one of our niggers did this do you Sheriff?" he asked.

"Naw Larry, I think they ran into somebody who didn't recognize who they thought were, nor did they care." he answered.

"I'll tell you one thing, I've seen these type of shootings once before in Hot Springs. Nine times out of ten, they are gangland slayings or copy cats." Deputy Stovall said.

"What would these fools know about gangs up north? I'll tell you the person that's going to be upset about this, and that's their boss, Harvey Sampson. Now he's gonna come up with all kind of theories and conclude that one of our black folk did this." The sheriff responded.

"Are you through with the bodies Sheriff? Can I move them now? Larry the coroner asked.

"You through Josh?"

"Yep, I got everything I need, pack-em-up Larry," Deputy Stovall answered.

"All right then, let's go break the news to old man Sampson."

It was odd, but not unexpected to see two other henchmen acting as guards on the Sampson entrance gate. They were not strangers, yet the sheriff realized he didn't actually know their names.

As they were most of the time, Harvey and his wife, Clara, were sitting on the porch when he drove up. His son, Petey came out in his wheelchair after hearing the sound of the police vehicle.

The old man and Clara were shocked at the news. Petey thought it was some kind of well-planned Negro plot to eliminate white people. He figured Sammy Parker came back into town with his gang and was just waiting for the most opportune time before launching another attack on the white race. It took his mother to tell quiet him down.

Harvey just stared at the Sheriff in that menacing way of his.

"I guess you are satisfied now. I done lost one son, another confined to a wheel chair, and now two of my men are dead. All while your office, by God Dan, just what in the hell do you do in that office? You should resign for all you haven't done while in office. That's all right. We gonna turn your office into an elected position. You just wait and see," he muttered through missing dentures on his top row.

The sheriff listened until Harvey and Clara were finished chewing him out for being in their words "a dad-gummed idiot". Afterwards, he politely bid the family goodbye. He got in the passenger side with Deputy Stovall driving past the guarded gate and onto the road back to Banks.

"You know Sheriff, I don't think they like you," Deputy Stovall said barely holding back the laughter.

"Oh hell, I never make their Christmas list."

It was no secret that Bob and Clarke were not well liked in the white community. The Sampson's attempt to make them some kind of martyrs fell on deaf ears. They were correctly identified for who they were a couple of two-bit crooks.

CHAPTER 9

1930-33 Hangovers, FDR Programs & Family Illness

Herbert Hoover had a good record as Secretary of Commerce under Presidents Harding and Coolidge. One could say he also earned his stripes working as an engineer, administrator, and humanitarian in public service positions. While campaigning in 1928 as the Republican Presidential nominee, Herbert Hoover, once said, "We in America today are nearer to the final triumph over poverty than ever before in the history of any land."

At that time, a lot of people of wealth in the U.S. were feeling superior about their investments and savings. After all, the country just went through the Roaring Twenties prosperity. Herbert Hoover was elected and took office in January of 1929. Most in the country thought his election would keep the status quo, businesses would continue to prosper, and everybody would benefit from that prosperity. In the world of monetary reality, as politicians of today so succinctly put it, substituting the words *we are* for *they were* and paraphrasing a quote, 'They were living in two Americas, those who had it and those who did not.'

The spring and summer of 1929 passed leaving a lot of people across America anxious and trying to watch their bottom line. October 29th was such an infamous day in America's financial world; they dubbed it 'Black Tuesday.' That was the day the Stock Market crashed.

President Herbert Hoover announced that he intended to keep the Federal budget balanced. He would cut taxes and expand spending on public work projects.

Most Arkansans may not have felt the stock market crash immediately because they were already in a poor economic state. Yet reverberations of the crash would find its way down the Mississippi River spreading even more economic troubles like the flood of 1927.

When bad economic times are present, it allows the growing of self-serving groups that prey on the suffering poor. The KKK, the organization in which Harvey Sampson and family were key players, was increasing in numbers, not only in the South but in the North too. By 1930, cities such as Dayton and Detroit had recruited new members who were concerned about urban issues.

Reportedly, Detroit had about 40, 000 members of record. Rapid social change, limited housing, and general competition for jobs were a serious problem for whites. They were annoyed with European immigrants; similar to New York's issued with the immigrant Irish people and others hitting their shores looking for a better life. The Klan was making their feelings known among the immigrants along with black or white Southerners arriving in their city.

This was supposedly a different Klan that had no connection to the KKK of post-Civil War Reconstruction. This Klan was on its surface just concern about getting its members its fair share of the pie, however small it was at the time. There were numerous groups of social clubs that allowed men to join and meet others like themselves with similar ideas and lifestyle. Men used these types of close knit social organizations to provide for their families in case the breadwinner could not or did not earn a weekly wage that fed his family. Organizations like the Elks were blueprints for the Klan's organization appeal to more and more whites in need.

In March, President Hoover infamously declared the United States had "passed the worst" of the depression. True to the Republican mantra, he noted the economy would sort itself out.

The public was tiring of Herbert Hoover's actions and inactions. Those who lost their homes were living in shanty towns they called "Hoovervilles". The food that was served in soup kitchens was called "Hoover Stew". People forced to use newspapers as a blanket dubbed them "Hoover Blankets". Jack rabbits, eaten for food were called "Hoover Hogs" and so on. From the public's standpoint, this was now Hoover's depression.

Meanwhile in Arkansas, a drought contributed to the problems during the summer of 1930 and lasted through the summer of the next year. It was reportedly so severe, especially with high unemployment (25% nationally), the need to feed their families brought about dangerous reactions from locals. Lonoke County area farmers, idle or unemployed, shot at a black road construction gang. One of Arkansas major crops, cotton decreased in production from 1.4 million bales in 1929 to 879,000 in 1930. For the same time spans, corn production decreased from 29 million bushels to 8.3 million bushels. The state itself was heavily in debt for taking on loans to build its highway systems during the early part of the decade.

The New Year arrived with a hangover from 1929. The United States, and indeed the world, was in 'The Great Depression'. Many economists say the straw that broke the camel's back was committed by the signing of the United States Hawley-Smoot Tariff Act into law on June, 17, 1930. The result raised the price on over 20,000 import goods. Americas trading partners retaliated by raising their prices too. In effect, it slowed down the import and export of affordable goods for consumers. These same consumers were suffering from unemployment and stagnant wages if they were lucky to have a job.

Like always and even with the world seemingly crumbling around them and at their feet, life and death went on in the Gravel Ridge community. Gracie would get pregnant in February and have the child on October 23, 1930, naming him Clarence D. This would mean the union of John and Gracie had produced three boys, Codis, Curtis, and Clarence D, and one girl named Lacireen.

There would be a double celebration at the Strong household. They would oddly enough celebrate in a double manner because it was the first child and first boy. Yes, at last, this year Colrolus and Lena had their first child, naming him D.C. Strong.

The only living Hall girl who had not produced was now Versia Boswell. Gracie and Lena sent her a letter after the boys were born. They did not tease, only wished her God Speed in having that baby she and her husband wanted so badly. Versia was indeed happy for her sisters and felt her day would come.

The Federal Government, under the Hoover administration was attempting to address the depression, but issues experienced by the world's European communities deepened the crisis. In 1931, they presented a program to Congress seeking the creation of the Reconstruction Finance Corporation. It was designed to aid business. Hoover asked for more help directed at farmers who were facing mortgage foreclosures. He wanted to lend states money to feed the unemployed. Yet, he also kept his core belief that the federal government was not in the business of personal care for its citizens. He felt that responsibility was a local issue and must be left up to the states, municipalities, and local volunteers. In his view, they were better equipped to feed their hungry while providing heat from the cold.

He nominated, John J. Parker, who was known for his anti-black viewpoint to the U.S. Supreme Court. His nomination was successfully opposed by the NAACP. This further strained an already tenuous support for Republicans among America's black population, especially in the Northern cities.

Hoover's positions and attempt at solving the nation's crises were viewed as too mild of a response to such a devastating problem. The President himself felt Congressional opposition to his plans and those individuals grandstanding for their own political gain were at fault. He felt they were casting him as a callous and cruel President. In the end, Herbert Hoover was cast as the 'scapegoat of the Depression'. With no help from black voters, who deserted the Republican Party in droves, he was soundly defeated by Franklin D Roosevelt in 1932.

The new administration wasted no time in proving to their black supporters their plight during this depression would be fully considered and acted upon in plans and execution to help those in need. There were a number of black leaders from all parts of the country, dubbed the "black cabinet" advising President Roosevelt. People like economist Robert C. Weaver, Pittsburg Courier editor Robert Vann, executive secretary of the National Urban League Eugene K. Jones, and William H. Hastie who went on to become the first black federal judge in 1937. Educator Mary McLeod Bethune served as the presidents National Youth Administration's director of Negro affairs.

In spite of national politics, life goes on in the Gravel Ridge community. Lena would still be waiting to have her first girl, when two years later she had her second son, Frank Strong, born in November of 1932. Needless to say, her husband, Colrolus was ecstatic. He thought about naming the second son Junior as he had thought when the first boy was born. Once again, the idea was squelched by his wife. She felt one Colrolus in the family was enough. Most strangers were already having problems pronouncing his name. Reluctantly, he agreed, so they gave their son a common name that everyone could pronounce.

With people dying, babies being born and many more people suffering, the Gravel Ridge community, the rest of the United States, just like all people throughout the world was still trying to climb out of a severe depression. Economic stability was the goal and mantra of all the aforementioned inhabitants, municipalities, state, federal, or world governments.

It was New Year's Day of 1933. The weather was cold with a slight wind blowing flakes off of snow drifts around the area. The county had just experienced a large snow fall but had no prediction of snow in the near future.

Unfortunately, neither national nor local politics were able to save the Hampton Farm. During January of 1993, John and Gracie lost the forty acres of land giving to them by Sallie and Sambo Hampton. A little over a year before, John had mortgaged the land with the little house on it trying to help his father save the bigger lot and acreage with the big house. He was somehow able to take out a loan at the Farmers Mercantile Bank.

236

The plan was for his father to help repay the note, with expectations that the crops from both John and Sambo's land would provide enough income from the open market. They even added to their cotton fields by planting more seed in other areas. Between the drought, and depression, those plans like many, many others in the county affecting white and black folk were not realized. Most around this community had lost land, were heavily indebted to the banks or just downright sick and tired of being sick and tired.

Sallie and Sambo, who had to sell off a substantial portion of the rest of their land, were barely hanging on to the big house and a few acres. Sambo could not pay his part of the loan. Nor did John didn't have the resources for payment. So the bank foreclosed on the property causing Gracie, John and family to move. The fact the little house had become too small for them and their four children plus Mae Ellen were of little solace.

Luckily, Lena and Colrolus had less of a problem with their holdings than the rest of Gravel Ridge. A lot of the acreage the Strong family owned was on the other side of the railroad tracks and deeper into the woods. There was less farm land than normal available on those properties. They bought it to raise stock, like cattle, horses, or goats. That is not to say they did not experience major problems during the depression. It simply meant their troubles had nothing to do with producing crops for resale like the local farmers. There was also more timber on those properties than on a farm.

Colrolus and Lena Strong had a four acre plot directly across from their house that was located on the Banks highway side of the tracks. The trees were so dense you could not see either house from the porch of the other home. The houses were approximately a hundred yards apart. There was a three bedroom unoccupied house on the lot. No one wanted to live that deep in the woods or that close to the railroad tracks.

Colrolus agreed to sell the house to John and his family for very little. The monthly payment amount varied and including relief if no money was available. It was a sweetheart of a deal designed to take care of a family member's needs.

The size of the house, two of the bedrooms were very small, with the parents' bedroom a normal size for the times, was perfect for the Hamptons. Although John was used to a larger area for farming, Gracie realize the total size of the house resembled the lot on which she and her siblings were raised. In fact, it was not that far, about a mile, from the old Frank and Harriett Hall place. It sat almost directly behind the house that Edgar and Viola Hall once rented. Both those houses were still standing and rented out to a couple of families that the Hamptons would meet soon enough.

John and his family moved into the house on the 16th of January, 1933. Codis would turn eight years old on the 3rd of February, Lacirene was six, Curtis three, and Clarence D two. Their live-in cousin, Mae Ellen would turn eighteen years old this coming August. She had moved with her deceased mother, Viola, parents' the year before last only to have those set of grandparents die last year, just before Christmas. Her grandfather died the day after Thanksgiving with her grandmother following a week later. Edgar's parents had passed the year she moved to Warren during the fall of 1931. At least she got to attend the colored high school in Warren for a year and a half. There had been so much death in her family she decided to move back where she was comfortable. In fact, she moved back with Gracie and John just in time to move with them to this house.

Spider had died a few months earlier, taking some of the spunk out of Oh No. Her two pups were now fully grown. They named one Blackie because he had the same color coat as Spider, and the other one Brownie. He had the same color coat as his mother, On No. Both dogs had turned out to be excellent hunting animals, yet they still retained the playfulness of their mother. All three dogs moved with the Hamptons to the new house.

They only had about a dozen chickens left; most had been killed for food during the last few winters. They brought along the same rooster that had grown up with them. They left Old Thunder grazing in the much smaller pastures of Sallie and Sambo Hampton. John never did have his own wagon team. The one he used belonged to his father. Unfortunately, Sambo had to sell the horses while trying to hold on to the big house and some land.

Colrolus was able to lend them a horse team and wagon to get around. The house already had a small barn on the property along with a well and a pump for water usage. John would have to build a small fence to hold animals, like hogs he expected to raise near the barn. He'd also have to build a hen house, and there was already a small smokehouse. Another good thing was the hunting; game was notable in the local woods which ran for miles to their left or right. There were raccoons, opossums, rabbits, squirrels and wild hogs. He could also lay traps in the density of the woods. Within a short walking distance was a small creek runoff from a lake which produced catfish, bullheads, carp, and other fish.

The front of the house had a porch which faced the narrow dirt road that ran right in front of it. There was a fence, partially covered with barbed wire to keep out wolves, and the like, that separated the house from the road with the tree line on the other side of the road. If one went to their right from the porch steps and followed the road swerving left it would lead to Colrolus and Lena house, after crossing the tracks.

If turning right instead of left at the fork, one would be headed for the house where Viola and Edgar once lived. That is the same house that Rand Tatum and his family moved to last year. If one stayed on that road after crossing a Len Jennings' farm property, you would run into the road to Banks.

Following the road to the left of the porch would take you to the few neighbors' houses. Staying on that road would carry you right to the vacant old Frank and Harriett Hall place. And of course leaving from that front porch would lead past the Tatum house (the old Edgar & Violet Hall rental); turning right onto the road coming from Gracie and John's would lead to the main road of Banks or to Hot Springs in the other direction.

So all in all, the house was in a good location. John and Gracie felt blessed to find such a place that fit their family and needs.

Having been in the house a few weeks, John was taking advantage of a mild winter. He was not wasting any time in adding on the structures or fencing needed to keep his present and future animals enclosed on this property. He also had to protect them from predators like bears or wolves. He managed to finish the hen house and barnyard structure by himself. I should say with the occasional help of his seven year old gofer, little Codis. If anything needed to be brought to his daddy, Codis would go and get it. That worked out fairly well as long as the items were not too heavy for the boy. So it went for the first three months.

March brought around the planting season. He needed a mule to pull his plow. He planned on putting in a few crops that would allow for the feeding of his family. John was able to buy a mule from Colrolus, at a discounted price, using some money he received from his father, Sambo. The only problem with that was the animal was not familiar with John and had the stereotypical stubborn streak.

He warned his kids and everybody to stay away from the mule because it was on the cantankerous side. One morning he forgot his own advice, walking directly behind the mule before leading him to the plowing section. The mule, startled by a mouse or something kicked John in the forehead knocking him backwards into the barn wall. He lay unconscious for about fifteen minutes until little Codis found him.

His son ran screaming to the get his mother, who was able to get John awake with a wet towel. She finally got him to his feet and into the bed. Besides a fleshy knot and small gash across his forehead, he seemed to be coming around, albeit ever so slowly. It took a couple of hours for John to regain his complete self of sense or his whereabouts. He could recognize the people in the room but had consistency of awareness problems. Every time he would try to stand up, he found his balance shaky. He would sit back down complaining of a headache. Finally, taking his wife's advice, he decided to rest for the day and see how he felt in the morning. For the first time in his life, he had been knocked down and had trouble getting back up.

March also brought about a change in political leaders at the national level. Franklin D Roosevelt was sworn in as President of the United States on March 4, 1933. A Democrat, he would help the people believe in themselves again.

He delivered his inaugural address to the American public by radio, media that Bradley County or many Arkansans did not have because electricity was not available in the rural areas of the state. Of course, large cities like Little Rock had access to electrical power. Nevertheless, the new president's words did get down to the masses of all color and creed one way or another.

The first paragraph of the speech was to address the issue itself, he said,

"I AM certain that my fellow Americans expect that on my induction into the Presidency I will address them with a candor and a decision which the present situation of our Nation impels. This is preeminently the time to speak the truth, the whole truth, frankly and boldly. Nor need we shrink from honestly facing conditions in our country today. This great Nation will endure as it has endured, will revive and will prosper. So, first of all, let me assert my firm belief that the only thing we have to fear is fear itself—nameless, unreasoning, unjustified terror which paralyzes needed efforts to convert retreat into advance. In every dark hour of our national life a leadership of frankness and vigor has met with that understanding and support of the people themselves which is essential to victory. I am convinced that you will again give that support to leadership in these critical days."

He went on to describe the nation's current predicament, telling a captive audience how the effects of the greatest depression this country has ever seen. The chief executive went on to tell the nation that some in our ranks have put profit before common sense. He explained why,

"Primarily this is because the rulers of the exchange of mankind's goods have failed, through their own stubbornness and their own incompetence, have admitted their failure, and abdicated. Practices of the unscrupulous money changers stand indicted in the court of public opinion, rejected by the hearts and minds of men."

He pretty much explained the problem with most business people, who forget about any moral obligation to concentrate on the business of making money. He said,

"True they have tried, but their efforts have been cast in the pattern of an outworn tradition. Faced by failure of credit they have proposed only the lending of more money. Stripped of the lure of profit by which to induce our people to follow their false leadership, they have resorted to exhortations, pleading tearfully for restored confidence. They know only the rules of a generation of self-seekers. They have no vision, and when there is no vision the people perish."

"The money changers have fled from their high seats in the temple of our civilization. We may now restore that temple to the ancient truths. The measure of the restoration lies in the extent to which we apply social values more noble than mere monetary profit.

Happiness lies not in the mere possession of money; it lies in the joy of achievement, in the thrill of creative effort. The joy and moral stimulation of work no longer must be forgotten in the mad chase of evanescent profits. These dark days will be worth all they cost us if they teach us that our true destiny is not to be ministered unto but to minister to ourselves and to our fellow men."

Reading the words of a newly elected President Roosevelt speech brings a resemblance to this author's mind. Parts, if not the greater part of this speech, could be given today by a politician who understands why the founding fathers were so adamant that the government should be of the people, for the people, and run by the people and not special interest groups. That is further illustrated by the President continuing by adding,

"Recognition of the falsity of material wealth as the standard of success goes hand in hand with the abandonment of the false belief that public office and high political position are to be valued only by the standards of pride of place and personal profit; and there must be an end to a conduct in banking and in business which too often has given to a sacred trust the likeness of callous and selfish wrongdoing. Small wonder that confidence languishes, for it thrives only on honesty, on honor,

on the sacredness of obligations, on faithful protection, on unselfish performance; without them it cannot live."

His words were that of encouragement. One got the feeling; this president understood the task at hand. The following words would also apply to today's political world in the United States.

"Finally, in our progress toward a resumption of work we require two safeguards against a return of the evils of the old order; there must be a strict supervision of all banking and credits and investments; there must be an end to speculation with other people's money, and there must be provision for an adequate but sound currency".

The president went on to lay out his ideas of how to get America's house in order once again. He emphasized that he accepted the will of the people that he should guide America out of this crisis. Yet, in almost every word he stated, it was the general public who would most help themselves. He called for members of Congress to do their part and the world of commerce to accept theirs. He told America to be prepared to go against the grain and try other avenues to help people help themselves. In the end, he assured all Americans that if there were no consensus on approaches, he would follow it up this way:

"For the trust reposed in me I will return the courage and the devotion that befit the time. I can do no less.

We face the arduous days that lie before us in the warm courage of the national unity; with the clear consciousness of seeking old and precious moral values; with the clean satisfaction that comes from the stern performance of duty by old and young alike. We aim at the assurance of a rounded and permanent national life.

We do not distrust the future of essential democracy. The people of the United States have not failed. In their need they have registered a mandate that they want direct, vigorous action. They have asked for discipline and direction under leadership. They have made me the present instrument of their wishes. In the spirit of the gift I take it.

In this dedication of a Nation we humbly ask the blessing of God. May He protect each and every one of us. May He guide me in the days to come."

It was a great speech, but still just a speech. Americans, including the world, were anxiously waiting what actions would be taken and would its leaders be able to bring their economies out of this downward spiral that had its grips on the world's throat.

For Sheriff Penelton's office, his manpower still consisted of himself and Deputy Stovall. Deputy Charlie Oats was still working part-time. The Sheriff had no problems in hiring him full time. He needed another full time person. However, the town's authorities did not have the money in the budget. So the town had to work in conjunction with other county law offices in cases of emergencies.

The sheriff, who at forty-eight years old, had gotten married to thirty-five year old Rebecca Doyle, was lucky they didn't have a family. Although Rebecca was still working in Dr. Purvis Clinic, her hours had been cut and she was more or less on call. People were still getting sick but could not pay for service. The doctor was treating them anyway, many times trading his services for something he needed, other times for free.

His father, Ben "Skeeter" Purvis, was having the same customer problems at his store. Shoppers were scarce and payments were long overdue. The shelves were not as full as in years past. No need to order product if you are not going to sell it. They manage to keep the necessities stocked, with that list going through a reevaluation process as the months passed.

McBain store was in the same boat, yet maintained its status as a meeting place for the Klan. The local Klan headquarters was still old man Sampson's place. McBain and his followers had become more visible and blatant. They now flew flags at his store and held parades down the small street of Banks. They passed out inflammatory flyers espousing white power, jobs for white people, help for whites first, and so on.

244

Banks' population was about the same as it was during World War 1. No noticeable drop, in fact a slight increase in the 200 plus population. It was the surrounding areas that took a hit during these hard times. White people were leaving the area, more so than blacks, during the depression.

Large parcel land owners like Harvey Sampson lost a part of their lands. He, like many others with similar sized farms in the area, had to sell off sections of their land. Those owners, where part of their land ran alongside the road to Banks such as Clem and Cora Parker, Len Jennings (who Frank Hall once worked for), and Papa Warner ending up selling parcels of their land to make ends meet while holding on to as much of their property as possible. The land now belonged to mostly private investors who were buying the land for little of nothing. Or banks, and not necessarily local or state banks.

Len Jennings, who actually owned the house and land that Edgar and Viola rented sold the lot to Rand Tatum (old man). Rand, his son Rand Jr, his wife Millie, and their son Rand Tatum III (Peanut) moved in last year from another place they lost through foreclosure. Mr. Jennings still owned the land on both sides of the little road that ran from the Tatum house to the main road of Banks. He also still maintained a good porting of his farm that was two miles or so up on the other side of the Banks' road.

Papa Warner took a hit to his investment at the Hole in the Bushes place. He had received no returns in the last few years. Neither had its owners, Henry J or Carrie Strong. The restaurant section of the place had been reduced to serving items like eggs, bacon, hamburger, fish and game meat shot in the local woods. At any point in time, even those items may or may not be available. The Strong's had covered up most of the patio dining area because they simply didn't need it.

The entertainment section was still there and on occasion when William "June-bug" Davis was in town, he would play there for free. This was his home. His folks were still part of the community. He felt he owed his community. He still had to eat and took to the road to earn money. No matter what, he always found the time to come back home to check on his folks, and play at the Hole in the Bushes.

Security was performed by family members and volunteers as the Strong's could not afford to pay anybody. They, like the rest of the community, were trying to hold on while continuing to provide a place where one could go to get away from their daily struggles.

President Roosevelt took office to find 13,000,000 Americans unemployed. Reportedly in his first 100 days, almost every bank across the nation was closed. He wasted no time in getting to work as he had promised. Congress passed his proposals to jumpstart business and agriculture. Sweeping reforms included relief to the unemployed, homeowners and farmers in danger of losing their assets. The Tennessee Valley Authority was established to carry out reforms or restructuring. Most were part of the New Deal.

For Arkansas, the New Deal was a lifeboat of sorts. The unemployment rate in this state was 37 percent. Black unemployment was two or three times the rate of whites. One third of the rural taxpayer's payments were delinquent. Half the manufactures were closed. $279 million dollars would be spent in the state by the Roosevelt administration between now and March 1938. The Federal Emergency Relief Administration or FERA was organized in 1933. On May 8th, the Agriculture Act was passed to encourage farmers to go against what their parents and they had been taught all their lives. They would be paid to decrease production by not growing certain crops.

In June of the year, he created the Public Works Administration PWA. The organization was aided in the construction of new buildings on the UCA campus under the School Building Aid Program.

Additional projects developed in Central Arkansas by PWA were Joseph Taylor Robinson Memorial Auditorium, Tower Building renovations, Quigley Stadium Camp, Ouachita Girl Scout Camp Historic District, among others.

The president created the Civil Works Administration (CWA) in November of 1933, from which 58,000 Arkansas had jobs a month later. These changes were small yet significantly required to start money circulating and restore people's confidence.

One of the biggest problems Arkansas had was in getting electricity to the rural areas of the state. Although the state had several power-generating facilities, distribution was the main hang up. The fact the rural homes were somewhat isolated back in the woods was a large obstacle. President Roosevelt's New Deal allowed funding for rural electrification. The Governor was now allowed to sign legislation that would give electric companies the ability to incorporate in Arkansas. Oddly enough, it would still be awhile before this state actually took advantage of the federal governments help offered.

May was a special month in the Hampton household. John and Gracie were married on May 4th, nine years and counting this year. Gracie's birth day was on the 13th, twenty-nine years old and counting. The anniversary date had passed but her birthdate was today, and John and the kids would try and do something special for her.

There was a cake baked by Mae Ellen. Gracie helped her cousin prepare the fried chicken, a rabbit, cooked in gravy, mashed potatoes, string beans, biscuits. Although Gracie, the guest of honor, prepared her sweet tea cakes, another one of her specialties.

They all sat down to a special dinner, having invited Colrolus and Lena too. John, who was still having headaches and visions problems since the mule kicked him the head, managed to smile through mild discomfort.

The house was full of kids, Codis, Lacireen, Curtis, and Clarence D. Lena brought her two boys DC and Frank. The oldest kid in the bunch was eight year old Codis with the rest of them as young as age six.

Colrolus remarked how John had made improvements to the house and grounds not leaving out the changes Gracie had made to the interior of the house. "You people have put in some work here," He said.

"Man, you just don't know. With us movin' in during the middle of January, we were still able to get some work done outside. Thank God for the clear weather," John replied.

"I got a letter from Versia yesterday Lena. Did you get one too?" Gracie asked.

"No girl, I might get my next week sometime. What did she have to say? How are things in Hot Springs?

"She was talkin' bout how the town was still making money through gambling despite the Depression. The town's mayor, McLauglin said he would run an open town when he got elected back in 1926 and is still doing it. She say Hot Springs is the place of be if you looking for gambling, women, wine, or maybe I should say moonshine and song. Codis take that thing out of Lacirene's hand," Gracie responded while eating and keeping an eye on the kids.

"John, when the last time you been down to Hot Springs?" Colrolus asked.

"Never, I can tell you that," Gracie interrupted. "Versia said the mayor is trying to get the Oaklawn Park Racetrack opened again."

"One thing you can say about him though, he got his town on the map for not only the baths but a safe retreat for gangsters. Jus' so long as they behave themselves. That town must be rolling in dough, even now." Lena added.

"Sammy Parker still down there doing his business too." John said.

"Yeah, whatever that is" a laughing Colrolus said.

"Boy . . . , that's it. Come over here DC, you too Frank. Sit down right here by me," Lena ordered motioning for her boys to sit next to her. "Well how's Versia and James doing?"

"Fine, she says. No sign of a child yet. They are thinking about adopting soon as times get better."

"At least they still have a job and that's a good thing," Colrolus said.

"Yeah, a couple of our local colored boys went down there looking for a job. We haven't heard how it went yet, but . . . John, John you goin' to sleep?"

"Naw honey, I wasn't sleep. I heard everything you said about the colored boys going to Hot Springs. Um not sleep. I tell you."

"Well, your eyes were sure 'nuff closed. Anyway, that's pretty much all she had to say, 'cept she and James were going to try and drive up around the fourth of July this year. They will let us know," Gracie said while noticing John closing his eyes again she put her finger over her mouth in a shhhh gesture and pointed to him. He had nodded off completely this time.

"He's been doing stuff like that ever since that mule kicked him in the head. Yawl think he should go see Doctor Purvis.?" She asked whispering.

"Well, see, I got a potion that is supposed to help in these kinds of cases, where people been kicked by horses or mules," Colrolus whispered.

"I don't know Colrolus. Him dropping off to sleep like that, he needs to see a doctor. Let the doctor tell us what's going on," Lena advised while whispering as she spoke.

"Okay then, I'll drive him into Banks tomorrow. You think he'll go?" he asked Gracie.

"He'll go or be tied down on the hood of the truck like a deer. We'll get him to go. Don't worry about that."

"Then I'll be by 'round 10:00 o'clock Monday morning to pick him up," Colrolus stated.

"Pick who up?" John asked after being awakened by the sound of the kids laughing and playing.

"Um gonna take you to town with me on Monday. While we there, you can see Doc Purvis about those headaches you been having," Colrolus answered.

John looked at Gracie, Lena and Colrolus for a hot second. He looked back at his wife again who had a serious expression on her face. "All right," He said resigned to the fact that Gracie was already on board with this. There was no need in refusing. Besides, he wanted to know what was going on himself.

They all talked, laughed continually admonishing their children through desert, and after dinner conversation. John didn't nod off anymore but one could tell, he was not quite himself either.

Colrolus was right on time Monday morning. In fact, it was a little before ten when he drove up to the Hamptons' house. John waved goodbye to the family, climbed into the Ford truck's passenger seat, and off they went towards the Banks highway.

They waved at Papa Warner as they went by. Traffic was very light on the road. A lot more people walking to and fro than normal. Neither Colrolus nor John could figure out why except maybe it was the cheapest way to get around these days. Then again, maybe a lot more people lost their horses and wagons too.

They arrived at Dr. Purvis' Clinic around 10:40, parking the truck alongside the building. They walked in and found the doctor sitting at his assistant's desk.

"Morning Doctor Purvis," Colrolus greeted.

"Morning Doc," John added.

"Good morning boys, Hi you' all doing this morning? Colrolus I ain't seen you in a long time. You neither John. You are Sambo's and Sallie's boy right?"

"Yes suh, I am."

"Good, what brings you boys to town?"

John detailed his explanation to Dr. Purvis when and where he was kicked by the mule. He told him of his mild headaches and passing dizziness. He felt tired a lot of the time and falls asleep as if he hasn't had enough sleep.

"Other than that, I feels find most of the time", he added.

The doctor led him to the examination area, asked him to take a seat and started a full visual exam of John's forehead, back of the head, and so on. The gash was no longer on his forehead but did leave a small scar. When he finished, he told John, he was going to have to take a few x-rays and forward them to Little Rock for an in-depth evaluation and report.

He did tell John, It was possible; he received a mild concussion when he got kicked. The symptoms were indicative of and warranted that kind of preliminary diagnosis. He gave him a dozen pills used for migraine headaches, asking that he use the medication if or when the pain last a long time.

"Take one every four hours. Just as you've described, the mild headaches do not last a long time. So you should not have to use many of these pills. You sure ain't going to run out of them before the x-ray report comes back. So come back and see me next Thursday for the results and another examination." Doctor Purvis concluded.

"In other words, to be continued," A smiling Colrolus said.

"That's right," he said. "Bring him back around the same time next Thursday." The doctor added.

"What's the charge, Doc? Colrolus asked.

"No charge, except tell Gracie to make me one of her apple pies and bring it with you on the next visit."

"Thanks Doc. We'll see you next time," John said.

"All right boys, you' all have a nice day, ya' hear?"

John's first thought after getting into the truck was of how glad he was that he came to the doctor. He was a little anxious about the report results but at least he would find out what is wrong with him. He could not wait to get home and tell Gracie.

The week went by without any major incidents with John as a result of the kick in the head. Occasionally, he had the mild headache that didn't last long. He also felt dizziness which lasted briefly too. Ironically, he did not fall asleep in the middle of conversations during this time. He never once had to use the pills given him.

On Thursday, Colrolus drove John back to Doctor Purvis' clinic for his return appointment. They carried along a fresh baked apple pie from Gracie, per the doctor's request. Unfortunately, he received a more ominous warning of symptoms that may or may not appear.

The doctor advised him the report indicated he suffered a mild traumatic brain injury. Although it may not be as serious as it sounds, there was caused for concern. The doctor read of possible symptoms that had yet to be experience by John. They included nausea, blurred vision, mental changes, irritability, anxiety, anger, difficulty concentrating among a few others. If any of these were experienced, John should return immediately for additional prescribed medication and more x-rays to look for additional damage.

Doctor Purvis told John to make sure he got plenty of rest to avoid feeling fatigued whenever possible. Sometimes, he said, the brain takes a while to fully recover from the trauma. Reminding him that it's only been a little over two months. He gave John a brochure detailing the aforementioned symptoms to take home, also advising the pills he initial gave him were still good. Otherwise, he felt, or maybe hoped, the worst was over.

John felt a little more anxious about Doctor Purvis latest diagnosis but was determined to follow his instructions. After all, what else could he do? He reported the findings to his wife, giving her the brochure for safe keeping.

She and John grasp hands and prayed to God that this would not develop into anything more serious than it currently was. They thanked God for all he had provided up to his point, realizing their future rest in his hands. They end the prayer with a hearty "amen" in unison.

Over the next couple of years, John, Gracie and Mae Ellen, with Colrolus, Lena's and others help, spent time breaking in the new property. They planted small crops for personal use. There was not enough room to plant cotton for market; however they planted small fruit trees such as apple, peaches and a pear tree so the fruit could be used for cooking and canning.

Being so close to the wood line also brought concern of wild animals wandering onto the property searching for food and attacking their mule. John set traps at various spots, not only hoping to catch game for food but to discourage other animals from wandering onto his property. He managed to get two small pigs and a mama hog from his father. He built a small pig pen to keep them enclosed. It was also designed to keep them from wandering off.

He got two more full grown hunting dogs, one from Papa Warner named Zeke and another one named Popo from Clem Parker. They along with Oh No, Brownie and Blackie patrolled the Hampton property, alerting the family of possible intruders, especially near the house. In addition to alerting those same possible intruders that they were on guard 24-7. It was clear to John and Gracie from the beginning that all their dogs had plenty of sense. They would take one look at the density of the tree line and deduce that if anything was out there, it would have to come into full view before they acted. Otherwise, all they were going to do was bark like crazy, bringing out John and or Gracie with loaded shotguns to deal with any adversary on four or two legs.

It was a quite a chore for the Hampton's to get acclimated to their new home. Growing up, both John and Gracie were used to having a large field of something to look out on. They had a lot more space in between their house and the timber line, even with clearing spots for planting. The surrounding area, excluding the tree line, or small road, was dotted with foliage, high grass, or weeds. With small and curious kids, it was always a chore to keep them from wandering into the woods, which was so close to their front door, or while playing hide and seek, getting confused and, God forbid, lost within the high grass outside the property boundaries. Both parents had to be strict with their children to ensure they obeyed their parents. The fact was, this was no different than the rest of the region, because during those days children did as they were told or else. Or else meant if a child did not mind a family grown-up, which in this household, twenty-year-old Mae Ellen was considered grown too, they were sent to get a switch from a bush on the property. A switch was a very small piece of the bushes growth, stripped of its leaves that left a flexible vine like piece that was used for whipping a disobedient child. Country parents found it was a very effective way to punish their child; even sending a child to get the switch was an effective way of having them to think differently before misbehaving again. Yet, we are still talking about children who have a way of finding themselves in compromising or dangerous situations, especially in this environment. Thus the concern.

Rural area children have to grow up quickly, learning to understand what is and isn't a safe act. They have to learn to be aware of their surroundings at all times. Kids being kids, they had their mishaps and unforgettable adventures but they also were able to adjust to living in the woods.

May of 1935 found Codis, now ten years old, nine year old Lacireen, six year old Curtis, two and half year old Clearance D all safe and sound. They were growing up like crazy and not at all intimidated by their surroundings.

Gracie had gotten pregnant and she had another boy this past January, naming him John T. Although the boy was delivered without any major problems, he turned out to be a sickly child. He was a fighter but could not keep his food down. The child passed a little over six weeks later from hunger. This was the second child Gracie lost and it clearly upset her. She told John, Mae Ellen and Lena, she saw this baby's death in a premonition, which added to her anxiety about having any more children.

She surprised her husband by announcing they should not have sex anymore because she was afraid to get pregnant. John accepted his wife's reasoning believing this was a period that would die out over a short time. At least that is what he thought.

As for himself, physically or mentally he was never quite the same as before the kick in the head. He could function with all body parts working, just not as sharp as before the accident. He discovered his concentration was not as sharp; he had occasional blurred vision although the dizzy spells had stopped. He had not gone back to Dr. Purvis because he felt no need to trouble him. Colrolus and Lena was as helpful as could be. It was nice being so close to them. They had added to their family too. Lena had another baby boy, Joe Strong last year. DC was now seven while his brother Frank was five years old. Whenever possible the Hampton and Strong cousins played, ate, and even went to church together.

Politically, national and local leaders were still dealing with the linger effects of the great depression. Last month the Works Progress Administration (WPA) was formed. It was designed to distribute various benefits, hire workers and implement various projects. These type federal organizations were able to reach past the local pecking order of discrimination and provide jobs to African Americans. This was good for the area; at least somebody was getting help, thereby benefiting the region itself.

The Federal Writers Project, a part of the WPA, was able to support the work of many black authors throughout the United States. Authors like Melvin B. Tolson, Arna Bontemps, Waters Turpin, and Zora Neale Hurston, to name a few were aided by this program.

The plight of sharecroppers in Arkansas became a national concern. The more publicity on what is happening in the deep south the better it was for everybody. The Farm Security Administration (FSA) began fighting rural poverty. Still for a lot of black folks, most of the help were being directed to white folk by the local establishment. If federal programs were not directly aimed at black folk, they would hardly see or reap any benefit from such programs. That is one reason, even though there were plenty white sharecroppers too, that particular profession became a national concern.

Given time, most business people who have a wealth of money will become dissatisfied with any government program that does not directly benefit them. By 1935, despite evidence of some recovery, wealthy businessmen and bankers were turning against President Roosevelt's New Deal programs. Among other issues, they did not like his concessions to the nation's labor force. The Congress of Industrial Organizations (CIO) was established and began to represent and organize labor unions to represent the workers. They also began to organize black workers into labor unions. Again, any move that interferes with their bottom line, profit, is not going to go over well with big business.

In August, President Roosevelt signed into law the Social Security Act. It meant heavier taxes on the wealthy. It allowed for more control over banks, as well as public utilities. There was also a work relief program for the unemployed. All acts that had a negative effect on rich folk bottom line.

The world was still reeling and trying to recover from the depression in 1936. Germany's Hitler, Italy's Mussolini, and Japan's Okada, followed by Hirota, formed an alliance that would later threaten the world order of peace. During the summer Olympics in Berlin, African-American Jesses Owens embarrassed Hitler by winning four gold medals. Hitler, who championed the idea that his great Aryan supermen was a super race of athletes and people, was noticeably agitated as he watched Owens celebrate his victories.

In the U.S., the depression was still hanging on while unemployment fell to 16.9% from a high of 25%. A gallon of gas was ten cents, average rental of a house was twenty-four dollars per month, hamburger meat was twelve cents per pound, and a Studebaker car cost six hundred and sixty-five dollars. The average wage for the year was $1,713. President Roosevelt was re-elected in 1936 by a wide margin leaving him with the impression he had a mandate to solve the nation's ills.

Meanwhile with each passing month or so, symptoms from John's mild traumatic brain injury began popping up on more than one occasion. Gracie maintained her vow not have sex while fearing another pregnancy may result in a third child's death.

Trying to cope with these new symptoms, raising a family by keeping the children out of danger, tending to farm chores, and the distancing of his wife was beginning to take a toll on John. He became more irritable towards everyone and angry at Gracie for what he believed was desertion at a time he needed her love and comfort.

He began wandering off for no apparent reason and seemed unaware of his surroundings at times. Colrolus took him back to the doctor who gave him mild sedative pills to help him sleep, advising him to get more rest. Doctor Purvis also told Colrolus that John's mild traumatic Brain Injury was taking a drastic turn for the worse. He asked if John and Gracie were having problems. He sent word to Gracie that her husband needed all the comfort she could provide at this time of need. The doctor had no magic pills or any known remedy for what John was going through at the time, so he relied on family love and support to help ease the concern.

Colrolus relayed Doctor Purvis words verbatim to Gracie. She was torn between a providing her love, loyalty, and wifely duties to her husband and a feeling, not a premonition, but a feeling, that if she got pregnant again, the child would die.

Over the next few months, she tried to show him that she loved him while still rejecting his sexual advances. She had also begun to put on weight as she snacked while cooking, among other things. John lost a few pounds from his already slender body size. This battle of a basic human need for John and Gracie, whether she realized it or not, was just as important for her state of mind too. They began to bicker at each other in front of May Ellen and the kids or whoever happened to be there when they argued.

Having seen their arguments almost come to blows several times, Lena and Colrolus became concerned. They, along with Mae Ellen were concerned for the kids as well as John and Gracie. Lena tried talking with Gracie about her problem. The conversation was always short. They could talk about anything, agreeing on most everything, except her position on marital sex. She was adamant about not having another dead child.

Colrolus himself had begun to look at Gracie through eyes of resentment. He could not understand, nor could Lena for the matter, why she felt having sex with her husband was never going to happen again.

He, like most men, including John knew there were ways to prevent a pregnancy. The most expedient being the purchase of a condom, which had been a standard issue to members of the military since 1931. The program was designed to prevent soldiers from catching sexual transmitted diseases while serving in the armed services. They were not visibly displayed but could be bought at Papa Warner's anytime.

"You know what?" Colrolus casually mentioning to Lena over a cup of coffee this particular Friday morning. "I bet you Doctor Purvis has a supply of those rubber things for his patients."

"You mean condoms," Lena corrected.

"Condoms, rubbers, whatever you want to call them. Those two people across the way need to go at it something fierce."

"Yeah I know. My sister is scared out of her mind that she's going to get pregnant again. Before I talk to her, why don't you take John in to see the doctor? If he don't have any, then buy them from Skeeter Purvis' store or Papa Warner. Somebody got them. We may even have to order them out of a catalog, but somebody got them."

"You right baby. Hell it don't make no sense no how the way Gracie is acting about this. I'll pick him up tomorrow. I'll drop you off at while picking John up. You talk to her, you hear?"

"Oooh wee, that's another reason why I married you. You scamp you," Lena playfully squealed.

"For my brains?"

"That was part of it," she answered, hugging him and planted a big kiss on Colrolus lips."

"Now, now, now, nowdon't you go startin' nothing you can't finish woman," her clearly excited husband said in a stuttering manner.

Just then, their oldest, seven year old DC, pulling five year old Frank by the hand ran into the kitchen area from outside. "Mama, we fed the chickens, can we eat now?" DC asked.

Lena laughed, getting up off Colrolus lap and replied, "Sure baby, you two sit down and I'll fix yo' plate. Where is yo' baby brother, still asleep?"

"Yes sum," The boys replied.

"I'll go check on 'em." Colrolus said slowly standing up and walking into the kids room where he saw three year old Joe Strong getting out of bed. Awaken by all the commotion; he grabbed his daddy hand while being led outside to the outhouse.

The next day, the entire family got into the truck and headed for the Hampton's place. Gracie was glad to see her sister and nephews. After a few waves from Colrolus to his and the Hampton family he and John took off for Doctor Purvis' office.

Since they were headed for Banks on this Saturday morning (March 27, 1937) they took the oldest boys, Codis and DC with them. The men were given a few other things to pick up at Skeeter Purvis' store and Papa Warner's on the way home.

John was in a pretty good mood because he wanted to see the doctor anyway. His mood turned to almost jovial when he found out why they would try to find some condoms for him to use while having sex with Gracie. He was told that her sister was going to speak with his wife about that possibility while they were in town. Colrolus had to speak in code and gibberish so that the boys would not know what they were talking about. At least that is what he thought. The boys themselves were enjoying the ride and sights so much, it probably didn't matter what they were talking about as long as ithis thoughts were interrupted by,

"Daddy, what is Uncle C talkin' about when he says condoms?" Twelve year old Codis asked.

"Never u mind boy. It's just some equipment for work." John answered while smiling and almost choking holding back laughter.

This was not the first time that Codis and DC had been to Banks but it certainly was a memorable trip. Although the town had not changed that much, especially during the depression, almost everything was new to the boys. Colrolus drove Codis and DC to the back of Skeeter's store where they found a couple of shopper's wagon teams. Kids were loading or milling around waiting on their folks. The men told them to wait there until they returned.

Doctor Purvis listened to the same and a couple of new symptoms John was experiencing. He told him his short temper and irritability may be symptoms too. He was very anxious to hear John's explanation of wandering off as if in a daze. John told him he would have neither recollection of when or why he left nor any indication of where he was going.

This in itself was troublesome to the doctor. His first thought was to admit him to a hospital for test. Since he would have to send him all the way to Little Rock, he decided to perform another round of test in the clinic. He took x-rays of his head and neck this time.

He was glad to hear about the sexual abstinence problem only because any decrease in anxiety could help his condition. He felt that a return to sexual activity may reduce some symptoms. He did have a supply of condoms, of which he gave john a half dozen and asked him to return the next week. The next time, he suggested they bring along Gracie.

Colrolus and John drove down to Skeeter's store, picked up a couple of items, and drove off with their boys. They pulled into Papa Warner's lot and parked the car. The boys went into the store to spend a few pennies on candy for themselves and their siblings. John went in to pick up a couple items he and Colrolus needed such as tobacco and Papa's syrup.

Papa Warner provided the latest community news as john returned to the porch and sat down with his brother-in-law. He reluctantly spoke of his wife Dora, suddenly dying in her sleep and how he missed her although his wife of three months was fitting in nicely with the family. Dora's death was still somewhat of a mystery. He said she looked great all day long. She wasn't complaining, so he thought she felt fine when she got into their bed on that early spring night of March, 1936. She was 54 years old and his heartbeat.

"She just went to sleep and never woke up," A somber Papa Warner concluded.

John and Colrolus remembered it well. The immediate family was almost speechless at her sudden death. The community sadly mourned the loss of such a valuable asset as one of their own, especially given the fact she was such a giving, God fearing church going good person.

"I tell you one thing. Fannie was there when I needed someone. I don' know where I'd be without her. She's a good woman too. Take time to know her and you will see," Papa said.

"Yep, there's nothin' like having a good woman by yo' side." Colrolus added.

"Amen to that." John said remembering how Gracie used to be.

The boys, as kids will do, found other kids of customers to speak with after putting their candy in the car. Finally Codis couldn't stand it. He saw Joel Warner over by the car shed. He walked over to the shed and asked where those pretty girls of Papa Warner's were? He received a chilling stare for his answer. Evidently he didn't realize that two of the girls were Joel's daughters. He decided he would catch them at school. No need to push the issue here, he thought.

"I heard you sweet on that one girl, ain't you?" DC asked Codis as they walked away.

"Boy, you don't know what you talkin' bout," Codis answered.

"Okay, but I heard her name is Doreatha Childs, one of them pretty grandchild girls of Papa Warner's."

"Would you shut up?" Codis whispered loudly as they walked back to the truck.

In all, they must have hung around Papa's store for about an hour. Finally they left for home full of news, carrying items requested by their wives, and their oldest sons who had a wonderful time hanging with dad and meeting new friends.

Gracie, who heard the plea from her sister to get back to a normal sex life with her husband, agreed that her abstinence had taken a toll on her marriage. Her stance was also self-depreciating as a wife and woman. She told Lena, the decision to stop having sex with her husband was the most traumatic act she has ever done. It tore at her religious beliefs while going against her desires as a woman. Yet the picture of having another dead child was even more imposing.

She would welcome the use of condoms by her husband as a way to avoid another pregnancy. She was also aware that during the act of sex a breakage could occur in the condom. Yet she welcomed this compromise as a way to heal the sexual rift in her marriage. It came just in time for the celebration of their thirteenth wedding anniversary on May 4th, 1937, just a few days away.

Together they decided to make the renewal of their lovemaking special, a time of recommitment, so they waited until the night of their anniversary. That particular night Mae Ellen would be staying at Lena's house working on a sewing project. They put the children to bed and talked a long while before they actually had sex. They renewed the love they had for each other. They begged for forgiveness from each other on how they were acting up to this point. They vowed to talk more to solve problems. Finally, they got reacquainted with each other's body and found out the touch from a person in love makes all things right. One tends to forget why an argument ensued, just concentrating on the here and now. Even tomorrow seems so far away when tonight is all that is real at the moment.

Afterwards, they lay in each other's arms satisfied they had gotten this part of their marriage back on track.

CHAPTER 10

Papa Warner's Grand Cuties

For Papa Warner, the smell of the early spring weather this March of 1938 brought about a time for contemplating of what has happened, what is happening, and what will happen because of the effort and work one puts in today. It's funny how time has passed allowing him and his former wife to enjoy the birth and growing up of their grandchildren.

Even after all of these years, at 59, he was still known as a man who would catch a young lovely in the fields or down at the Hole in the Bushes place, and try to put a move on them. Whether he was successful or not was a matter for debate.

He went wild shortly after his first wife died in her sleep year before last. The chase after this woman or that one didn't last long. Thanks to the presence of Fannie Mormon, whom he married in January of last year, he was able to come out of his widower's funk while maintaining enough business savvy to keep a steady hand on his holdings during the national and his personal depression.

Even so, the last few years haven't been kind to his businesses or personal life. Being a Mason also helped him through the trying times. If not for that organization, the Warner Empire would have been hit harder. The fact that he has family labor to work and manage the different entities has been a tremendous asset. Credit must also be given to his number one son, Joel Johnson, who is his second in command. Joel has stayed by his father's side, even when he agreed with other family members that not all of Papa's decisions were right.

Yet there have been and continue to be major problems. His family member wages, which Papa Warner pays and has used as a bargaining chip, can be adjusted to fit any situation. At least that is the way Papa sees it. It has become hard for some family members to get items they needed during this depression because of Papa's habit of keeping all supplies under his direct distribution. At times, his children, who all were still living and working on the Johnson land, felt they needed more food or something than the man in charge would distribute. Papa refused to bend his self-imposed rules. It was the direct cause of a couple of his older children, excluding Joel and his family, to move away to places like California and Milwaukee.

Papa refused to bend and still ran a tight ship. He began to wear a whistle to summon those working in the many different areas of the farm. Whenever he wanted to have a meeting at the main house, he would blow his whistle. The entire clan knew that a meeting was being conducted and they better find a way to get there in a hurry.

He still made Syrup, grew cotton, albeit on smaller fields, performed auto-repair, made coffins for community funerals, fixed wagons, repaired shoes, and was the local blacksmith. To this day, including some grandchildren, with very few outside assistance, perform the work on the farm producing product and income.

To the community, his store was still the place where one finds new products or inventions, job openings, and so on. He could explain the benefits of the New Deal programs, especially if black folk were able to get them or not. In other words, depression or not, Papa Warner's store was still a vital informational, catalog ordering, post office for some, retail products and service outlet for this community.

He and his deceased wife had taken in two of their daughter Edna's children. They were still living in the house with Papa and new wife Fannie. At 44 years old, Fannie has fit in very nicely with the household and remaining family members living on the property. She is smart enough to realize she can never replace his first wife. She doesn't have the talent Dora had or the respect of the community at this point. Yet, she is a woman who is motherly enough to be a very capable person in her own right.

Papa and Dora's daughter, Edna, was separated from husband Edward Childs. She is courting another man in another county and thinking of leaving Arkansas. Meanwhile, twelve year old Doreatha Childs and her ten year old sister, Gertie Mae Childs, were growing up as normal girls in their grandfather's house. It should be said, there was no special privileges for them either, other than a nickname. Doreatha was called "Do", pronounced Doe and her sister, Gertie Mae, was called "Nookie".

Papa's oldest son, Joel Johnson, his wife, Viola, and their children, eleven year old Georgia M, ten year old Virgie L, and his nine year old son JO, was living on the property. The girls, Georgia Mae (nicknamed Beeka), Virgie, Do, and Nookie were all light brown skin and pretty girls. They all had long black hair breaded in pigtails. Nookie's hair was really fine and straight, similar to white folks' hair. Her and Do's father, Edward Childs was a mulatto. They were called the "Papa Warner Cuties" by the local boys and a few other things by the local girls. They stuck together waking to and from school. Most all the local boys were chasing those cuties. It was said; some of the other girls were jealous and wanted to fight them because their potential boy friends were running after the Warner grandchildren too.

They all started out attending the same community one room school house, Gravel Ridge. Parents, John Hampton, Gracie Hall, Joel Johnson, Viola Ross, and Edna Johnson, along with the rest of the community's young parents, were students of this school. Following their parents, John and Gracie's kids, other neighbor's children, are attending this school. It still serves this area as the first to eighth grade learning facility. Students who want to go further will have to go to the black high school in Warren.

In the past year they built another school, calling it Oaklawn, almost directly next to the old school. The Works Progress Administration (WPA), part of President Roosevelt's New Deal, in conjunction with other organizations funded the construction of the new school. Arkansas school consolidation and education reform was directed at closing down the one-room schoolhouses. Afterwards, they finally tore down Gravel Ridge. It was getting to be uninhabitable.

Oaklawn had two rooms but no door to separate the two rooms. This year they added a rec room and another classroom, still separated by an opened door. Like Gravel Ridge, the new school accepted six year olds into the first grade, offering classes up to the eighth grade. Some said they saw a few of the books their parents used while doing their school work. After all, the schools did not fully escape the tentacles of the great depression.

The county, with funding from the government (WPA) had put in a baseball field in between the Oaklawn Methodist Church and Oaklawn School. The eleven and twelve year old boys used it. It was also large enough for semi-pro games too. Gravel Ridge, which was renamed to Banks, had their local baseball players such as Joel Johnson, John and Monroe Hampton. They played visiting teams from inside and outside the county. It was a great place to see Negro baseball players.

It had been an eventful summer for the Warner Cuties. Another summer of avoiding some and allowing the boys you like to talk to you. Unlike some of the younger boys who chased after them, the girls were growing up fast.

On this particular November day, a few days before Thanksgiving, Doreatha (Do), Gertie Mae (Nookie), Georgia Mae (Beeka) and Virgie had on their red winter boots. They grabbed their homework, lunch pails, and headed out walking along the fence line between the Warner property and the road to Banks. They were going in the opposite direction of the town of Banks.

The red boots was a family tradition. It was also a trademark of the Cuties. Originally Papa Warner would make sure he had enough red boots to supply the girls in his family during the winter. The color was a way of signifying those who wore them were members of the Warner family. He would not sell red booths to any other family in the community. That's not to say, those families could not buy them somewhere else, but mostly the community relented to Papa's wishes and bought other colors for their girls. This didn't make certain girls happy either, who couldn't understand why they could not wear red boots. On rare occasions, you might see a non-Warner girl wearing a pair, but it was very seldom that happened.

This was a cold winter day. The girls were wrapped up tight as they walked along the six mile route taken to get to the Oaklawn School. Georgia Mae and Virgie's brother, J O, was bringing up the rear. After walking as far as they could along the two rail fence line of the Warner property, they stepped through it to cross the road. They continued to walk on the other side facing the oncoming traffic.

The girls had been taught to be extra cautious and look for danger in every corner. That is another reason they stuck so closely together. They also had to be aware of the farmland houses they had to pass on the way to and from school. Most was owned by white folk. Sometimes their family members would sit on the porch watching and staring at the girls. Some older black girls walking alone have been grabbed by white men of all ages who were looking for a good time. The white men found them to be easy targets if caught walking alone. After all, this was the south, and the word of a white man ruled against almost any person of color.

The Klan was still meeting regularly at various locations. They continued to meet, burning crosses on old man Sampson's property. Some whites continued trying to intimidate black folk when it was to their advantage or they wanted something from them. There were still 'whites only' signs on facilities from Banks to Warren, through Little Rock and throughout Arkansas. Signs were on stores, cafes, private property, service places, even outhouses at gas stations.

The girls were walking to a segregated school that was part of a segregated school system. Black folks still lived with the code and coped with how to survived and thrive in this type of environment. So yes, the girls and anyone of the same color had to be aware of their surroundings at all times, especially walking to and from anywhere in this region.

Yet, they were still young girls and while they walked along they carried on young girl conversations.

"Pretty soon we gonna see Lacirene and her brothers walking to school," Georgia Mae said.

"She's a friendly girl who don't hang around with that Marjorie bunch," Doreatha added.

"Uh huh, Marjorie Tatum likes that Calvin Hampton boy and he like you Georgia Mae. That's why she always after you," Virgie teased. "JO you better come on here and stop fooling around, or um gonna tell daddy."

"I see the way you look at Codis. I think you do like him, don't you? I know he likes you," Georgia Mae said laughing and teasing her cousin Do.

"You like him?" her sister Nookie asked as Do couldn't help but smile when thinking about the boy.

"See there Do, I know you liked him. Ain't it funny he is older than his uncle Calvin Hampton?" Georgia Mae asked while still teasing Doreatha.

"All I know is yawl better watch out before your brother gets left behind and lost. He better come on here, 'cause he is gonna get in trouble when Aunt Viola gets a hold of his behind," Warned Doreatha, "And stop calling me Do, I want yawl to call me by my full name, Doreatha not Do. Especially you Nookie, cause you started it."

"Aw shut up Do, here comes yo' beau, Mister Codis Hampton, now," Nookie teased.

"He's all right. There's his sister Lacirene and that mannish little brother of theirs, Curtis," Added Georgia Mae.

"You got that right. I caught that little scamp lying on the classroom floor trying to look up my dress. He acted like he was picking up a pencil," Virgie told the girls.

"Did you tell the teacher?" Doreatha asked.

"Nooooo, but I popped him across the head one time. He got up laughing, asking me why I hit him. I told him to do it again and he'll get worse."

The girls broke out laughing. Virgie was like the policeman of the group. She was quick to slap or pop someone for teasing her or just making her mad. Just like now, she got tired of telling her little brother JO, to keep up with them so she placed him in front of her and pushed him along whenever he slowed down.

The Hampton kids had caught up to them by now with Codis walking alongside Doreatha and sort of whispering to her to avoid the rest of the kids from hearing their conversation. Lacirene was walking alongside Georgia Mae followed by Virgie bringing up the rear watching JO and Curtis horse around while she pushed them both along fast enough to keep up with the others. They only had about a half a mile to go before reaching the school.

As the months passed, Codis and Doreatha became more and more serious about each other. Even the kids in school were aware of their budding love affair. In fact, after school Codis had gotten into a scuffle or two over Doreatha. Boys will be boys as more than a few sought the attention of Do. She was a quiet and reserved cutie, known as the smartest one although all the cuties were smart. Why she liked Codis was a mystery to some, they just hit it off from the very start.

The other girls, like Georgia Mae, Virgie, and Nookie were still playing the field. They had not settled on one special boy. In Georgia Mae's case, she didn't like any of her boy classmates in that way. Virgie was too busy fighting them off to like them and Nookie was still too young and not serious enough about that like or love stuff. She just liked to play.

Thanksgiving, Christmas, New Year's passed with most in the region still trying to recover from the Depression, so celebrations were muted or normal according to a particular family's financial condition. Valentine's Day, 1939 arrived and vanished with the entire school body anticipating the planting season break. Again, this is where the schools shut down and let the children stay home to work in the fields with their parents or help in some fashion with the spring planting season. This was a grown-ups idea because this is one time their kids would much rather go to school. Nevertheless, March 1st rolled on a Wednesday; Oaklawn will join other rural Arkansas schools and close for a three and a half month recess, reopening in mid-June. This year they are schedule to return on June 12th.

You could tell by the activity and restlessness of the kids that this was the last day of school before the break. Kids were asked to maintain their reading levels by reading any paper, with parents' permission, mail order catalog, or books they have or can afford to buy during the break.

They were also asked to practice their penmanship whenever they could by writing letters or keeping a diary of some sort of their life during the planting season. Georgia Mae, Lacirene and Doreatha were in the sixth and seventh grade group. Surprise, Codis, along with (his younger Uncle) Calvin, and cousin DC Strong, was in their group too. Virgie and Nookie were in the fifth and sixth grades group. Curtis and JO were in the fourth and fifth year group. The third and second year grades rounded out the multiple grade groups. The single groups were the first or eight grades, which meant it was either your first or last year at Oaklawn.

On the way home that evening, they all knew that this was a special time for kids who would only see each other sparingly if at all during this break. Just in case, Codis made his angry face at any potential suitor of Doreatha as a warning. Therefore most of the kids let sweetheart couples have their last walk home together for the break.

The other cuties, Virgie who would pop you if you messed with her at any time, Nookie playfully laughing with two boys, and Georgia Mae trying to convince Calvin Hampton there was no future between them, were walking in the crowd toward their route home.

When they arrived at the fork in the road, Codis and Doreatha hugged each other and waved goodbye. Codis sister, Lacirene waved goodbye to a potential beau who was new to the school and area. They and little brother Curtis peeled off, headed in the direction of their home walking with their cousins, DC and Frank Strong.

"Well child, here we go. Back to slavery days; chop that cotton, plant those tomatoes, boil that water, canned that jam, do this, do that, go to bed, wake up, and start all over again." Ain't that 'bout it Do?" Georgia Mae asked Doreatha and any of the other girls who felt like answering.

"That's it. No more school work, just work, with no time to play," she answered.

"You think anybody can get that whistle off of Papa Warner this year?" Virgie asked.

"Not if you wanna live," Nookie responded.

"Did Mama Fannie tell you girls where you would be working this spring?" Georgia asked.

"Not yet?" Doreatha answered.

"Shhhh! look at them two white boys over there staring at us," Virgie offered on a more serious note. "JO, you better get you behind up here like mama told you. You want me to tell her you wouldn't listen? You don't want me to have to come back there now, do you?"

"Awwwwwwww, um coming," JO answered running to catch up with the girls.

The two white boys sitting on the porch of a house across the field stared at the kids walking while the kids watched them out of the corner of their eyes. They walked off the porch and headed for the group. Virgie, who carried a big stick to ward off anything and anybody, like the rest of the girls, picked up there pace. The girls and JO began to jog toward the opened field gate leading to the Banks' road. They looked back to see that the boys had stopped. They slowed down to a fast pace after reaching the road.

They felt the boys were just trying to scare them. They were not that scared but just could not take a chance on something major happening. This happened often to the girls, usually from the same two white boys. This year, for some reason, it happened quite a bit more than normal. A couple of them just couldn't understand why and said so out loud.

"Some of us have grown over the last year. They see our breast's got bigger," Doreatha explained. "They think we more woman now than little girls."

"You mean we got bigger tits," a laughing Georgia Mae added.

"Ooooooo weeeee, um gonna tell JO said laughing and teasing.

"Boy shut up 'fore I smack you one," warned Georgia Mae.

"I told you, she'll pop you, didn't I?" Virgie asked JO.

"Whoooooo, I know you gonna miss you some Codis ain't you Do? Georgia Mae asked Doreatha. "I know you going to miss him sniffing round you all the time. Trying to sneak a kiss 'thout nobody looking."

"Foot! I ain't gonna miss that boy. I got a lot of stuff to do 'thout thinking about his butt," She lied while trying to look angry with her reply. "Anyways," she continued rolling her eyes. "Who was that boy Lacirene was talking to? I have never seen him before."

"I think his name is R.T. One of 'dem Tatum's, R.T. Tatum, He moved over from Lanark. He just started school a couple of weeks ago," Georgia Mae said.

"Come on girls we better hurry, before Mama Fannie wonders where we are and why we are late," Doreatha urged.

With that the cuties and JO picked up the pace. They were almost running to the house after they reached the Johnson property fence line. They could hear Papa Warner's whistle blowing for a meeting. They knew it wasn't for them but decided they better show up at the big house anyway. That would at least show their parents they were home from school.

Harvey Sampson was one of the farmers who were able to take advantage of the Agricultural Adjustment Act (AAA) passed in 1933. It's the act that paid some farmers to reduce certain crop output, with cotton being the main crop of seven others. Designed to raise the valid of crops, the measure favored the large growers at the expense of the sharecroppers. The Supreme Court declared the act unconstitutional in 1936. It failed because it taxed one farmer to pay another. This year Congress would take up the matter again, and pass a second AAA with funding coming from the general taxation. For Harvey, it meant that he was going to get paid anyway. Besides, his wealth was pretty set because he inherited most of it.

For years, old man Sampson has served as a Grand Dragon of the Ku Klux Klan. His family and employees have tried to buy, steal, or even intimidate black folk, in this and other Arkansas counties, off their land, sometimes committing acts out of spite and hatred. He lost one son through violence with another one crippled for life. He has not changed; only harden his attitudes toward people of color and Sheriff Dan Penelton of Banks.

He still blames the sheriff for letting Sammy Parker get away from Bradley County after his sons ambushed young Parker and his cousin. The old man has been trying to get the sheriff kicked out of office ever since then, with the help of McBain, the Banks' store owner. It has not worked so far.

In Bradley County, as in all Arkansas counties, the sheriff is elected and can be removed by losing such an election. This does not apply to small towns. The towns' public servants, such as the mayor, councilmen if needed, treasure—tax collector are appointed by its citizens. An appointment can be a lifetime job as long as the individual pleases their constituents'.

That was the problem for Harvey Sampson and like-minded McBain. Sheriff Penelton is still, after all these years, known as a fair and impartial man. The only people that don't see him that way are Sampson, McBain, and friends. They tried to kill him and that didn't work. No one can prove it was them, but the Sheriff is pretty sure of it. So try as they might to replace him, they have failed. Yet, they keep trying. The 48 year old sheriff has served in the same position for over 27 years with a three year break for World War I.

This morning just before daybreak, as he has every third Saturday of the month for the last year, Harvey is sending his son, Petey, to town. He will have breakfast at the café, meet with McBain and others regarding family business. For Petey, it's a chance to get out of the house and ride in a car. He is able to sit in the back seat of a car while being driven by a driver. Petey has also welcomed the importance of participating in the family finances.

The car, driven by Petey's chauffeur, Allan Grassley with his cousin Paul Grassley left the Sampson's house about half an hour ago. Ironically, about two miles just outside Banks and at about the same spot the sheriff's deputy had been killed, multiple shots rang out. So many shots were fired at the Sampson vehicle, its front tires were punctured, and causing the car to spin out of control flipping once and landing overturned on the other side of the embankment.

Once the car landed, additional shots were fired, hitting the gas tank, which causes an explosion which could be seen miles away in the early morning.

Another car pulled out of the bushes alongside of the road drove down to a filled in break on the embankment and sped off in the opposite direction of the town. There were no witnesses this time. There were no one coming or going to Banks except the Sampson car.

Papa Warner and Joel were on their way to open up the store. They heard the explosion and could see the glow from the flames lighting up the sky from their vantage point. They saw a vehicle go past them with two men in it, but could not tell if the men were black or white. In fact, it could have been a man and a woman or two women. All they saw was two figures in the front seat.

Joel got in their truck and drove up to see if anyone got hurt. Papa Warner asked him to go alone while he opened up the store. When he got there, Deputy Stovall was already there. A Banks fire truck was using water from a tanker to put out the fire. An ambulance was also at the scene.

He saw the ambulance driver and his aide place a body on the stretcher, slide it into the back of the ambulance and drove off headed for Banks. They might have to go to Warren if the injury is really serious.

There were a couple of other people standing around, Joel's guess was they were people on the road who may or may not have seen anything. Joel asked one of the men if he knew who was involved.

"Petey Sampson and two other men," he answered.

"Did they all get out? Was it an auto crash or were they drunk?" Joel asked.

The white stranger looked at Joel as if he was asking too many questions and walked away and stood next to another white man.

The Sheriff drove up to the scene now. Joel knew he had better come back with some answers or Papa would be fit to be tied. He walked over to sheriff's vehicle as he was getting out and being briefed by Deputy Stovall.

"Morning Sheriff," the deputy began, "It was Petey Sampson and a couple of other people in the car. Amazingly, he is alive and on his way to the hospital in Warren. We think he was thrown from the car when it flipped. The other two men are dead from gun shots wounds. From the looks of the vehicle, the weapon was some kind of automatic or machine gun. Maybe one of those tommy guns you see in the movies. They meant to kill everyThe Sheriff stopped his deputy from reporting because he saw Joel standing behind them.

"Hey you, come here a minute."

"Yes suh," Joel said as he walked up to the Sheriff.

"Did you see anything that could help us?"

"No suh, we saw the explosion after it happened but we were just coming out of our house across the road from the store," Joel answered.

"Right, I know you. You're Papa Warner's son, right?"

"Yes suh."

"Well, is that all you saw, nobody on the road or anything?"

"Yes suh, that's it. Oh yeah, we did see a car coming from that way, but couldn't tell you who was driving it."

"Can you describe this vehicle?"

"Well, I don't know suh. It happened so fast. It was just a Ford model something or the other. I do remember the Ford emblem. I think it was black or maybe dark gray. You can ask Papa, he might remember more than I do."

"All right Joel. Thanks boy. You tell him we will be out to see him as soon as we leave here. For now you go on and tell him what I said."

"Yes suh," Joel answered, and walked back to his truck and took off heading for the store.

After Joel left and the law officers were sure no one was listening, Deputy Stovall finished his report. Sheriff, we need to get the bullets but there was a lot of firepower directed at that car. Petey must have the lives of a cat."

"Yes he does, because one has to figure they were trying to kill him."

It would take a while for the heat to subside for a more intense examination of the car. The sheriff enlisted one of the firemen to say with the car until he and the deputy returned.

The sheriff and deputy drove down to Papa Warner's. He gave them all the additional information he had which was no more than Joel told them. So the officers left his store and drove up to the Sampson place.

Petey's folks were shocked and devastated. They just could not figure who was trying to kill their son. The old man and his wife, Clara told the sheriff they would have to see him later. The Sampson's took off in a hurry using another chauffeur to drive them to the Warren Hospital. He wanted to meet with the Sheriff upon his return from the hospital.

Both men stopped at the scene of the shooting on the way back to Banks. The fireman was still there poking around in the ashes. The two dead bodies were removed and transported to Banks. The trunk of the car had popped open during its rolling ejecting Petey's wheel chair in the process. The spot where Petey was found was marked.

Deputy Stovall had already examined and pulled the clues for the spot of the shooting. This time they were able to take pictures of the vehicle's tire tracks, men's foot prints that told them it was two men. The car was leaking oil which was not too much evidence. They figured it might have been the same car seen by Papa and Joel.

The sheriff had reached one conclusion. There was one clear piece of evidence that was not found at this scene or the Bob and Clarke shooting. Somebody doesn't like the Sampson's or their people and was trying to wipe them out. That, in itself, pretty much widened the suspects list.

There was another meeting going on that day. It was at the Hampton household between Colrolus, Lena, Gracie, Sambo and Sallie. The subject was what to do with John. The kids had all been asked to do specific chores or simply find something to do while their parents' dealt with a serious issue. It was Mae Ellen's job to insure the kids found something else to do. The oldest Hampton kids knew the meeting had to do with their father. Some of them had been enlisted to keep an eye on John with no success. You simply cannot expect a man's teenage children to suddenly become their father's boss. It had finally come to a time when something was going to have to be done.

Six months had gone by since these same people met about the same subject. At the time, it was Dr. Purvis diagnosis that John's brain had developed severe complications from the kick by the mule some years ago. The fact that he was depressive, aggressive, angry, subject to a loss of awareness of surroundings, sometime all at one time, caused the doctor to suggest that Gracie send him to a mental institution for 24-7 care. The Doctor provided the name of such an institution that was located in Pulaski County, Little Rock.

His wife, Gracie, was almost traumatized at Dr. Purvis' suggestion. What about his family? How long would he have to stay there? Does the hospital have a colored's only section, and is the hospital staff segregated? Would he be allowed home visits or could the family visit him, and most importantly, will he ever be able to return home? Will he ever be the same again? The short answer to a lot of those questions was to hope for the best. The doctor told her, the hospital was somewhat segregated and, like all public facilities in the state, there may be one or two black people on the staff in menial jobs. The managerial positions were staffed by white people. As far as the answer to the bigger question, the doctor simply didn't know if John would ever be the same again. That would be up to God.

That was six months ago. John's mind had deteriorated even further since then. He stayed at his parents' home for a while after the last diagnoses. That lasted a few weeks, because he has this tendency to wander off onto other people's property. Sometime he would come back with a neighbor's chicken where he'd broken its neck. He would do this in anticipation of having his wife prepare it for dinner. Sambo had a hard time explaining that to one of his neighbors even after giving the neighbor a live replacement. No matter how he tried to downplay the incident, the neighbor suggests his son should be locked up before he causes real harm to someone else's property. After that, they brought John back home.

Keep in mind that John himself can never recall those incidents, so he didn't take personal responsibility for his own actions. He is sort of sleepwalking at the time. A tearful Gracie relayed the latest deadly incident to this worried group of family members.

Almost a month ago, his son Codis followed him on one of these excursions. He had to physically stop him from taking one of Mr. Jennings mid-sized pigs. He was chasing the animal with a large stick he picked up with the intent to kill it for his supper table. Codis could tell that was his intention by the things he was yelling as he chased the pig.

The frightened pig took off running back to his pig pen which was located across the Banks' road and back onto the main farm of Mr. Jennings. John must of chased that pig about a mile with Codis running behind him yelling for his father to stop, wake up, and come back home.

This happened shortly after day break when people were tending to their early morning chores. One could just imagine the thoughts going through Mr. Jennings and his sons, Cal and Hal's mind when they spotted the commotion of their pig squealing, gasping for breath, and running for its life, with two darkies chasing after it. The men were just walking toward their timber line to check on traps and shoot game for their table. Their first reaction was to kill a thief. If it had not been for Codis yelling, "Don't shoot, wait! Don't shoot!" John would have died at the hands of white men protecting their property.

All of a sudden John stopped in his tracks with Codis tackling him to the ground as the Jennings men ran up to the scene. The pig kept running until reaching the safety of its pig pen on the side of the Jennings barn.

Codis told his mama that his father woke up from his sleep walking or whatever when he was tackled. He got up wondering how he got there and wanted to know what in the hell was going on. Mr. Jennings, dumbfounded at this development after being told by Codis what actually happened, told the boy to get his father off his property. He also gave a final warning, that if he or his family saw John on his property again, stealing or not, they would shoot to kill.

Codis and his father walked back toward their home. John never said another word to his son while walking back home. Codis tried talking to him but got no response. Mr. Jennings had a reputation as a fair man with colored folk. This was the man that Gracie's father worked for all those years. He might call a black person a nigger. It would not be out of hatred for his race, but more so because that is the way white folk talk down here in the south. Yet, you could also believe him when he said the next time John was caught on his property they would shoot to kill him.

Gracie told of a couple other incidents. He almost set the barn on fire for no apparent reason except to be out of his mind at the time. They caught him firing his shotgun at the wood line in front of the house. When asked what he was shooting at, he told them he saw some crackers with sheets over their heads carrying torches and setting the woods on fire. He yelled they are trying to burn us out. After Gracie took the shotgun he sat down on the porch and just stared off into the woods.

They tried to chain him up to the barn to keep him from wandering off. No one could watch him all the time. The kids and his wife were growing afraid of what he might do next.

In the end, they all agreed, John Hampton would have to be placed in the hospital as Dr. Purvis suggested. Colrolus would drive up to Banks, check in with Dr. Purvis, and go on to the hospital's mental ward in Little Rock from there. Sambo would ride with him. They decided to keep John's hands and feet tied so that he would not run away. That is the way they had him tied now, except he was also tied to the chair in the bedroom waiting for the final decision of this meeting.

One by one, family members went in to see him. They tried to talk to him and got no response. He just stared at them as if to say, why have you tied me up like an animal.

The kids were called back in to tell them their father/uncle was sick and would have to be taken to the hospital. They should say goodbye now because Colrolus and Sambo would be leaving soon, taking John with them.

It was a tearful farewell by everyone in the family including Mae Ellen. Through it all, John's expression was one of "what the hell is everyone crying for and why am I tied up?" Colrolus pulled his vehicle onto the little road with his passengers headed for Pulaski County, Little Rock by way of the Banks highway to Banks at about 10:00am on March 18, 1939.

A week had gone by after the ambush and killing of Petey Sampson's driver and aide, when Sheriff Penelton got a report that Petey was being released that following Monday. The report indicated there was no more permanent damages to the victim's body other than a broken right arm from being thrown from the vehicle as it rolled over. His shoulder on the same side had to be popped back into place. He also had a few scratches and bruises but that was it. Petey was a lucky man even though he was an invalid.

The sheriff had taken a statement from Harvey and Clara Sampson at the hospital last week, although it was brief. The Sampson couple did not want to have anything to do with the sheriff but answered his questions anyway. No, they did not know who wanted to see Petey dead. No, they were not aware of anybody who hated them enough to want to kill them. No, they were not aware of any possible enemies made from family or business dealings. Maybe you ought to be asking questions in the nigger section of the Banks community, he was told. Other than that, they wanted their privacy, which would start with him leaving them alone while they look after their son.

"It's odd that these people, who have caused so much anxiety among black folk in this community, think they have no enemies," The sheriff said to Deputy Stovall. "The days of black people not responded to intimidation, even threats on their property or lives, are over."

"You're right Sheriff. You want a cup of this coffee?"

"Will you please, sir?" Sheriff Penelton requested as the Deputy poured the liquid into a cup placing it on the sheriff's desk.

Taking a seat in front of the desk, the Deputy placed his cup on an empty chair beside him so as not to disturb the Sampson's Evidence Report on his boss's office desk.

"My, my, they actually told you they didn't have any enemies around here?"

"Son, I just don't understand these Klan folks. They do not and have not come to grips with the fact that life before the Civil War is over. Black folk, just like white folk, want to be left alone and not bothered while they scratch out a living in these here parts."

"I don't care who you talk to, everybody knows the Sampson's are KKK. So do we start bringing in every colored man and woman 'round here for questioning?"

"Naw, but I tell you who I do wanna talk to; there are two to three people. One is the Belin family; I've heard there is strong hate from two of their boys who vowed to get even with Bob, Clarke and Petey. I wanna see the Parker's and their son Rollie. Then, there is the Longs boy whose family suspect the Sampson's of burning down their barn last year."

"You want me to go with you?"

"Naw, I'm gonna head out to Belin's place in about an hour. I'll probably stop off at the Parker place first. You stick around here and call in that new deputy, Bob Stillwell to watch the office while you makes the rounds."

"All right, Bob is working out fine, ain't he?"

"Yes he is. I'm glad you found him for us."

Rollie Parker, his wife Willa, and their 19 year old son had moved in with Clem and Cora after losing part of the Parker farm during this Depression. His parents were getting up in age and he felt better about being closer to them.

They welcomed the Sheriffs visit. Sitting out on the porch, they served him lemonade while answering his questions. No, they had no ill feelings toward the Sampson family. Yes they could still see occasional KKK cross burnings near the woods of the Sampson place. No, nobody from that place has bothered them. Yes, they heard about the ambush but had nothing to do with that. In fact, sometime they feel sorry for Petey and the whole family. Other times, they just don't want anything to do with them because they are mean people. Finally, no they haven't heard from their son Sammy. They don't know whether he is dead or alive.

Sheriff Penelton left the Parker place thinking he had gotten honest answers all except the part about their son Sammy. He was sure they knew where he was but was not about to tell him.

He had no better luck at the Belin's place. Answers did not come as openly as it had at the Parker farm. The Sheriff found several discrepancies in Jessie and Alice Belin's answers, especially about two of their boys, who were nowhere to be found during his visit. There were a few major issues that required clarification. So much so that he told them he would return for a follow-up next week. He made himself a mental note to bring along his Deputy.

He stopped by Papa Warner's on the way back to Banks. Nothing new there, the men talked about the current rumors and goings on in the community. Sheriff Penelton asked Papa his opinion on the Belin family. "Mostly nice people but a few hothead sons," Papa answered. The Sheriff told him about the expected release of Petey Sampson from the hospital.

While he were there talking, Nookie and Virgie were sent down from the house to the store. Fannie asked them to bring back some flour for making biscuits and crust for a peach cobbler. She sent them both so they could take a break from work for a moment. Doreatha and Georgia Mae were already there helping Joel clean up the store and restocking the shelves. The sheriff commented on how pretty all four girls were, laughing with Papa at the thought of having to keep the boys away with a big stick.

"Those gals gettin' so big, um gonna have to change up. I think um gonna have to sit here with my shotgun so I can get these young whippersnappers attention. You know, boys today think they know all the tricks. They just think they're the slickest thangs' there is. Slicker than grease, but I got something for 'em. I keep tellin' 'em, you don't know me," Papa said laughing out loud at the thought of trying to keep boys away for his grand girls.

"Yeah, by God, good luck with that my friend," Sheriff Penelton added, laughing just as hard as Papa. One got the feeling; both men were remembering when they were youngsters.

The store was not as busy with customers these days. Still, there were a few people milling around, coming and going, picking up the latest news and items or service they needed.

The Sheriff left with the understanding that if anything came up regarding Papa or Joel recognizing the car they saw driving down the road on the day of the ambush, they would alert the sheriff's office. He stopped off at the ambush scene just to walk around the area grounds. He didn't see anything new, nor did he expect too. Satisfied, he drove off toward his office to check in with his new deputy.

Codis, the oldest boy, were trying to take over as the man of the family. At least as much as a fourteen year old boy can take charge for his father. Thirteen year old Lacirene was helping Mae Ellen and her mother with the cooking, sewing, plus taken on new chores that normally fell to Codis.

The garden crops had to be planted. In areas around the house and barn, foliage had grown up over the winter had to be removed. New ground had to be plowed using the same animal that kicked John. This was especially hard for Cods because there were times when he wanted to kill that mule. Yet, the animal was solely needed to plow the small areas they intended to plant the crops they needed for survival.

The entire family was trying to adjust to a life without their father. Curtis, and Clarence D, helped where ever they could lend a hand. They were told by Gracie, their Aunt Lena and Uncle Colrolus, grandparents Sambo and Sallie that they were going to have to chip in to do their part to see that this family endured. Emotionally it had already taken a toll, even with John's limited capacity to work towards the end. Still they all agreed, even while the younger ones didn't understand. They knew it would be up to them from here on out. Sadly, their father was away, they all looked forward to visiting him at the hospital one day.

They all tried to make their mother feel loved on this day, her and John's anniversary. They could tell she missed her husband. They also understood how she felt because they felt the same way about the absence of their father.

CHAPTER 11

A Mixture of Southern Attitude, National Progress & War

T he Great Depression eventually touched each and every person's life in this area and facilitated some type of change from their economic normalcy. It has been ten years since the country saw and experience the crashing of US Financial Market. Ten million US workers were still unemployed despite President Roosevelt's New Deal. To this day it continues to affect this region which was well behind the national norm at the very start of the Depression.

Nationally, while many still suffer, families are sitting down daily to listen to the latest news and weather broadcast on the radio in their living rooms. The newscast is followed by their favorite drama, comedy, or variety show. Their status or wealth doesn't matter; most everyone has access to a radio. It also provides instant communication of political news, local and national programs to assist the needed, job offerings, other pertinent information one might need to know. There is something new called the commercial where advertisers pay for time to peddle their wares. Families are learning to take a break during this time to go to their indoor bathroom, hurrying back so as not to miss the show.

This year of 1939 will also see the start of regular television broadcast in the United States. The new media will allow one to actually see a person presenting news, weather, or performing through a small screen in their living room.

Family members can call other members of the family or friends on the telephone to talk about what they heard or saw or just keep in touch while sharing information. The telephone has become an essential instrument in the family house as a way of communicating with whomever.

All three of these vital mediums call for the family serviced to have access to electricity.

To date, there is still no electricity reaching the masses in almost all rural areas of Arkansas. Indoor plumbing is a luxury not felt by all, as evidence by the many outhouses that dot the landscape from county to county. State resources and capability to raise funds to help its citizens are at an all-time low despite the help of the federal government. People are still recovering from floods, heavy rains, droughts, and other natural disasters that have hit the state, counties and some communities.

Time stops for no one. Obviously, this comes as no big surprise to anyone. What is unusual here is how some world events never seem to faze this community, county or region while others have a devastating affect because it immediately lowers or raises a family's economic position.

The majority of people in this and other southern states want to hold on to their heritage. They want to remember, while honoring their relatives that came before them. They want to note, tell, and retell the heroic acts of their forefathers to their children and their children's children. The way those same forefathers were the first to blaze their way through the wilderness forging a life out of nothing taking on all comers with the enthusiasm and will of a survivor should be honored. So they justify their inclination to hold on to their past as a way of not dismissing their heritage.

The problem occurs when they mix facts with fiction. First of all, most history books have verified that many of these so called wilderness areas were already occupied by American Indians. There was a difference in opinion about natural resources. The

Indians wanted to leave nature as it is while settlers wanted to build, reroute waterways, kill game for sport, fence in land and claim it now belongs to the person who built the fence. That was a major difference in a people's way of accomplishments that caused friction and fighting among those who were here in the first place and those who came later. The result often ended with the newcomer wiping out the Indians who they claimed to be savages because they didn't understand or refuse to accept the settler's version of progress.

Many also try and disallow the contributions of another race of people as if their only existence was to serve the white man. The South's foregathers relegated them as chattel, less than human but nevertheless let them cook their food, raise and sometimes nurse their children. They allowed, in fact encourage, them to procreate in order to increase their own personal wealth. Sometimes the offspring was sold for much needed funds, or willed to a relative by a dying owner. All the while they denied these people, who were less than human beings in their eyes, the rights of being a normal citizen of the world.

In essence, professing to be Christens, they knowingly repudiated the entire black race's status as a child of God. This, when their own bible, Galatians 3:28 says "There is neither Jew nor Greek, there is neither slave nor free, there is no male and female, for you are all one in Christ Jesus."

There were other places that pointed out the need for all men to be free. The founding fathers of the United States of America, in all their wisdom, wrote in The Declaration of Independence, "We hold these truths to be self-evident, that all men are created equal, that they are endowed by their Creator with certain unalienable Rights that among these are Life, Liberty and the pursuit of Happiness." Throughout history, many Southern people and other supporters of slavery have simply said this does not apply to people of color.

Again, this shows a tendency to mix fact with fiction, choosing which ever version is expedient to satisfy ones goals in life or merely just to raise one group of peoples personal status over another. It would be wrong for anyone to chastise another being for longing to document or even hold their great grandparents in grandeur. One should always be aware of their history. However, that history should be supported by fact and not embellished to make a person out to be more than they were or erase something they did because it makes them look like bad people.

There lies the crux of a lot of southern white people's attitude. They want to remember their relatives and friends as good people. After all, they are the offspring of the same and love their people. It is very hard to love someone when that someone commits a horrendous crime against man or the word of God. It presents a conflict that oftentimes the individual just don't want to deal with. Therefore it's simpler to disregard certain facts of an ancestor's life because it would tarnish the memory of who they were.

Meanwhile on the national stage, all New Yorkers were celebrating with hosting of the World's Fair this year, 1939. The north eastern part of the country was suffering from a drought that caused crop failure with personal hardship. The Daughters of the Constitution denied the U.S.'s most famous contralto a chance to perform at Constitution Hall. Marian Anderson ended up singing before 75000 people, with First Lady Eleanor Roosevelt greeting her before attending her concert.

There are other major changes going on in the world this year that will touch Arkansas and rest of the United States in the near future. Russia invaded Finland. Hitler's Nazi's attacked Poland on the first of September. Two days later, Britain, France, Australia, New Zealand, and India declared war on Germany. This in effect was the beginning of World War II. The United States decided to remain neutral, yet began to rearm for war. Congress amended the Neutrality Acts in order to send military aid to countries in Europe.

Meeting at a convention, the American Psychological Association place the question of Hitler's sanity on the agenda. Charles E. Lindbergh receives a metal from Hitler in October. This may have come as a result of Lindbergh's blaming a potential war with the US on "the British, the Jews, and the Roosevelt Administration."

In November, an assassination attempt on the Furor failed by 12 minutes. A bomb exploded twelve minutes after he left the hall after giving a speech to his most loyal followers. Those who had been with him through the earlier years were there to celebrate with him. The bomb was placed in a pillar behind the speaker's platform where Hitler gave the speech. The Nazi Party blamed the bombing on British secret agents in an attempt to stir up the people of Germany for war with the British. It actually looked like an anti-Nazi movement was responsible.

By 1940, the rearming of the US forcers caused a noticeable ease in the Great Depression. The average American worker was earning more, able to afford buying more, which helped the sellers' bottom line, causing them to order more stock and hire more workers. Manufactures were now able to make more items for the open market; because they were selling more, which also allowed them hire more workers. All of these actions and more added fuel to the American Economy.

A brand new Radio would cost $16.95, gas was 18 cents per gallon, and the average price for a new car was $850. Bread cost 8 cents a loaf, milk 34 cents a gallon, and a postage stamp cost 3 cents. One could rent a house for $30 per month and the average wage per year was $1,725.00. The minimum wage was 30 cents per hour.

The new medium, television, whose sales were very slow even as RCA reduced its price on its latest model from an original $600 in 1939 to $395 in the early part of 1940. Programing was still a problem. Around the last of March, RCA offered huge discounts to its employees for its TT-5, TRK-5, and TRK-12. The TT-5's normal selling price of $199.50 was discounted to $75.00. The only stipulation being the employee had to keep it for one year.

This year, Germany would invade Denmark, Norway, France, Luxembourg Belgium and the Netherlands. Italy, Hitler's ally, declared war on the United Kingdom and France. The US conducted its first peace time draft in the latter part of the year. Peace could be a tenuous term considering that the rest of the world, including the United States' main ally, Britain is fighting for their very survival.

Gracie thought the best way to ensure her kids would not have any adverse reaction to their father's condition when they visited, was for her to visit him first. She would be able to see his current condition, maybe talk to the doctors before she allow visitation from her children. She asked Colrolus to drive her up to the hospital's mental ward on Wednesday, the first of May. Lena went along for support and to see her brother-in-law for herself. May Ellen was left behind to watch after the Hampton kids, including their visiting cousins, the Strong's.

The visit turned out to be short, because John had no recollection of who they were. He didn't recognize his sister, brother-in-law or his wife. He was able to speak but it was gibberish and no one could understand what he was trying to say.

He, himself, seemed to be trying to make sense of it all. It was as if he were trying to ask them who they were. At one point he smiled, pointed to Gracie, and said a few words while looking at her oh so sincerely. He would say something, look at the blank expression on his wife and the others' faces and finally give up. He was aware enough to understand he was trying to communicate with people who didn't understand what he said. Then a look of sadness would come over his face. He would retreat back into his own world of silence looking down at his hands.

Once, he looked back into their faces as if he had thought of another way to communicate but realized if they can't understand him talking then, that's it. Finally, he turned angry, started shaking his head back and forth until a standby attendant came and got him.

The attendant begged the visitors' pardon. "I've got to returned John to his room before this gets out of hand," He said.

Gracie, with tears in her eyes nodded her head in agreement. They all watched as the attendant went through an open door of the visiting room with a resigned John Hampton walking beside him.

Reaching the outside of the hospital, Gracie was the first to speak. "I don't know if I can stand to see him like that, his kids shouldn'tthey just can't see him acting like that."

Lena, who really had no other words, agreed, "You're right."

"Well, my God. I just don't know what to say about that. You think he knows who he is?" asked Colrolus.

"He might, but I sure as hell don't know who he is. I just need to pray for him. It's almost as if he may as well have died when that damn mule kicked him." Gracie said while sobbing and standing in place right outside the hospital door.

"You mean we all need to pray for him. It just don't look like he'll ever be right in the head again," Lena added.

They got back in the truck and drove back towards Banks in almost silence. Neither of them could wrap their head around what they just saw. Collectively, they were not expecting much, but they certainly were expecting more than they got.

Gracie had no idea how she was going to explain this to her kids who were old enough to comprehend but too emotionally involved to fully understand.

"Aw hell's bells, how can they understand if I don' understand it myself," She said out loud to no one in particular. "I think you're right Lena. He may not ever be the same."

The vehicle turned off the Banks highway onto the little road leading to Gracie's house. It had been a revealing yet disappointing trip as far as substance goes. She knew her kids would be on pins and needles waiting to hear about their father's progress. In a child's mind a hospital is a place where one goes to get better not worse. As Gracie thought before, her children were not going to be able to hide their disappointment in not being able to visit John. Plus there is a possibility that he may never be released from the hospital because of a kick in the head by a mule.

The Hole in the Bushes place owners Henry J, his wife Carrie Strong, Rev Payne from the Gravel Ridge First Baptist Church, and Rev Morris Davis from the Oaklawn Methodist Church along with other prominent members of the black community decided to sponsor a Variety Show Extravaganza. They scheduled it for June 15th, the end of the planting season and just before the children returned to school after break.

The Hole in the Bushes would host the event. It would be patterning after the old minstrel shows, although you won't find any white folk in blackface at this show. They would have some local folk dress up as clowns, performing tricks for the little children. Games and prizes for winning sack races and other games would be available for the little ones up through ten years old. They have scheduled that program for in the morning after 10:00am lasting until 1:00pm.

Part II would be for the 13 to 17 year olds, beginning at 2:00pm and ending at 5:00 p.m. Scheduled were a dance contest, a singing contest, and girls could prepare shared picnic basket with special treats available from the organizers. It would be up to the girls via ladies choice on who to share their basket with.

Finally, Part III will be for ages 18 on up. They will be entertained by William 'June-bug' Davis and a couple of his road buddies. Folks could dance, let their hair down and just enjoy themselves.

It was the community's way of letting off built up steam. They wanted to provide an alternative to all the problems and worries of the past few years. More importantly, they wanted to celebrate a good planting season, a hope of better days ahead in spite of the rumblings of war.

It only cost a quarter to get in to any of the venue parts. The performers all donated their time for the cause. A lot of grown-ups were there all day. They supervised their own, and other younger children, then the teenagers before eagerly sending them home. That allowed them to relax and enjoy the night's entertainment.

Just as they do for their church affairs, people brought special dishes to the different affairs. The little kids had a ball, laughing, running, screaming, and eating until they were practically exhausted. For some of the little ones, this was the first time seeing people wearing makeup while dressed up as clowns. They were treated to skits of puppet shows, etc. It was like a circus, not that they had ever seen a circus. Colrolus performed with three of his show horses. Lena assisted her husband in the act that thrilled and awed the youngsters.

Part II brought out the teenagers in their entire splendor. One could tell the girls thought of this as a special occasion to show off a recently made dress, catalog ordered shoes and themselves for everyone to see. They came to listen to local talent sing and dance. They, too, wanted to enjoy themselves as did the boys.

The parings of couples could tell you who liked who in those days. Dora Marjorie Tatum shared her lunch box with Calvin Hampton while throwing dagger eyes at Virgie who was with a boy name Edward long. Georgia Mae was with Edward's brother Melvin. Lacirene had corralled R.T. Tatum, Doreatha had Codis, and her sister Nookie chose one of the Belin boys, Willie Hayes. Nookie and Virgie were let in because they were a few months from 13. You better believe they were closely watched by their older sisters.

They danced and enjoyed the talent show. A couple of them sang church songs because that was all they knew. It was just a great time for a break at the normal end of a good planting season.

Later on that evening, June-bug did his thing. He still played his brand of blues, experimenting with different riffs on his guitar. He had a drummer and a bass player with him. They put on a show playing some of the latest Jazz and blues recordings by artist such as Ma Rainey, Bessie Smith, and Billie Holliday. Most in the crowd was not aware that the majority of June bug's music was from women artist because they had never heard the originals. When there is no electricity, there is no radio. Without the use of a radio, there is a blackout of popular music in the area.

Since June-bug was putting a man's spin on it, they thought that was how each song was supposed to sound. You have to give him credit, he had a readymade audience eager to dance and holler at anything he and his little band played. He was not taking advantage; he put on a show that the original song artist would have loved. In the end, his style of blues would be dubbed the Memphis blues up by other new artist playing the chitterling circuit. It was a jam for the band playing before a listening and dancing audience.

Twenty-four year old Mae Ellen attended with her date, Robert Preston who lived in Warren. She met him in high school while living there. Every now and then he'd come down or she'd go up there to visit. Not so much, now that both sets of grandparents have died. To a casual observer, they seem to really like each other, although when closely watched, their dates always seem to end in some kind of disagreement between them. It was like mixing coal oil with gasoline, although both are liquids, they just didn't quite gel and there could be a spark under any conditions. It was rumored that the Preston boy came from a family of wife beaters, so he was not very well received by the locals. Especially in light of the fact, that everyone in this community was aware of how Mae Ellen's parents were killed. They all watched out for her just as much as they would their very own family.

All the festivities, including the grown-ups night jam went over without any problems. There was a little shouting between one of the couples, whose male date had a little too much homebrewed beer, but all in all a good time was had by everyone.

It was a cool September's day even though the sky was clear with the sun shining bright as Gracie remembered it. The older kids were outside doing chores leaving Mae Ellen in the house with their mother. There was a knock on the door. As Gracie opened the door she saw Curtis and Clarence standing at the foot of the front porch steps. The boys must have seen the runner coming because they were curiously wondering and waiting to see why this fellow was stopping by their house.

Papa Warner had sent a runner to the Hampton's house with a hand written message. It was from the hospital stating that John Hampton died on September 9, and the body must be picked up as soon as possible for burial. That was it, other than providing the name of a supervisory attendant to ask for and the hours in which to pick up the body.

Gracie dropped to her knees, partly in grief but also in shock. She just couldn't get it into her mind that her husband of sixteen years was dead. The fact that she had to learn about it from a handwritten note was equally devastating. It was then she noticed Mae Ellen crying, with Curtis and Clarence rushing to her side to see what was wrong.

"I'll be all right, um all right. Boys go get you sister and brother. Tell them to come in the house; I need to tell yawl something," She said.

"Thank you." She told the runner who was one of Papa Warner's grandchildren. The boy, who looked to be about fourteen, was riding a bike, which was lying at the foot of the porch stairs.

"You want somethin' to drink or Mae Ellen managed to ask.

"No, ma'am, I got to get back. Did you want me to tell Papa anything?" He asked Gracie.

"No honey, 'cept thanks for his troubles. Mae Ellen, give this boy two of those tea cakes on the table."

The boy thanked Gracie for the tea cakes treat. Gracie's tea cakes were somewhat equivalent to the scones of today. He picked up his bike and rode off back toward Papa Warner's store.

Gracie sat down at the kitchen table and poured herself a cup of coffee. She was trying to compose herself before the other children came into the house.

Codis came running through the door first, followed by Lacirene and the other two boys. "Mama, Mama, what's the matter? What happen to you? What's wrong mama?" he asked almost hysterically.

Tears began to flow from her eyes again as she asked her kids to have a seat and calm down a minute. By now most of the older ones had guessed it had something to do with their father but anxiously waited on their mother to say the words.

"There's no way to say it 'cept to say it outright. Your daddy has died in that there hospital. That's what the message said. We have to pick up his body to bury him." Gracie concluded.

You could have literally heard a pin drop at that moment until the sound of Lacirene crying broke the silence.

The boys just kind of looked at each other. Curtis had tears in his eyes, Codis and Clarence didn't. It seemed like Codis had expected this for some time now. Curtis did too, but it still hurt to hear the news. Clarence wasn't quite sure how to react; eventually he began to cry as well.

They all sat around that table for an hour or so, eating tea cakes, talking about their daddy, and trying to decide where they will go from here. Although, and Gracie reminded them, they had already moved on without their father. They do that each and every day to keep a roof over their heads. Finally she sent Curtis and Clarence over to Colrolus and her sister's house asking them to stop by as soon as they could.

Once the Strong's got to the house and was told what happened, it was decided that Curtis would be the only one going with Colrolus to pick up the body. He was the first one to volunteer; besides the other kids had some other daily chores to complete around the farm. Gracie sent Codis to tell Reverend Payne what happened because he would preside over the funeral services.

On the way, Colrolus stopped at Papa Warner's for cold drinks and ran into Calvin Hampton, Johns younger brother. He was there to see if there was any other news. They all learned the original message came from Sheriff Penelton. He, as the local official of Banks, received a wire message from the Hospital. Papa had also sent the same message to John's parents, Sambo and Sallie. Afterwards, fourteen year old Calvin went along with his twelve year old nephew, Curtis and Colrolus to pick up Johns body two days after he died.

They arrived at the hospital entrance, where the guards directed them toward the mental ward after Colrolus told him why he was there. He drove the pickup around to the ward's supply delivery and acceptance doorway. He presented his ID and message to pick up the body. They were told to wait in the truck.

Within a few minutes, two black men appeared carrying a stretcher with a body on it. They asked where the vehicle was parked. Colrolus pointed toward his truck a few feet away from the doorway. The attendants put the body in the bed or the truck and asked if they had something to cover it with as they needed the hospital blanket that was wrapped around him.

"Naw," replied an obvious disturbed Colrolus.

"All right boss, we'll just leave the blanket with you. We'll tell them it got stained or somethin'," One of the men said.

Colrolus didn't say anything to the boys but he noticed the head on the body was very loose as if the neck was broke. He'd seen this kind of movement on a dead person before. Say a person who were hanged or had gotten their neck broke in an accident. At that moment, he made up his mind to take the body and have it examined by Doc Purvis and Sheriff Penelton.

Unfortunately, they almost ran into a horse team on the drive back, which ended with them running off the road into a ditch with John's body falling halfway out of the truck. They got the heavy body back in and started out again for the Doctors or Sheriff's office.

They finally got to Banks, driving directly to the Sheriff's office. He took a swift exam and sent his deputy for Doctor Purvis. The doctor confirmed that John's neck was broken, but could not say when it happened. Yes it could have been broken before he was picked up or the force-off into the ditch could have contributed to the body's condition. There was no way of proving when it happened.

Colrolus didn't like it but understood why the doctor said it in that way. You needed absolute proof before accusing an institution of foul play, especially in a case like this. The boys were angry and felt the family had been let down by Colrolus. The Sheriff gave them a full explanation of the law when it became to burden of proof. They were still upset but understood what they were being told.

John was buried at Oaklawn Cemetery a few days later on September 15, 1940, almost a week after he died in the hospital. It was a solemn affair attended by a host of family and community people. All four brothers were there; his mother and father, his widow, children and Mae Ellen were present. Sheriff Penelton and his wife Rebecca attended, because he "liked the way that boy played baseball". Doctor Purvis attended with them. The Parkers, Cora, Clem, Rollie and his immediate family, was there. Doreatha and Nookie Childs came with her uncle Joel Johnson, his wife Viola, and their children, Georgia Mae, Virgie, and JO. Why even Papa Warner and his wife, Fannie, was there.

"And now a man's life has ended," Reverend Payne said as the pall bearers lowered John Hampton into his grave. "Some may see it as a premature ending. And ahmaybe in our eyes it was. Yet, we must remember, God decides when he wants one of his children to come on home. And ah, just as important, he and only he, decides how the end must come. Lord, let John Hampton finally rest in peace. Amen."

A final sendoff was held after the burial back at the church. People once again offered their condolence to the family, letting them know if anything was needed, they should not hesitate to ask.

That night while everybody in the Hampton household was asleep, Codis wrestled with who was to blame for this tragedy. They could not prove someone in the hospital broke his father's neck. Uncle Colrolus knew his neck was broke when they picked him up. Why didn't the sheriff at least investigate what happened. The boy was so overcome with grief and anger about how and why it happened he could not go to sleep.

He started to wake up Curtis but found he'd never gone to sleep either.

"Come on," he told him. "Grab that lantern and light it."

Curtis had some idea what was going to happen, so he went with the flow. Not only because it was his brother but because he believed it to be the right thing to do.

A single shot rang out causing Gracie to jump out of her bed. She grabbed her shotgun running to the sound of the shot, which came from the back door. She called for Mae Ellen, Codis, Curtis, and Lacirene. She heard her oldest daughter voice.

"What was that shot, mama? Is someone shooting at us?" Lacirene asked.

Before she knew it while already upset, Gracie flung opened the door only to level her shotgun at Codis and Curtis returning to the house.

"Boy, what the hell yawl doing out there in the middle of the night? Was that yawl shooting? Was it a wild animal? Answer me!" Gracie insisted.

Codis climbed the short back steps leading to the kitchen with Curtis right behind him. He was carrying the rifle that his uncle Colrolus had bought for him to hunt small game. He didn't immediately answer or even look at his mama. He did say as he walked by her,

"We gonna need a new mule, Mama." He continued on to his room putting the rifle back in its place up on the wall bracket.

Realizing what he meant, she hugged a shocked Lacirene asking Mae Ellen to take her back to bed in their room. She would be on in a minute. She turned to Curtis who was standing there still holding the lit lantern.

"Is he dead Curtis?"

"Mama, that mule is dead. He looked like he was waiting for it to happen. He fell after being shot between the eyes. He ain't breathing. That mule is dead, mama." With that he handed the lantern to his mother and headed for the boy's room to go back to bed. "Codis say we'll bury him in the morning," was the last words he said to his mama before disappearing into the darkness of the room.

This was also an election year. It was a month away, due to be held in early November of 1940. Franklin D Roosevelt (FDR) broke with tradition and was running for a third term. His administration had fought the Great Depression and was now facing the possibility of America officially entering World War II. The fact that he ran for a third term became a major issue.

Wendell Willkie, his Republican opponent shouted to any and every one that FDR failed to end the Depression and was more than eager to enter the war. For his part, the president promised there would be no involvement with foreign wars if he were re-elected.

On November 5, 1940, labor unions, urban political machines, along with ethnic voters and the traditionally Democratic South (at the time), gave FDR a very comfortable victory over his Republican challenger.

There should have been no underestimating the importance of First Lady, Anna Eleanor Roosevelt by his side during the last two terms and during that election. One should also not discount the influence this lady, who champion the needs of the underprivileged from all creeds, races, and nations, had on her husband. She was known as the eyes and ears of the President, was loved by the masses and hated by special interest for placing the interest of the common man ahead of the rich and wealthy.

FDR gave a rousing speech on this January 6, 1941. He enunciated his "four freedoms" message to the US Congress, American People and the world. It was the backdrop to his proposal of lend-lease legislation. It was a program designed to transfer war supplies to nations where defense of their sovereignty was vital to the defense of the United States in World War II. Shipments would include food, machinery, and services.

He stated that Four Freedoms should prevail everywhere in the world, freedom of speech and expression, freedom of worship, freedom from want, and freedom from fear. They were substantially incorporated in the Atlantic Charter.

The Lend-Lease Act, passed by the Congress gave the President power to transfer, lend, sell or lease war materials. He would be allowed to set the terms for aid. The U.S. would accept repayment "in kind or property, or any other direct or indirect benefit which the President deems satisfactory."

National Unemployment fell to 9.9%. The industrial boom that occurred as a result of the start of World War II in Europe last year ended the Depression. The practice of hiring whites over blacks continued as US workers found jobs. Discrimination throughout the country was a major problem for the FDR administration. A. Philip Randolph, head of the Brotherhood of Sleeping Car Porters, was attempting to organize a mass protest march on Washington. The march, scheduled for June 25, 1941, was intended to protest the discrimination in hiring among other things.

In response, FDR issued an Executive Order (#8802) banning "discrimination in the employment of workers in defense industries or government." He also established a Fair Employment Practices Committee (FEPC) to investigate violations of the Order. This one act did not stop widespread discrimination; however African-Americans were able to gain employment at better wages, in a wider selection of occupations than before EO 8802.

Throughout the year, The US was still reluctant to directly enter the war. That would change with a most cowardly attack on US forces.

On December 7, 1941 the Japanese attacked Pearl Harbor almost wiping out the American Pacific fleet. Eight battleships anchored along "Battleship Row" were severely damaged including two, the Oklahoma and the Arizona, which were sunk.

Three cruisers and the same number of destroyers were also heavily damaged.

The early Sunday morning attack destroyed almost 350 American warplanes on the island of Oahu. 2,400 US servicemen were killed and another 1,200 more were wounded. The attack would be viewed as a success by Japan and its allies. During the first years of World War II, it hampered the capability of the US to respond to the expansion of Japanese reach in the Pacific. Japans Minister of War; Hideki Tojo had struck a crippling, but not fatal blow, to the US forces.

Within two days, On December 9, 1941, the United States declared war on Japan. Two days later, Germany and Italy announced they were at war with the United States. America immediately responded by declaring war on the remaining two Axis powers.

All commercial production of television equipment in the United States was banned for the remainder of the war. NBC canceled it commercial schedule. TV is allowed to broadcast, but on a very limited basis at a few select stations. England has already banned it TV broadcasting in its entirety until after the war.

Merry Christmas 1941, the world's 3 most ruthless dictators gave you their present, World War II. And just so you don't feel left out, America, you are invited to participate in this grand battle for world supremacy. "We will crush all our enemies like a bug," so say Hitler, Mussolini and Tojo. At least that was the plan. However, sometimes the best laid plans are flawed from the very beginning. It would take a while, amid the loss of countless lives and property, but in the end, freedoms bell will still ring free.

Over the next few years, America and the world would be consumed with bringing World War II to an end with a victory. U.S. manufacturers modified their production lines to turn out weapons of war. They joined other entities as the mobilization of war efforts across the country. In a little over a month by July 30, Germany U Boats had sunk 96 allied ships. Although the three Axis powers of Japan, Germany and Italy had a head start and racked up battle victories in the early years of the war, by late

1942 America and its allies began to even the score and in many ways turn the tide by initiating several offenses of their own.

Twenty-five countries around the world began rejecting the dictator's claim to supremacy by joining the U.S. and signing a united declaration against the Axis powers. Twenty-eight nations pledge not to separately accept peace with the Axis. The US and British government establishes the United Nations.

Hitler's Nazi regime calls for the extermination of Europe's Jews as the "final solution". They issue a decree ordering all Jewish pregnant women in the Kovino ghetto executed. Reportedly some 1,500 Jews are gassed in Auschwitz. 5,000 Rovno Polish Jews from the Ukraine were executed by the Nazis. 300,000 Warsaw ghetto Jews are sent to the Nazi's Treblinka extermination camp. Nazi's exterminate 10,000 Minsk, Belorussia ghetto Jews. The German SS kills some 25,000 Minsk, Belorussia Jews. Nazi's murder some 16,000 Pinsk, Soviet Union Jews. By mid-November Russia launches its winter offensive against the Germans along their front. Over one million Russians ruptured the German lines.

The US Congress advises FDR that all US citizens of Japanese descent should be jailed to prevent them from opposing the war effort. This was followed by an FDR order to detain and intern all west-coast Japanese-Americans. The U.S. begins rationing food. Sugar and gasoline soon join the items that are rationed in the US.

Black Americans Jackie Robinson and Nate Moreland request a tryout with the Chicago White Sox baseball team and are granted permission to do so. Joe Louis, a Black heavyweight fighter knocks out Buddy Baer in round 1 to gain the heavyweight boxing title. He later knocks out Abe Simon in New York City to retain his title.

On May 20 of 1942, the United States Navy permits its first black recruits to serve. Sambo and Sallie's youngest son, Calvin Hampton would enlist in February of 1945 receiving an honorable discharge on June 9, 1946. The first detachment of the US Women's Army Auxiliary Corps (WAC's) began basic training.

The first independent US bombers are sent out on a raid in Europe. They attack Rouen, France. On October 12, 1942, the U.S. Navy defeated the Japanese during the Battle of Cap Esperance. U.S. and British forces under General Eisenhower land in French North Africa to begin Operation Torch. Hitler orders his African corps, led by German Field Marshal E. Rommel to fight to the last man. The battle of Guadalcanal begins in mid-November of 1942.

Over the last five months, the US and its allies had sunk 108 U Boats in August, 98 in September, 94 in October, 109 in November and 60 in December. It was reasoned that the number was so low in December because Hitler was running out of boats. Resources were being channeled elsewhere on a priority basis.

Back on October the 20th, Southern black leaders met in Durham, North Carolina. From this meeting an idea was form to construct the Durham Manifesto calling for fundamental changes in race relations. Jessie Ames, a white moderate at the convention of Southern Conference on Race Relations, asked Gordon B. Hancock, a black sociologist and also a moderate to conduct a meeting. The feeling was that voices of white and black southern moderates were being drowned out by more the radical black and white supremacists.

There were seventy-five prominent African-American professionals were invited and residing in the South at the time. Reportedly of which fifty-seven actually attended the meeting, while others provided their support by letter or telegrams. Those in attendance were split into seven committee groups tasked to present remedies and solutions to problems as a way to provide a framework that addressed the needs and requirements of Black people in America.

By the end of the day, they were unable to merge those ideas into a suitable worded document. Fisk University sociologist Charles S. Johnson was selected to lead the drafting of the document committee. The members met in Atlanta, Georgia, on November 6 and Richmond, Virginia, on November 26, 1942, all falling in behind different concerns that would center around three specific sets of ideas.

It was left to Mr. Johnson to verbalize and put to paper a cohesive statement that would address the concerns of all. The final version's was entitled, "A Statement by Southern Negroes" and released on December 15, 1942. Mr. Johnson wrote in his preamble regarding integration, Members of this body were "fundamentally opposed to the principle and practice of compulsory segregation," and that they regarded "it as both sensible and timely to address ourselves now to the current problems of racial discrimination and neglect and to ways in which we may cooperate" while improving race relations.

The document, known as the "Durham Manifesto", went on to spell out specific ways in which to accomplished the goals. It stirred a lot of interest in some quarters and lack of interest in others. Some viewed it as going too far and others not far enough. Those perspectives were the opinions of white, black, liberals, and conservatives alike. One thing it did accomplish, was to capsulate a people's concerns and their recommendations on how to fix it. That alone, made it a worthwhile and inspiring document.

There was a very important event that took place in Arkansas in 1942. The capability to distribution electricity into its not so accessible and somewhat isolated rural areas had been a glaring problem for Arkansans to date. The electric cooperatives pooled their resources, forming a statewide association. It would enable the state to finally set up electrical distribution points throughout its rural areas.

By January of 1943, there were signs that the Axis of powers were beginning to realize that this war was not going to be the cakewalk they envisioned. On January 13, Adolf Hitler declares "Total War." What he meant by that is unclear as we look back on history. The guess here is a strong resistance from those you aim to conquer, losses of personnel, equipment, and confidence will make an unstable person say strange things.

The Soviet Union announces they have broken the long Nazi siege of Leningrad, Russia. The U.S. Joint Chiefs of Staff make plans to invade Sicily. Hitler's same "fight to death" orders to

Nazi troops at Stalingrad, Russia, are the same as he said to Rommel in Africa. The battle ends with the surrender of the German Army. The Russian winter had contributed to bogging them down, plus their will to fight was coming into question. Elsewhere, the Japanese evacuate Guadalcanal suffering heavy losses. The U.S. 8th Army sweeps through North Africa all the way to Tunisia.

Meanwhile in our little community of Banks, life was slowly moving forward. Residents had relatives serving in War. Some had seen their economic problems get better at the ending of the Depression because of federal programs and the war itself. There were other notable changes in and around the town of Banks. And then again, some things just stayed the same.

There were not that many KKK demonstrations on the Sampson Farm these days. Most of the younger members were in the military. The old guard or older members was trying to keep their presence visible within the community in other ways other than outright large assemblies where they'd set afire a cross.

Since they did not know who might be wishing them ill health resulting in ambushing their son and others, they decided to tone it down. Of course there were other reasons too, nevertheless Harvey Sampson and his bunch had been pretty quiet the last couple of years.

The fact that Sheriff Penelton had a few unsolved murders and shootings on his record had not gone unnoticed by a lot of people in the community. He had yet to find the perpetrators in the Petey Samson attack that ending with the killing of his driver and aide. In the case where Deputy Paul Krause was killed, there was movement. Deputy Stovall had arrested one Paul Unger on a charge of drunken disorderly conduct a year earlier. In his state of mind, he let slip his knowledge of Bob and Clarke as the shooters that killed the deputy and wounded the sheriff.

That bit of knowledge helped, but unfortunately, both suspects were killed in a gangster style ambush a few days after they were released on bail. The Sheriff and Deputy Stovall took a sober Mr. Unger's statement and confession where he pointed out the guilt of Bob and Clarke for the record. He was fined and released from the drunk and disorderly charge. Paul Unger had since disappeared from the Banks area with no one knowing his whereabouts.

Sheriff Penelton turned sixty-two years old this year. A new mayor and tax collector was appointed last year. The sheriff, seeing the handwriting on the wall, announced that this would be his last year. He told them he would officially leave office by next year in April. They have agreed that his hand-picked successor, Deputy Josh Stovall would take his place. The new Sheriff would hire another deputy or two just before or after being sworn in.

The Sheriff and his wife Rebecca were looking forward to his retirement. She still helps out Dr. Morgan Purvis, Skeeter's son, on occasion but is training another girl to take her place.

The Sheriff's best friend, Ben "Skeeter" Purvis, died a few years ago at the age of seventy-eight. Gladys, his sixty-eight old wife, and Deputy Stovall's aunt still runs the store with their daughter Beverly Purvis. Miss Bev, as she is called, got married and divorced inside of five years while never stopping to help run the store except when she took off to have her son, Randy Scott. He is currently in the Army, stationed somewhere overseas.

McBain and some of his kin were still running his store. He was getting up in age, too, thinking of turning the store over to one of his sons. There would be no change of attitude as he, like the Sampson's, family members are pure Klan.

Like almost twenty-six years ago, there has been no noticeable change in the layout, population numbers, or overall locations in Banks, Arkansas. It has practically stayed the same except one change in the landscape. Electric poles have been placed along the highway between Banks and Warren and closer inland at some places. This has allowed for electricity to reach the town of Banks. The problem of reaching into the surrounding rural areas is an ongoing task.

Papa Warner's farmhouse is still directly across the Banks' highway from his store. He has gotten older with time too. At sixty-four he was still running his businesses. His son, Joel, has remained with him as second in command.

His 'Grand Cuties' as they were known are almost full grown women. A couple of years ago they were attacked by those two much older white boys whose house they always passed on the way to and from school. The girls managed to fight them off but it was a tussle that day. The young men suffered scratches and bruised from the girl's nails and the stick that Virgie and her brother JO carried with them. They told their father Joel and Papa Warner about it, fearing the white boys would make some other claim. Nothing was said or reported as far as Papa heard.

Doreatha (17 year old Do) and Gertie Mae Childs (15 year old Nookie) were seeing boys who they liked, Codis Hampton and Willie Hayes Belin respectively. They and everyone around them knew the boys were just as serious about them.

Georgia Mae (17 years old) and Virgie (15 years old) were seeing boys too, yet were unsure as to how serious they themselves were.

There was no shortage of suitors and true to his word, Papa Warner has taken to placing a shotgun on a man-made rack right on the wall in back of where he continues to sit on the porch during the day.

Papa & Fannie Warner's, the Len & Mae Jennings, Harvey & Clara Sampson, Clem and Cora Parker places are still located along that six mile stretch of highway from Banks to the little turn off road on the left leading past the old Viola & Edgar rental (occupied by Rand Tatum) down to Gracie Hampton's farm.

While the children of John and Gracie were still trying to help in any way they could to fill in for their missing father, boys will be boys. Gracie, with Mae Ellen's help, would cook tea cakes, pies and cakes to generate income or use the treats as barter to get items needed like baking supplies or other items needed around the house. Like all kids, her boys had a sweet tooth. She started by locking up the sweets in a cupboard to keep them away from her kids right after baking. She would put the key in her apron pocket for safekeeping. Giving up on getting that key, Curtis had the bright idea to take the screws off the cupboard door. The youngsters would take some of the treats, and replace the cupboard door.

This went on for an about a month until Gracie got tired of having to bake enough to allow for her kids to take some from the cupboard. Besides that, the screw holes that attached the door to the cupboard was beginning to wear from all the unscrewing and screwing back shut. One day at supper she made the following announcement,

"It seems like there is a rat in this here house that has a way of getting into my bakery cupboard. That old rat takes tea cakes; slices of cake and in a few cases took a whole apple pie. Um pretty sure if yawl had seen any crumbs left by the rat as he pulled, say like that heavy pie across the floor to its hideout, yawl would tell me. Huh?"

"Yes sum." Each and every one of her kids said almost in unison, with most nodding their head to make sure Gracie understood them.

"Well, that's good. Yawl so good to your old mama, knowing she work so hard to bake them sweets to get the things we need 'round here. I tell you what though, Um gon have to cut down on the sweets I serve at the table to make up for anymore that old rat steal."

"Don't you worry Mama, we gon' catch that rat. I don't think him gon' be round here much longer," Curtis said.

Codis looked at Curtis, looked at Lacirene, both shook their head. Clarence D didn't even look up from the table. Their "Yes sum," was almost the loudest along with Curtis.

After that, Gracie didn't have any more problems with treats missing from her cupboard. There was another incident where Curtis was responsible. Curtis, forever the more hyper one, put too much wood in the stove one morning. He was trying to get the fire started quicker and poured lamp coal oil over the wood. He lit it and went outside to join the rest of the family who were tending to their morning chores.

They were lucky that day; lucky that they were all outside as the house caught on fire. It started from the excess wood soaked in coal oil enabling the flames to burst through the sides of the round iron cooking plates that, when in place, act as a burner on the stove. In his anxiousness to really get the fire started, he left one of the iron cooking plates halfway off the burner holes placement. That normally would provide air to feed the fire if it was primed correctly in the first place. With flames already shooting up as high as three to four feet, it helped to spread the fire throughout the house.

Gracie sent Clarence D to Colrolus house for help. The Strong's arrival helped the Hampton's contain the fire, with each person throwing one bucket of water after another on it at a time. They manage to stop the entire house from burning down. However they lost clothes, food, some furniture, business documents and the use of the house for bout thirty days until they could rebuild the areas that need to be refurbished. It just reminded them of how vulnerable they were living in a rural area deep in the woods.

Addressing a sanitary maintenance issue, Codis and Curtis had to move the outhouse. They knew it had to be moved, because they could smell it when inside the house. Even though they were downwind of the old Edgar and Viola rental (now occupied by Rand Tatum) about 100 yards from their back door, they knew the Tatum's outhouse was facing their back door. Foliage and high weeds were in between the two houses, yet there was always a possibility they smelled the Tatum's outhouse. In the country, a family can tell their outhouse from another family's by the different odors. If you use it and are around your family outhouse enough, you become familiar with the aroma.

The Hampton boys actually added another slot onto their outhouse, enlarged the structure before placing it over the newly four foot deep hole which was more that several feet away from its original spot. They put lime in the newly dug hole to keep snakes away looking for heat in the winter. They had to avoid using too much lime otherwise they would poison the ground that might reach out to the well water. The other fear from users, especially women, was placing their butts directly on the seat of the outhouse. Black widows or other type spiders like to hang under the wooden surface around the hole and was known to bite those who sat down directly onto the seat.

The dirt from the new spot was used to fill in the old spot hole. Nature would take its course making the old spot a pile of compost where grass and other foliage would grow.

Other small structures on the place had to be maintained, like the smokehouse. This is where they kept their game killed from hunting trips, meat they barter for or fish they caught during the summer. In order to smoke the meat, Gracie and the boys used a small wood burning stove which was a kept in the smoke house. By its use, and keeping it slightly warm, the dry air from a very slow hardwood fire performs the actual act of drying the meats.

The events of the war or actions caused by war was happening so fast these days, life must have seemed like it was moving at warped speed to some. To newly made widows, moms and dads who lost sons and other kin, or whose relatives were still fighting in harm's way, time probably seem to stand still at times.

During the early part of April, 1943, while trying to keep inflation in check, FDR froze wages and prices, prohibiting workers from changing jobs unless the war effort necessitated the change, and bars rate increases to common carriers and public utility companies. In June he signs the first withholding tax bill law. It's known as W-2 day.

The Nazi's Hermann Goering division in Tunisia North Africa surrenders. Allies conduct a ten day bombing mission on Hamburg Germany on June 24th. Benito Mussolini was captured by Italian Resistance on July 25 trying to escape the country dressed as a soldier.

In California, a mob of 60 jumped on and beat up anybody they perceived to be Hispanic which was dubbed the Zoot Suit Riots. The attackers were from the Los Angeles Naval Reserve Armory. A black Race riot occurred in Beaumont, Texas where two people died. 35 were killed in a Detroit race riot whereas another race riot occurred, this time in Harlem.

The race riots were bound to happen because black people were seeing German and Italian prisoners-of-war treated better than black servicemen or women. These same service people had been treated with more respect overseas during World I and II.

The bottom line was that the new Negro was not like their old subservient parents and grandparents. No disrespect to their ancestors, they insisted or demanded to be treated equally. They felt they'd earned it by putting their lives on the line for their country.

There was also no doubt in their mind; they felt this was their country. They felt insulted that some in this county couldn't or even would not ever see them as equals. They would no longer wait for change and felt if change was going to come, they would have to accomplish it themselves.

There were various triggers that started each riot. In Harlem, on August 1, 1943, Robert Bandy, a black US Army soldier attempted to prevent a NYPD police officer from striking a black woman for the second time while arresting her for disturbing the peace.

The officer who saw this as an interference with his arrest pulled his service revolver and fired at Bandy, hitting him in the shoulder. Bandy was taken to a nearby hospital with a flesh wound. Some, who witnessed the incident, were joined by others forming a crowd at the hospital, the hotel, and police headquarters.

Keeping in mind that there reportedly were some 3,000 Negroes eventually involved in this riot. Somebody in one of the crowds shouted that a Negro soldier had been killed setting off a violent response. The end result was approximately 5 million dollars in property damage, six people died, and almost 400 were injured and many more arrested.

The Detroit trigger was different in some ways but the causes were similar. The KKK had established itself as the voice for white supremacy rights in this industrial city since 1920. The white dividing lines for living quarters were militantly guarded since World War II. Employer had hired a ready pool of black labor from the South to work in these growing factories that had mobilized for the war. Yet the city was in not ready for the large influx of new people looking for housing. The city's growing and bulging 200,000 black residents were cramped into a 60 square block ghetto called Paradise Valley. Sine there were so many people, the sanitary conditions were abysmal. Obviously, this was just one of the problems.

There were the old reasons given by the KKK, segregationist, and outright racist as to why they don't want a black person in the same room with them. In 1943, as in 2013, you could just go down the list in your head and you will get the same picture. Because when you strip away the rhetoric and lies, they undoubtedly boil down to racial intolerance. You could say the same thing about the causes in Los Angeles, Mobile, Alabama and Beaumont, Texas; same reasons just different areas in the US.

As for the Detroit trigger itself, it began at an integrated amusement park. On June 20, 1943 at Belle Isle, it was a hot muggy summer evening. Reportedly there were multiple fights between white and black teenagers. The white teenagers were joined by sailors who were from a nearby Naval Armory. While headed for home later on, heated rhetoric in traffic jams and congestion at the ferry docs brought on more violence. It's reported that 200 Negroes and white sailors began fighting.

Shortly thereafter a crowd of 5,000 white residents formed at the mainland entrance to the bridge waiting to attack black vacationers wishing to cross. Events escalated from there. With crowds of either race increasing, based on rumors or shouts from their own, the riot spread into the city. The mayor was late in asking for help, finally getting the aid of 6000 federal troops on the second evening of the riots.

The end result, 25 black people (17 by white policemen) and 9 white people had been killed while 700 individuals were counted as injured. Property damaged was close to $2 million.

Michigan Governor Kelly appointed a fact-finding a committee, whose members seem to have their mind slanted toward what they heard instead of actually finding out the facts. Their conclusions were not a surprise; it was the fault of the city's black population.

Never to miss exploiting their enemies problems, Vichy radio, controlled by the Germans, broadcast stated "The internal disorganization of a country torn by social injustice, race hatreds, regional disputes, the violence of an irritated proletariat, and the gangsterism of a capitalistic police." These were the same people who called for the extermination of Europe's Jews as the "final solution".

Racist in our own country were quick to comment. Mississippi's Jackson Daily News blamed the race riots on First Lady Eleanor Roosevelt by questioning her views on social equality. "In Detroit, a city noted for the growing impudence and insolence of its Negro population, an attempt was made to put your preachments into practice, Mrs. Roosevelt." This was no doubt a reference to the fact that Belle Isle was an integrated amusement park. Unlike Mississippi whose outhouses were segregated.

The actual reasons for these type riots have been noted leaving one to draw their own conclusion. With that said there is one constant when reading or studying world history. Many of the largest, smartest, and most powerful countries and societies in world history downfalls have come from within rather than from outside enemies. The old adage of a divided house does not stand rings true. Sadly some in the United States, think those in the house should all be of one color.

Meanwhile there was good news for this particular author. Codis Hampton married his sweetheart, Doreatha Childs on September 11, 1943. Although records from that era indicate he was 21 and his bride 18, he was actually 18 and she was 17 years old at the time. They took up residence in a small rented house on a farm in Bradley County. They were married on the same day they applied for the license, which says they had a private wedding with a few family members.

Doreatha became pregnant at the beginning of the New Year having the baby on August 16, 1944.The young couple named the child after his father, Codis Hampton Jr. The birth happened in Banks, Bradley County Arkansas. Codis were working in the Public Works arena and Doreatha was a housewife. Both had plans for a better future and would soon leave the area headed north.

The following December, on the 16th, Doreatha's sister Gertie Mae (Nookie) Childs married her childhood sweetheart Willie

Hayes Belin. They would settle in Banks, Bradley County for a lifetime of love, bearing children and enjoying life.

What was it like at the beginning of a new year? You could buy a car for $1,250; gasoline was 21 cents per gallon, a new house cost $10,000, a postage stamp was 3 cents, milk was 62 cents per gallon and bread was 9 cents a loaf. The minimum wage was 40 cents per hour with a yearly average salary of $2,900.

On January 13, 1945, Lacirene became the second child to leave Gracie Hampton's household. She married her sweetheart R.T. Tatum settling in Banks, Bradley County for a lifetime of happy memories.

A better job and future beckoned the South's younger residents including those in the Banks community. Cities like Detroit, Milwaukee, and other northern places offered a much better standard or living than young black couples were seeing in Arkansas. Codis and Doreatha Hampton took advantage and moved to Milwaukee, Wisconsin in February of that year. They were following Codis Uncles Monroe, Peach, David Jr., Lemon and Calvin who had moved there earlier.

The war came to an end with a few incidents of note. German forces surrendered in Italy on April 29, 1945. Having been beaten down and stopped at every turn they tried to implement, a week or so later they surrender in Western Europe May 7, 1945. The next day, they surrendered to the Soviets at the Eastern Front. A stubborn German Arm Group Centre held out and resisted in Prague until May 11, 1945. Allied leaders met in Potsdam, Germany to confirmed earlier surrender agreements on July 11, 1945.

Yet even earlier in the year, there was another major event that took center stage for the United States of America and its allies. President Franklin D Roosevelt died on April 12, 1945. He died of a massive cerebral hemorrhage. The longest serving president America has ever had; the statesman who led this country through the Great Depression and World War II passed on this day. He would be missed by a lot of people around the world. He would be missed more, if one can really say that, by America. For the country lost a great leader of all people that day. He died where he often went for a vacation and or rest at the "Little White House" retreat in Warm Springs, Georgia.

The next day a funeral cortege was formed to take the president back to the train station for the trip back to Washington. Graham Jackson, a black man, who played his accordion for FDR on many of his trips down there, played 'Going Home' as the procession began to move. With the procession moving around the semi-circle driveway and onto the street headed for the train station, the bareheaded accordion player, with tears rolling down both cheeks, played 'Nearer, My God, To Thee.'

CHAPTER 12

The Aftermath of Winning a War While Losing a beloved Statesman

V ice President Harry S Truman took office immediately after the death of FDR. He had not been in office long enough to be in the loop on certain important issues. He was not aware of any developments of the atomic bomb.

Yet as President, he was called upon to make the most difficult decision in his lifetime. He asked Japan to surrender and when they rejected him, he made the decision to drop the atomic bomb on Hiroshima and Nagasaki, Japan. The Japanese surrendered shortly thereafter.

A message was sent to all who needed to know, this president would take all steps required to keep wartime surrender agreements in places. He would also have no qualms about using whatever force that was available for him to protect the interest of the United States of America.

Japan officially surrendered by signing their agreement aboard the deck of the USS Missouri on September 2, 1945. The Axis powers had been defeated. In the wake of their defeat, countless lives were lost. Germany attempted to wipe out an entire race of people, the Jews. An enormous amount of personal and military property across the globe had been destroyed. Fathers, mothers would never see sons or daughters again. World landmarks were changed by bombers and personnel battles. The grab for world dominance by the Axis did not succeed and the entire universe was a better place for it.

Before and during the early part of 1940, Sambo and Sallie's household went through the kids growing up and moving on period. After their kids had grown and move out and to Milwaukee, they decided to join them in the city by late 1941 or early 1942.

Lemon and his wife Lula, John and Gracie moved out on their own.

Monroe Hampton married Mittie Lou Belin (sister to Oddie Lee Belin) on August 1, 1925. They moved to Milwaukee back in 1939 or early 1940.

David Jr moved to Warren where he lived until 1942. He left Warren that year for Milwaukee, Wis. His wife, the former Oddie Lee Belin died in August of 1948. Shortly after that he moved to Minneapolis, Minnesota where he remained until suffering from ill health. His family brought him back to Milwaukee in December of 1980, where he passed on January 15, 1981.

Van D (Peach) Hampton married Vernese Harmon on August 11, 1934, in Banks. He worked in a saw mill for 39 cents per hour until deciding he wanted better for his family. They moved to Milwaukee in 1940 where he got a job making 79 cents per hour. He later married Ruby. He died in Milwaukee on February 9, 1998.

Calvin Hampton married Dora Marjorie Tatum in 1945. They moved to Milwaukee shortly thereafter where he decided to enlist in the armed services. He served in the US Navy enlisting on February 23, 1945. He was honorably discharged on June 9, 1946. Calvin and Marjorie went on to have two children during their marriage. His wife and son, Johnny Lee preceded him in death. He died in Milwaukee on June 19, 2012. He was 86 years old.

Back in those days, a black man could get a job almost one day after arrival. That's what led to a lot of people's decision to leave the Banks community.

In 1946, consumer prices continued to rise for most items. A car's average price was $1,120; gasoline was 21 cents per gallon, a house cost $5,600 while the average salary had increase to $3,150. The minimum was 40 cents per hour. Bread was 10 cents per loaf, milk was 70 cents a gallon, and a postage stamp still had a price of 3 cents.

Jobs are hard to find for those returning from the war. This was the period of the Baby boomers as more people are getting married and having babies.

RCA and the television industry began to make a comeback with a brand new model, 630-TS that sold 10,000 sets that year. 20th Century Fox movie studio head, Darryl F. Zanuck was quoted as saying "Television won't be able to hold on to any market it captures after the first six months. People will soon get tired of staring at a plywood box every night." He must have had a hidden agenda to say such a thing.

The first televised fight broadcast on television was held June 19 between Heavyweight Champion Joe Louis and Billy Conn. It was seen by a record 140,000 people in bars and clubs across the nation that offered TV viewing to its customers. The following year, the Lewis-Walcott fight was seen by 1,000,000 TV viewers.

Gracie had two of her children still living with her, 17 year old Curtis, and 15 year old Clearance D plus her cousin and friend, Mae Ellen Hall. The oldest two children are married and living on their own. Her daughter Lacirene and her husband R.T. Tatum got the old Edgar-Viola, Rand Tatum place. It turned out; Rand Tatum was a cousin of R.T. He decided to move his family to Detroit and left the house for R.T, who was more than happy to get it.

Willie Hayes Belin and his wife Nookie (Gertie Mae Childs) took over the old Harriett and Frank Hall place and had settle in to start raising a family. This house is up the road from where Lacirene and R.T. is living.

There is another house in back of the Belin's, down another little road (about a quarter of a city block) where one of Willie Hayes' sisters, Pansy Belin-Davis lives with her husband, Willie Davis, and children.

Gracie's sister Lena and Colrolus Strong still live around the bend and across the rail road tracks from her house. The woods are still densely populated with timber outside her front door and porch. The Strong's children, DC were 16, Frank 14, and Joe the youngest was 12 years old.

Her oldest sister, Versia still lives in Hot Springs with her husband, James Boswell. They have been married twenty-eight years now. They never did have any children and are still working at the Arlington Hotel. They have made a comfortable living for themselves. The hotel itself still remains one of the favorite places to stay when visiting Hot Springs for the baths. The city still offers gambling to visitors and residents.

Some of the permanent residents and friends of Al Capone, who still visited a few times after his release from prison in 1939, were aware of his current physical and mental state. His physician and a Baltimore psychiatrist reached the conclusion that Capone had the mentality of a 12 year old. He is currently in seclusion at his Palm Island estate in Biscayne Bay outside of Miami, Florida. By January 1947 he died of a stroke and pneumonia.

The man who had made such an impression on Sammy Parker would die after his black protégé in Hot Springs. Years ago, it was Capone, Lucky Luciano and friends who impressed young Sammy with their lifestyle.

He started out shinning their shoes, but quickly became their personal runner. He ran normal errands such as delivering and picking up laundry, eventually graduating to ordering and picking up booze from the local moonshiners of the dry county.

Sammy asked a lot of questions about the numbers game, finally setting up his own little racket among the black folk in Hot Springs and Garland County. He told his heroes a year afterwards. Some of their white friends in the area started playing and it grew into a very lucrative business for Sammy and his partner, Big CC.

Capone always liked the fact Sammy came with his own personal bodyguard, Big CC. It was one of the gangsters who tacked on the nickname Big to CC's name. CC was already a nickname given to him by Sammy after they first met in that boxcar headed for Hot Springs. Sammy asked him his name. He responded by jokingly referring to himself as Calvin Coolidge, the US President at the time. Sammy started calling him CC for short.

It was Sammy and Big CC that planned and carried out the ambushed that killed Bob Longley and Clarke Riley. They used the presents from their gangster friends that became their new toys, tommy guns, during their ambush of Petey Sampson, killing his driver and aide.

Sammy, at forty-six years of age, still harbored a burning hatred for Petey Sampson. He still wanted to kill him. He has never forgotten that Petey, his brother Walt Sampson and their friend Bob Longley ambushed him and his cousin Elmo Parker in the woods. Walt was killed during the gunfight. They also killed Elmo that day, impaling him to a tree with a hail of bullets. He can never get that scene out of his mind. He also believes that it was that trio who sit fire to the little cabin that resulted in the death of Lummie Hall, his first and only love. He referred to the fire as the murder of his girlfriend.

It was an early Sunday morning before daybreak on March 3, 1946. He picked that day to finally even the score with Petey Samson and whoever else got in the way. Of course, he'd heard about the St. Valentine's Day Massacre. He was emboldened by the last attack on Petey. They got away with it. His only regret, Petey did not die and he needed to correct that error.

This time it will be different. They will not wait in ambush for him to come down the road; they would simply drive up to his house and kill him. Sammy knew from the reports he'd gotten from several sources in Bradley County that the Sampson KKK staff was next to zero. There were no more regular meetings on the grounds as a show of force. Petey was still wheel chair bound and probably sleeping in the same room he and his deceased brother used as kids. Sammy knew the layout like the back of his hand. Petey will never know how close Sammy came to shooting him in that room even before this day.

The gray four-door 1944 Ford deluxe sedan made its way up the highway headed for Banks in Bradley County. The fact there was nothing unusual about the vehicle was by design. It was just a car on the road that happened to be carrying four Negroes in it on the way to visit relatives in the Banks area. Big CC was in the back seat with Sammy Parker. Two of Sammy's men were in the front seat. Eddie Johnson, the driver and Larry Harrison, sitting across from Eddie. They all were heading for the Samson farm.

Sammy figured four was enough considering the Tommy gun fire power they had plus each was armed with a pistol too.

"This ought to be a Goddamn 'nough men to take care of that little shit. Um gonna tear his head off with my little tommy here," He said to nobody in particular.

"You've waiting a long time for this, Sam. I hope these folks are where they supposed to be," Big CC said.

"You Goddamn skippy, they are in bed right now waiting on the sun to rise. Um gonna make sure it rise and fall on the same damn day for Petey."

"How far is this farm again Boss?" Eddie asked.

"All total 'bout 80 miles or so, just take your time and drive. We got 'bout 20 more miles to go," Big CC answered. "The turn off gonna be on your left. I know it when I see it, so keep yo' eyes peeled."

They were hoping to get there an hour before daybreak; probably catching old man Sampson sitting up while his wife fixed coffee and breakfast. The road was dark as the Ford came within ten miles of its destination.

Finally the Sampson farm road turnoff came into view. Sammy recognized it by the trees on both sides of the little road. He still couldn't see the little Sampson Farms sign from this side of the road because of the trees, but he was sure it was their destination.

"Kill the lights and turn left onto that little road and stop the car," Sammy ordered.

Eddie slowed down, turning off the lights and turned into the road and immediately stopped the vehicle. They could see the white gate that spanned the width of the road a few yards in front of them. At one time there were guards, now there were none even though the gate was still closed. Eddie moved the car in for a closer look. They could see for sure now that there was no one on the gate. Everyone except the driver got out of the car at Sammy's instruction.

Turn the car around, heading back out then get out and meet us at this gate. Again, Eddie did as he was told.

Each man, dressed in slacks, dark shirt, and short jacket while wearing combat boots with their pants leg tucked inside the boot, stepped inside the gate area. Big CC had opened and tied the gate to a tree, preventing its closing. The men made their way up the short distance to just outside the front porch.

Sammy directed Big CC and Eddie to stand guard at the front door entrance of the porch just as planned. They took their positions, kneeling down on one knee, with Tommy guns at the ready for anyone coming out of that front door.

Meanwhile Sammy and Larry went around to the bedroom window where he expected to find Petey. He quietly moved to the window, after motioning for Larry to stay there in a spot to watch his back. The house, wired for electricity, night lamp was on in the room. He could see the wheel chair sitting beside the bed but could not see exactly who was in the bed.

Big CC heard a growl and turned to his left to see a German Sheppard growling at the unexpected visitors. Never one to mess up a planned operation over the years, they had thought of this too. He held his right hand out to calm Eddie, with the weapon in his left hand. He barely moved the rest of his body as he took the bone, with pieces of meat out of the bag he had draped over his shoulder. The meat on the bone was dotted with small doses of a homemade animal sedative to put any dog to sleep within seconds of it reaching the animals mouth. He threw the dog the doctored bone.

"Here Fido, have a threat," He whispered as the dog grabbed the bone, backed up and fell out cold as he began to chew on the meat morsels. Both men smiled as they seen the results of their quick thinking and planning.

Sammy was just about to knock on the window to wake up Petey or whoever was in that bed when he heard a growl to his right. He saw another German Sheppard dog growling at him. He took the same type bone concoction from his bag and tossed it over toward the dog. To his surprised a third dog suddenly appeared it looked like an old hound dog. The third dog grabbed the bone and ran off behind another structure with his prize.

The other German Sheppard, now really pissed, began to bark and growl while moving toward Sammy, who had no more bones. Feeling he had no choice, he fired a short burst at the dog. The automatic gun fire rang out into the still morning air as the dog groaned from being shot and fell over dead.

The sudden noise of gunfire woke up Petey; he sat up in his bed, looking confused. Sammy, turning his attention back to the bedroom, for just a second, looked at Petey's horrified facial expression at seeing the face of Sammy Parker outside his bedroom window. Quickly pointing the weapon at Petey, he fired through the window, causing a violent reaction from Petey's body being riddled with bullets from the automatic weapon. His body was finally thrown backwards from the bullets impact.

Sammy turned, motioned for Larry to follow, and ran toward the front porch where Big CC and Eddie were firing their weapons at the figures who once stood on the front porch. At the sound of gunfire, a big white guy, they took to be a guard came to the front door with a shotgun. Quickly stepping outside of the screen door, he took aim at the closer of the two men standing in the Sampson's front yard.

Clara Sampson ran out the screen door followed by her husband, Harvey. Big CC's one second hesitation to fire because of seeing the women cost Eddie his life. The guard opened fire with his shotgun sending Eddie sprawling backwards. A startled and hit Eddie fired his weapon in the air before hitting the ground. Big CC opened fire, killing the guard, Clara and her husband who was standing behind her.

Sammy and Larry got there just as Big CC stopped firing. He looked at Eddie and shook his head letting the others know there was no life in that body.

"Let's go," He yelled. The three men ran back to their car. Larry got behind the wheel, started the car and began driving the short distance back toward the Banks highway.

Ironically, Sheriff Penelton and Deputy Josh Stovall was driving from Banks, heading to Hot Springs. A friend of Josh had given him a description of a Negro gangster working the numbers game around Hot Springs. Josh had no idea it was the same Sammy Parker that the Sheriff had been talking about for years. That is not until he was able to get Sammy's fingerprints. The fingerprints were taken some time ago. They arrested him, with others, at an all-night black juke joint near Hot Springs. They let him go after he paid a fine but fingerprinted him in the process. It wasn't clear if they took a mug shot or not. He gave his name as Stanley Parks, which was the name he often went by in Hot Springs.

On a hunch, because of the similarities in the two names, the Sheriff checked the fingerprints which matched Sammy Parkers. They decided to drive down to Hot Springs because it was Sunday and a slow day. They wanted to see and hear more about this character, find out if anybody had a mug shot or picture, or at the very least, find out if they had his current address. They figured to be back by noontime.

Both men heard the automatic gunfire coming from the Sampson place, knowing it was not hunters; the officers were intending to pull into the Sampson's property. They were as surprised to see this speeding car darting out into the road in front of them as the occupants inside the car were at spotting the Banks' Sheriff's patrol car.

Once Big CC and Sammy saw the patrol car, they pointed the weapons at the two officers and pulled the triggers. Unfortunately, they did not think they would need the guns anymore and didn't reload the weapons with new drum magazines. The two men pulled the guns back inside the window and drew their pistols. They never got off a shot. Seeing them wave those Tommy guns around, caused the Sheriff and Deputy to pull their service revolvers.

Firing at the vehicle as it made the hard right turn onto the road, there were about six shots fired by the officers. One shot hit Big CC and another tore through the back glass passenger window, shattering it going out the other window leaving a hole but the window intact. The third, fourth, fifth or sixth shots must have missed the targets, but one of the last shots hit the driver's side rear tire.

The tire blew out, causing the car to violently swerve from side to side as Larry desperately tried to gain control of the car. The sheriff grabbed a rifle out of the patrol car and fired two more shots at the careening Ford. One bullet shattered the back window and the other caught Larry on the side of his head as the car turned exposing the driver. The bullet went through the open driver's window, which had been rolled down by someone for some reason or another.

With Larry letting go of the steering wheel, the car suddenly jerked to its left causing it to roll over three times, finally coming to a rest on its side in the embankment on the Sampson Farm side of the road. The Sheriff and Deputy sprinted the fifty yards or so to check on survivors. There were none.

It didn't stop the two men from laboriously dragged all three men from the vehicle, across the road, and away from the car simple because, they knew they had only a few minutes before the vehicle caught on fire. Without those bodies, who they were and why they were here would be lost. The only time it took both of them to carry a body was with Big CC. Exhausted they sat down on the ground for a moment. The car, gas leaking into the ditch, burst into flames just as they plopped down on the edge of the left embankment.

It took almost the rest of the day, but the sheriff, Banks' coroner, roadside helpers containing the fire with a lot of assistance from the County Sheriff's office in Warren, including their coroner helping out the guy from Banks, and Dr. Purvis to finally wrap up the evidence gathering. Information found on the bodies of Larry, Sammy Parker and Big CC, plus the ID found on Eddies body at the Sampson's house cleared up a lot of mysteries for Sheriff Penelton's office, especially when he got the full report on Hot Springs' Stanly Parks yet born in Bradley County as Sammy Parker. Big CC turned out to be Ralph Smith from Harlem, wanted for assault with a deadly weapon, robbery and burglary. Eddie and Larry were Hot Springs natives with no serious arrest records.

The Parker Family was shocked. Although they figured, they had lost a son some years ago, they still held out hope that some good may come of it. Clem had heard some of the whispers and noticed how some people stopped taking when he walked into a place like Papa Warner's. Now he knew. Rollie, too, had heard the same whisperings as his father. He knew, like his mother and father, that Sammy was in Hot Springs, but also like the rest of the family felt that he should keep his distance because his brother was still wanted for questioning here in Bradley County.

He also didn't want to give any clues to the Sampson's or any of their KKK connections. The way he made his living was a shock, the fact he hated Petey Sampson wasn't.

The Bradley county community was surprised although a few of them had heard and talked about the rumors. When contacted by Gracie, Versia and James were not shocked. They knew Sammy was involved in unlawful ways of making money. They were taken aback at his visits and killings in Bradley County.

This time Deputy Stovall made the rounds and gave out information. Although the Sheriff had notified the Parkers, the Deputy made one more stop to offer his condolences too. He stopped by the Jennings Farm and Papa Warner's, providing a full report at each place he stopped. He, at Sheriff Penelton's request let them know that he would be the new Sheriff by the end of next month. Most already knew.

One major issue on the sheriffs to be mind was how the public at large felt about the incident. Ninety-nine point nine percent of the black people accepted it as Deputy Stovall expected. They felt a sense of loss for all involved and hope this incident would not rile up the KKK.

As also expected, white people had a different take on the issue. Some wondered out loud and verbalize the need for revenge on local Negroes for killing people. They wondered how they should respond to such a bold attack on the Sampson family. Some kind of message must be sent to the darkies that this type of action will not stand. Most of those who felt that way were friends of the Sampson and shared their views on race relations.

There were some white people who knew of the Sampson's connection with the KKK and yet felt that black people should know they can't get away with murdering a white family in their own home like that. Deputy Stovall reminded them all, that the perpetrators did not get away with it. It was like a jolt for some when he brought them back to the finality of the killings. Those who were responsible are dead at the hands of the law and God. That realization calmed a lot of the 90% revenge mongers. The other ten percent would only be satisfied if all black people were wiped from the earth or at least cleared out of Bradley County.

The deputy reminded that small percentage of folks that the law applies equally to each and every one of us. All in all in it was a good experience for all the people he spoke with to understand the incoming sheriff's views on how to apply the law.

We have said this often because it is true. Life goes on. No incident halts life from moving forward as we know it. No wars or man-made, nature driven, or act of God catastrophes halt the evolvement of life. There are moments in time when the speed of life is slow or fast, depending on one's perspective, but we can all be sure of one thing, tomorrow always comes unless its Gods will to prevent that from happening to mankind.

And so it was for Gracie, and her family. By the end of 1946, President Truman officially declared an end to World War II, by a Presidential Proclamation on December 31st.

CHAPTER 13

Little Hamp Revisits His Place of Birth

O ver the years Gracie had become somewhat callous and was known for being difficult to deal with. Some say she had gone from a sweet innocent young girl to mean quick tempered old woman.

One could understand how a single mother must be the rock in the family, especially in a segregated South. Given where she and her family lived, one could also understand why she had to be tough to fend for herself and those she loved. In some ways, she took on the personality of a frontier woman blazing a trail for others to follow.

She had to be a teacher after school was out, a mother when one of own was physically or emotionally hurt, a strong, kind, or stern disciplinarian whenever a situation presented itself. She had to provide the voice of wisdom and experience to young folks who thought they had the answers to all problems. But most of all, she had to be the protector of her family when it came to dealing with people, especially local white folk.

After her husband left the home, she maybe a little grudgingly, took on all those and other roles. As time went on, she realized that she could not be hesitant in making decisions. She had to convince some by proving that she was neither weak nor reluctant to do whatever was necessary for her and family to survive. Those who dared to challenge her authority found they'd better arm themselves because it would be a fight to the death.

Even at 34 years of age, her live-in cousin and friend, Mae Ellen looked to Gracie as more of a mother than the woman who brought her into this world. Not only because she had been with Gracie longer than she'd known her biological mother and father, Viola and Edgar Hall. It's because they acted more like mother and daughter than related friends. The relationship had evolved. Gracie, being eleven years older, eagerly taken on the role of Mae Ellen's protector and advisor in all matters. In fact, the Hampton children considered her more of a big sister than cousin.

To some, Gracie was a sweet old lady who made the best tea cakes and other sweet treats. She was just as nice as she had to be to get her way. A testament of her character all depended on who were providing the information.

For me, Codis Jr., as a young wide eyed five year old kid, she was just Grandma. I was sent south because my father and mother, who were still living in Milwaukee, were going through a separation period which finally ended in divorce. The story I got from my mother was she took me down there for my Grandmother to keep until she could find a steady job. She later came to pick me up and Grandma would not let her have me until her and my father got back together. My mother told Grandma that she would have me until I got grown because there was no hope of her and daddy getting back together. Mama said she started to call the police but was talked out of it by Mae Ellen and other relatives. They were afraid that Grandma Gracie might shoot the first person that stepped on her land trying to take me out of her house. Once again, my grandmother's reputation preceded her.

When I got there around August 31, 1949, my Uncle Curtis and Clarence D had moved out. Mae Ellen and Grandmother were the only ones living in the house.

I remember specific events that happened while I was there. Although I may not be able to correctly identify the date and time, I can honestly say it is as I remembered it to be. One such incident was after going fishing with my Uncle Colrolus, Aunt Lena, Cousins Frank or Joe Strong I decided I liked this fishing thing.

I may have asked if anybody was going fishing that day. Grandma probably told me there was no one to take me that particular day. Being somewhat of a take care of my own wishes kind of kid, I decided to build a fishing pond in our back yard.

I can almost picture Grandma asking what I was doing as she saw me digging the hole. I'm sure I told her I was making a pond so I can fish. Can you imagine a grandmother telling a young boy that's not possible? Well, she didn't, probably thinking, let him find out.

I went on to dig this hole. I didn't have a shovel, so I used a hoe, and anything around that was sharp enough to break the ground. I had to be sure it was not something that was needed by Grandma. I didn't want to break something like that otherwise, I would get in trouble. I used the top of an old can to scrape around the bottom of the hole to smooth out the rough areas.

Finally, I had a pretty wide hole that may have been about one and a half foot deep to two feet deep in its deepest spots. Then I made several trips to the well to get water under the watchful and amusing eye of my grandmother. Maybe even with her help in getting the water. I filled up the hole and went to get a piece of strong long flexible tree branch to act as a fishing pole. I tied a string onto it, placed a hook on the end of the string, bated it with a live worm, and sat there trying to catch a fish for the longest time.

I am not sure of the questions I asked Granma as to why there were no fish in my pond; but I never did catch a fish. The next day, I ran out to fish again, only to find that all the water in my pond was gone. Weather it was Grandma, or my Mae Ellen, somebody told me that no matter how much water I put into that hole, eventually the ground would soak it up. That was surly a lesson I learned and remember to this day.

A Few days later, after going to a real lake to fish, I had caught a small to medium sized turtle. Never one to let something go to waste, I put more water in my back yard hole and placed the turtle in the pond. It seemed happy.

The next day I ran out to see how the turtle was doing and of course the ground had soaked up the water again. My turtle was nowhere to be found either. To my recollection, that is when I gave the whole idea a lot of thought with the conclusion that I needed to find something else for me to do.

We attended church on Sundays. Aunt Lena and Uncle Colrolus would pick us up in the horse team wagon. We hardly ever saw his truck. That is where I learned the art of preaching. I liked the way the Preacher had everyone's attention. Kids quickly pick up grown folk mannerism and habits. There were many times I found myself standing on the front porch of Grandmas house. I would look out into the mass of trees and began my sermon. I saw the trees as my congregation and the porch as my pulpit. I stormed, stomping my feet and clapping my hand like a preacher and telling my story to the trees.

I would beg them to repent and try to repeat to them what our preacher would have told us. It probably would be the latest sermon from our preacher I'd heard. I can truly say I had a very attentive listening audience.

Normally there were no interruption or pause in my delivery, except on occasions when I would hear some kind of reply coming back from the congregation. It normally came from the sound of some curious animal wondering why this little human was jumping up and down and shouting from the porch. I did notice, once I stopped and stood still for a minute or two, the noise in the woods would go away. Do you see what I mean by adapting to your environment?

Anyway, church service would continue with me singing hymns and gospel lyrics I learned in the real church. Of course, the church would end with me, as the preacher dismissing the congregation with a prayer, normally "Our Father, who art in Heaven . . ."

Now that I am a much older and I never thought about it before, but I bet my Grandma and Mae Ellen was rolling on the floor inside the house at this little boy preaching to the trees. I can almost hear my grandmother saying out loud to my aunt, "He's probably going to grow up to be a preacher one day." Sorry grandma, that didn't happen.

There is nothing but good memories from my time down there. The only bad memories I had was when I missed my mother and father. I used to play with lady bugs, catch lightening bugs in a jar. Somebody gave me a little black dog that I ran around the grounds with. It was the only dog on the place. All the others that belonged to Grandpa John had died over the years. There were plenty of cats. The local residents let them run around to keep the rat population under control.

My Cousin, Frank Strong or his brother DC gave me a horse. I can't remember which one it was but either way, I bet Uncle Colrolus had something to do with it. I'd probably been down there almost a year. It was a beautiful brown horse with black stockings, black mane and tail. I was too little to ride him but it was my job to take care of him. And that I did.

We could not go far because the safe grounds for a little boy were limited. I am pretty sure that is where I go my fear of snakes. I was always scared of being bitten, probably because I don't remember hearing of any good endings to that situation. Even though there were some snakes that were harmless. I just felt there was no need for me to identify which was which.

There were times when I was able to visit other relatives close by, like my Aunt Lacirene. Normally, somebody would come and get me to walk the distance to her house. The bushes and other foliage were pretty high along that little road. You never know what or who was hiding there. To a kid it looks pretty scary, since whatever might attack you would be upon you in a second.

I always enjoyed going up the road from her house to visit my Aunt Nookie and her husband Uncle Willie Hayes Belin. They had kids older and younger than I was. Bill was the son I played with the most. Aunt Nookie tells the tale that when Grandma would send me up to play with bill she always had me carry a lunch pail. She says Bill would try to trick me out of my lunch by asking to see what I had. They say my answer would always be the same. While looking to see what I had for lunch I would say to Bill, "Go on now Bill, this is my lunch." Each time Bill would try to get some of my food, like tea cakes. I would say, "Go on now Bill. I done told you. This is my lunch." Eventually, I might share something but kids will be kids. Aunt Nookie would say, "let him have his lunch, Bill." And within a short time she would hear me say out loud and louder, "Go on now Bill. I ain't playing now. Go on, this is my lunch." That always amused my Aunt Nookie while watching that kind of "Give me that! No, No!" kind or exchange between two kids.

Spring time of 1950 rolled around while I was settling into the country life. There was a homecoming celebration held in the community. That is where people who had left the area and state return to visit relatives, old neighbors and friends.

Mae Ellen tells the story of how I almost got her a serious wiping. She says we all returned home after the homecoming festivities. Grandma wanted to know why Mae Ellen disappeared for such a long time. She said her and Grandma went back and forth for a while until I jumped in saying "She was kissing that man named Robert." Shocked that I saw her, Mae Ellen tried to deny it. But she was caught red handed.

Grandma was so angry; she had tears in her eyes as she shouted at her. "Everybody in Banks knows that Robert Preston is married with two kids and one more on the way. What you messing 'round with him for?" During the heated argument, it turned out his family still lived in Warren. He still was a women chasing wife beater just like the rest of the brothers, including his daddy, or so Grandma said.

She said finally, Grandma told her "to go get the switch, 'cause you gon' get a whupping." Shocked that Gracie would even think about whipping her, Mae Ellen who was all of thirty-five years old was not going to take a whipping from anybody, not even Gracie. She told her she would leave and went to her room to put a few clothes in a bag. Evidently Grandma went and got the switch because as Mae Ellen came out of the room, she popped her two or three times with it. Not wanting to fight her cousin Mae Ellen dropped the clothing bag and ran out to the front porch, down the stairs, and toward Lacirene's house. Gracie was yelling after her, "I'll whip you 'til you're forty."

She stayed with Lacirene a couple of days and returned to Grandma's house on day three. The cousins made up after Gracie promised "never again" would she try to whip Mae Ellen. The relationship had taken a serious turn after that incident. Mae Ellen knew it was time to move on or otherwise Gracie would never expect her to leave home.

Sometime during that summer, I was doing my chores and noticed the chickens were eating my horse's food from his trough. I'd walked outside the barnyard gate and was headed toward the front porch. When I looked back and saw the chickens, I yelled, "Get away from his food". Of course the chickens ignored me. I took off running to scare them away and forgot about the string of barbwire strung across the top and middle of the fence.

I ran smack into that barbwire splitting the skin of my left cheek open wide enough that they could see my teeth or so they say. All I remember was I yelled so loud that time, I startled the chickens and my horse.

They took me to a doctor. He cleaned the cut and bandaged what felt like the entire left side of my face. To this day, I still have a two inch scar on the left side of my cheek to remind me of that incident. I remember all the time I was growing up, especially after I became a teenage and a man. Every time someone would ask how I got this scar, I tell them the truth. Yet, the toughs in the street wanted to believe it came from a personal or gang fight. In other words, that somebody cut me. I remember two guys having a conversation about it right in front of me. "Hey man who cut you? That's a dangerous looking scar you got there. What did you do man?" Before I could answer the other guy said, "I would not want to mess with the guy who made that scar." They both laughed and walked away, so sure of themselves on how my scar came to be. I just let it go. I didn't want to spoil their fun and imagination.

I have no memory of that horse after my accident. I believe and am almost positive that Grandma told DC or Frank to come get that horse. She felt since I could not ride him yet, I didn't need him. That hurt me so bad; I no longer wanted to stay with Grandma. Over the years, I have sort of blocked what happened after that out of my memory. I do remembering asking her what happen to the horse. This was some time after she moved to Milwaukee. She really didn't want to talk about it. All she said was they came and got him.

The last and most vivid memory I have of living with Grandma was the time I was in the back yard. It was in the fall of 1950 and a cooler yet mild kind of day. It was either late August or early September. That particular day, I was just looking for something to do. The dog was still there but he was just lying down somewhere. I was lonely and wondering if I was ever going to see my parents again. I had just turned six years old. I sat down on the back steps and looked toward Aunt Lacirene house. The foliage was low enough plus they had turned a large section of it into a garden. One could see past her house on the little road that ran toward the Banks highway. It had to be in the afternoon because the sun was in the middle of the sky.

Looking in Banks road direction, I could barely make out this figure of a man walking. I picked up the sight of his figure before he reached Aunt Lacirene's. I suppose, I looked away and started daydreaming. Intuition is a strong emotion and will make you wonder. My eyes turned toward this individual once again. By this time he was at my aunts but I could not see him or her. Her house was blocking my view. I turned my thoughts away again. I don't know how long it was but I never moved from those back steps. The man reappeared and might be coming in our direction. I thought I saw him riding a bike or something when he left my Aunts. I had to wait awhile for him to come into view again because of the high foliage along that little road leading to our house from my aunt's. I remember thinking he could have kept straight and might not be coming our way. I wondered who he was. Maybe he was from Grandpa Warner's store. Then I saw him just as though I was standing in front of him. It was him, riding a bike and coming our way. It was my father. At this point, I can't honestly tell you what I did because I cannot remember.

I do know the man was Codis Hampton, my father riding on a bike he had bought me for my birthday. He looked funny as a man riding on a kid's bike to me. I can't say what my emotions were at that exact moment, but I do know this. There was no pretty of sight or no one I wanted to see more at this particular time in my life than my father. And there he was riding a bike while heading my way. I don't really think I said anything, because I wanted to be sure, I wasn't dreaming.

I ran around to the front of the house and was standing there when he rode up giving me that Hampton smile that said 'hey there'. He did say "happy birthday boy." The man called me boy up through my 35th birthday. He put the bike in my hands and I lost control, crying with happiness.

I don't remember the conversations after that. I don't know what he and Grandma talked about. I don't remember if he took me for a ride, if I tried to ride or what happened. I don't know whether he stayed the night or if it was the next day when he left. I can say when Codis Hampton left returning to Milwaukee the next day or the day after; I was in the car with him. The bike and my clothes were in the trunk and he was taking me home.

Of course I had mixed emotions. I saw the sad look on my most favorite Grandma's face. I also wanted that horse and would have liked to take my dog with me, too. I still don't remember whose car it was, my Uncle Curtis or my fathers. It wasn't my business and it really didn't matter. I've forgotten which uncle drove down to Arkansas with him but I know it was either Calvin or Curtis. I was just glad I was in the car with my father too.

CHAPTER 14

What's Next and What Should I Do?

N
o one can say exactly what was going through Gracie's mind. Yet the reality of her family growing up and moving out left one cold fact. She was getting older, had no husband, and was being left to attend to four acres of land by herself.

There was no doubt that people who loved and cared about her well-being lived nearby. Her daughter, Lacirene to her front, her sister Lena to her rear was the closest but they had a husband and immediate family responsibilities. No matter how one put it they were not in the same house as Gracie. Add that to the now tenuous relationship between her and Mae Ellen. It was a fact of life that had to weigh heavy on her mind.

Her youngest son who had moved out earlier to be close to his employment got married to Gertharene Campbell day of May 9, 1951. The small private affair took place in Warren, Arkansas. Shortly thereafter, they too left for Milwaukee, Wisconsin for the same reasons as those before them, a higher paying job and better life.

A month later, Gracie, Mae Ellen, her sisters Versia and Lena were sitting on the front porch of her house working jointly on a quilt that Gracie had almost finished. Gracie's sister's husbands, Colrolus and James were out working on chores around the little farm that Gracie and Mae Ellen just could not get too.

"Girl I don't know how you all do it. I mean, I know how Lena does it, besides always carrying that old shotgun, she has a husband and her boys living with her," Versia remarked.

"What do you mean? What are you talking about?" Gracie asked.

"I mean living so deep in and close to these woods. I can almost feel the animals and that 'thing' watching my every move."

"Oh shoot. I thought you was talkin' 'bout something. I carry my shotgun wherever I go too. It's right next to my bed at night. Ain't nothing gon' bother us."

"Yeah baby, we been living down here all this time. I know these woods like the back of my hand. Um subject to see it before it sees me and shame on whatever it is if I can get a shot off," Lena added.

"Yeah, well what about the Thing? You know that Thing that always make a racket and chases people away from fishing holes." Versia asked.

"First of all, ain't nobody ever seen this Thing, as the folks call it. Furthermore' it's just an old tale where somebody's trying to scare kids or grown folks away from something they don't want seen." Gracie countered.

"I don't care what you say. Me and Rollie was fishing over by the Parkers' pond, at least back in the days when they had the pond, and we caught a glimpse of that thing out the corner of our eyes. It looked like a big hairy monster. Girl I peed on myself before we both took off running," Versia added.

"You been telling that same story for years," Gracie said getting irritable about the conversation.

"Well, I got to admit; I saw the Thing when I was a little girl. Daddy took me fishing with him one time. Daddy shot at but missed, I guess," Lena said.

"That's the first time um hearing this. Where was I at?" Gracie asked.

"I don't remember. Maybe you stayed at home with mama that day. It looked hairy just like Versia said. Girl, I had not thought about that in years." Lena added.

"All right, all right then, that still don't escape the fact that you living down here next to these woods with nobody but Mae Ellen in the house." Versia said.

"Would you hush Versia? Don't remind me, not that um superstitious or anything." Gracie said.

They talked and quilted about an hour before the men reappeared. They all sat down to a nice Saturday diner after going inside the house. Gracie and Mae Ellen were glad to have visitors, especially family.

After their company left, and while they were cleaning up the remaining dishes that her sisters didn't wash. Mae Ellen, who had heard all the talk about moving north and saw Codis, Curtis, and Clarence do it, not to think of uncles and cousins who had left the south wanted to ask Gracie the big question too. It had been on her mind for some time. She was just waiting until the right moment. Finally she just decided to ask Gracie.

"Gracie, um 35 and getting older by the day. I don't want to stay down here either. I mean I love ya, but I wanna go up to Milwaukee too. I'll find me a job and send you some money so you can hire somebody to help you run this place."

Gracie figured it had been on Mae Ellen's mind for some time too. Try as she might, she could not find a reason to deny her cousin and friend. She was pretty sure, if she did not agree; she would take matters into her own hands and leave home. Gracie did not want to think about what she would do in this house by herself. Nevertheless, she would not deny Mae Ellen's wish because she felt she had no other choice. So she made a bargain while stalling for a little more time.

"I tell you what," she started. "You stay with your old cousin through this winter, helping me out 'round here and I'll pay for your trip up there around this time next year.

"Oh, Gracie!" an excited Mae Ellen squealed while hugging and kissing Gracie on the cheek. "Thank you, I didn't want to hurt you or leave you alone but I've got to get on with my life. Thank you Cuz."

Mae Ellen may have had other reasons for wanting to move north. She was still a young enough country woman with all the natural curiosities that come with it. The selections of young singles in this and surrounded communities were limited because of black migration.

She was also a new breed of black woman; one who was more independent than that of her predecessors. She saw herself as more than just a housewife. There were more educational and career opportunities available up north. Even though there were black colleges available in other parts of the South, it was still the segregated south. The good paying jobs for Negroes were in the north as were the chance for her to finally finish high school before going on to college. In her mind, she had overstayed her time in the south and with Gracie. She was just wasting her life away if she remained in Banks.

Throughout the rest of the year there was more goings than comings in Banks' black community. The exodus has slowed somewhat because the war has ended, competition for jobs has increase with armed service personnel returning to civilian life. Plus there are some who just want to stay in the South. The country was on a new roads building exercise to accommodate for all the additional cars and vehicles on the roads these days.

There is one other major consideration black people took into account when deciding whether to leave their place of birth or stay. That was the difference in the standard of living when comparing North, East, or West to the South.

A few isolated areas in Bradley County are just now getting electricity. The comfort of having running water in one's house alone can make the difference. Running water means flushing toilets, hot baths, ability to have hot water through a kitchen or bathroom faucet is worth the move in itself.

A couple of months before June of 1952, the month Gracie had agreed to pay for her trip north, Mae Ellen found out she was pregnant. She went to see Doc Purvis for verification, so there was no doubt about it. The baby was due to arrive in January of the New Year. That was just part of her problem. The father was Robert Preston; the same married man with three kids who lived with his family in Warren. There was no doubt about that either. He is the only man she has allowed to make love to her within the last couple of years. They'd managed to keep their affair a secret up to this point. In fact, he was another reason she wanted to leave the area and get a fresh start away from him.

Over the next few weeks she was going out of her mind, while trying to make a decision. Should she move north without telling anyone of her pregnancy? How would she survive up there? She knew her cousins, Codis and Curtis would be mad at her. She figured Clarence, with his funny ways, would have nothing to do with her. Should she tell Gracie? The thought of that scene sent chills through her body. Gracie would have a "hissy fit" and want her to continue to stay with her, she thought. It was just too much to think about now. She figured she had until around the last of May to make up her mind. She probably would begin to show after that. Although she still might be able to hide it, she could not see herself going to Milwaukee and dropping that bombshell on the fellows.

As it always is with secrets they have a way of being exposed if anyone is paying attention. This one was no different. Lacirene and her mother just happened to see Dr. Purvis in Papa Warner's over a week ago. He unsuspectedly asked how the expecting mother was doing, while simultaneously trying to soothe what he thought might have been a concern of Gracie. "You tell that gal, she should come on back and see me on occasion. Just to be sure things are working out. Gracie, she is sho' lucky to have you to help out with the baby after it comes. Gotta' run, now you tell her what I said, you hear? You all take care."

With that, Doctor Purvis left the store heading for his automobile. Gracie and Lacirene stood there, speechless for almost a minute until their thoughts were interrupted by the store clerk. "Will that be all, Miss Gracie?"

RT was waiting by his truck to take the ladies home and sense something was wrong on the ride back to Gracie's place and then back up to his and Lacirene's house. He figured when somebody wanted him to know what was wrong, his wife would tell him, so he went on about his business after they got back home.

A week went by before Gracie could no longer stand the secrecy, during which time she'd watched Mae Ellen closely for signs of her pregnancy. She wore loose clothing, so there was no visible baby bump. There was also no sign of morning sickness that Gracie witnessed. This particular morning they were setting at the kitchen table chatting about this, that and the other when Gracie casually asked, "When is the baby due?"

The room, without anyone speaking, screamed silence. Mae Ellen looked at her friend, confidant, and almost mother-like cousin with such a surprised expression at first, followed by a hurtful look on her face, feeling as if she had let Gracie down. After a minute, all she could do was shake her head. The elephant in the room was now dancing on the table. Teardrops streamed down this fully grown woman's face as she relayed the entire affair with Robert Preston to Gracie. She ended with, "I wanted to tell you but I knew you would not understand. I just didn't want you to hate me."

There was more silence as the elephant disappeared into thin air. Finally Gracie, hurt, confused, and disappointed in her ward of all these years, suppressed her instinct to go off on Mae Ellen. After all what was done was done. She smile at the thought of having a baby in the house and ended the conversation, at least for now with, "Don't worry, we'll get by."

This let the expecting mom to know she still had a problem because if Gracie thought she and the baby were going to stay in this house, she was wrong. She had not dismissed the thought of moving to Milwaukee. She just figured to carry her new born baby with her next spring. Mae Ellen would pick another time and date to drop that on Gracie.

Spring arrived and went just as fast as it seemed to arrive. The summer was hot and muggy, even more so for Mae Ellen who had yet to tell Gracie of her plans to move to Milwaukee after the baby's birth. Through the winter months, she was emboldened by the letters she received from Curtis and Codis. Simply put, she and the baby would be better off in Milwaukee, where sanitation issues for newborns were not a crapshoot. Public transportation was plentiful. They would help her get a family babysitter while she worked to improve her financial wellbeing. She could stay with Curtis, who was a bachelor living alone until she decided upon what she wanted to do.

She finally told Robert, the baby's father, and received the reaction she expected. He would be no help to the health and welfare of the child, but he still wanted to continue the affair.

That was the day she officially broke it off with him while Gracie looked on from the porch with her shotgun in her arms. A shaken Robert left the area without incident.

A month later, on January 15, 1953, she gave birth, with the help of a local midwife, to a baby boy. She named him John, after Gracie's deceased husband. He was an active little baby from the very start. Mae Ellen called him little Johnny Hall. She was happy because most everyone said the cute little fellow looked like her. Gracie was also ecstatic about the birth. She was spoiling the child by holding him so much when he wasn't in his mother's arms. This only reassured Mae Ellen that she needed to move this baby away, the sooner the better. She was a 37 year woman with a newborn, yet afraid to tell her cousin that she, along with little Johnny were going to leave Arkansas. The anxiety when just thinking of how Gracie may react was taking a toll on her nerves, even the baby's god mother (Gracie) was beginning to take notice.

Codis Senior and Doreatha were divorced. Last year, he married Rosalie Miller from Fountain Hill Arkansas. They and his son Codis Junior. was living in an upstairs flat on 12th and Juneau in Milwaukee. As stated, Curtis was a bachelor and had his own little apartment.

Mae Ellen wrote Codis and Curtis asking them to come and get her. Everyone around Banks knew of Gracie's vow to help raise the child and really wanted no part of challenging her viewpoint. Like their pregnant cousin, both Codis and Curtis knew that Gracie would not want her to live anyplace else, especially now that there would be a baby in the house.

By early spring, around April 7, 1953, the brothers were on their way south to pick up Mae Ellen at her request. She had written them a couple of letters describing how she was being treated. She was restricted from going out with men while she was with child. She could not even go out by herself, especially to the Hole in the Bushes place. Even now, Gracie seems to overlook the fact that she was a grown woman by treating her more and more as if she was a minor child with a child. Their relationship had taken a drastic turn since news of the pregnancy, up through the delivery and after Johnny's birth.

After arriving at the house, they tried to talk their mother into letting Mae Ellen return with them. They promised her and the baby boy would be in good hands staying with Curtis until she was able to be on her own. It didn't matter; Gracie would not agree to let her leave the house. Taking matters into their own hands, Curtis stood up and told Mae Ellen,

"Come on; let's just get in the car."

"What about my clothes and things?"

"Get your baby, and just get in the car," Codis said as he got up from the chair.

Shocked at the nerve of her sons, Gracie grabbed her shotgun as the two men, Mae Ellen carrying the baby all ran and got inside the vehicle. She followed them outside yelling at her them.

"Mae Ellen, you get that baby back in that house. I ain't playing with yawl. I'll blow a hole through you with this gun."

The men were still surprised to see their mother level her shotgun at them. Gracie was mad, torn between keeping Mae Ellen with her and having to kill a child of hers to do it. She fired a warning shot just over the top of the car. She stood at the ground just at the end of front porch steps with the full intention of using the weapon. Taking aim once again while Codis began backing the car up the little road. He really had no room to turn the vehicle around and had to be very careful backing up on that soft dirt road. It was still somewhat moist from the winter weather. Now was not the time to get stuck in mud.

It was a scary sight for all, as Curtis yelled for Codis to hurry up before they get shot. Codis turned his head to look backwards after looking in the rear view mirror, then turned back to see his mother aiming at the car. Unsure whether she would really shoot them, yet feeling confident she would not shoot into the car carrying the baby, he kept backing up slowly. Gracie kept walking toward them, seemingly to get a better shot.

Gracie watched as Codis finally reached a spot he could turn around, did so and sped off carrying Mae Ellen and little Johnny back to Milwaukee. Her hands was sweating and shaking. Tears were beginning to roll down her cheeks. In all her life, she had never felt as alone as at that exact moment. She could not believe her own children would defy her wishes. Slowly, she walked back to an empty house. For the first time in her life she also felt old and out of place. She shook her head while trying to picture if she, her sisters or brother would have ever defied her mother or father's wishes.

At this point, she didn't know how to feel, what to say or what to think about the situation. She was also relieved, because at one point she intended to fire that shot into the car. She just didn't have it in her to harm or possible kill one of her own or harm that baby. She just could not pull that trigger. For that at least, she said out loud looking up to the heavens, "Thank God."

Gathering herself, wiping the tears from her face with the back of her apron, she replaced the spent shell in the double barrel weapon. Walking back out the front door, still carrying the shotgun, Gracie headed toward Lena's house. She needed to talk to someone on her level, with her type of upbringing, someone who could possibly make sense of it all.

Lena had never seen her sister so distraught. She had only seen this type of expression on her face once, which was at their mother's funeral.

"Gracie, what's the matter with you? What done happened? Where's Mae Ellen and the baby?" she asked as her sister sat down at the kitchen table.

"They just took her. My loving sons, Codis and Curtis, they drove all the way down here to take Mae Ellen back to Milwaukee. They told her to get in the car and she did. She just got in the car without a word. Then they drove off. No goodbye . . . she didn't even carry a clean pair of draws with her, no other clothes . . . nothing. She just got in the car and left with her brothers. I just don't understand . . . who . . . these children we raised . . . are, today."

"Gracie, wait . . . Joe, gon' back out and find you something to do. Tell yo' daddy I'll call 'em when I need yawl in here. Wait a minute, tell Colrolus . . . ,"

"No, no . . . I don' want him to see me like this," Gracie, crying uncontrollably, asked of Lena.

"Don't bother your daddy; just tell him I'll talk to him after 'while. Now go on Joe," Lena instructed. "Honey, you didn't shoot nobody did you?"

"I almost did. I was going to shoot him as he backed that damn car up, but . . . I just couldn't do it. He's my oldest son, Lena. I couldn't shoot none of them. And if I'd of hit that baby . . . . But they sho' don't care nothin' 'bout me like I do them."

"Aw Honey, they care, they just young and dumb. Can I get you something? Coffee, water . . ."

"Yeah, can you bring my family back home?" she asked pounding her fist on the table. "Oh, um sorry sis . . . I just, um sorry," she continued, while using her apron to wipe away the tears streaming down her face.

"If they want to go, they are old enough, and there is nothing you can do about it. All though, you'd think they'd have mo' respect for you than to just do what they did. We never woulda' did our folks like that. Um so sorry, honey, I don' know what to say 'bout that."

"Lena, ain't nothing to say. I can't say or do nothing 'bout it. Just like you say," Gracie said regaining her composure. "Maybe, I'll surprise all their asses. Maybe, I'll move to Milwaukee too."

They continued to talk for about an hour, until Colrolus walked into the house. Sensing something was wrong, he immediately hugged his sister-in-law. He poured him a cup of coffee and sat down at the table with them. Gracie managed to tell him what happened, while holding back her tears. The more she talk about her boys taking Mae Ellen and the baby, a move to Milwaukee seemed like a good way to keep an eye on her family. She didn't have to live with either one of her sons or Mae Ellen. That is, if Mae Ellen ever got a place of her own.

"I can live by myself. I don't have to be a burden to none of them chillen," she said.

"Maybe you can rent your house out to somebody. That would help you with expenses to live up north," Colrolus offered.

"Yeah, but whose gonna help you get set up if you don't want to ask yo' children?" Lena asked.

"Monroe and Mittie Lue's up there, they helped almost everybody from here that move to Milwaukee," Gracie answered.

"I don't have to live with them either, but they can help me find a place of my own."

"All John's brothers, with their wives and kids, are up there. And don't forget, so is Sambo and Sallie," Colrolus said.

"That's right, and you got other kin folk up there. I betcha you can get set up without asking any help from your chillen. It'll serve them right for treating you like they did. And . . . and you can be right there in the city with them if they want to see you. Or, if you want to go see them," Lena added.

The three of them talked for about another half hour until there was a knock at the back door. "Can I come in too?" Joe asked.

"Oh, um so sorry baby, come on in," Lena answered her youngest son, who had grown into a 19 year old young man.

"Son, after you eat, gon' and take that mare up to D.C.'s house for me. Tell him he should put her in with that new stallion he got and see what happens," Colrolus told Joe.

"Okay daddy," Joe said as he sat down at the table too.

Lena got up and fixed everybody scrambled eggs, and pieces of bacon. She served the food with fresh biscuits she had baked that morning. She opened a fresh jar of apple jelly she canned last year. They eat and talked about other children growing up and moving away. They talked about the changing attitudes of children today and how different it was from how they grew up. Joe added to the conversation, when he felt they needed a youngster's opinion. He understood why they were having this discussion when he heard his cousins, Codis and Curtis, had picked up Mae Ellen, baby Johnny and took them to Milwaukee. Figuring this was a good time for him to leave, he said goodbye to all, kissing his mama and Aunt Gracie before heading out the door.

"See yawl later," was his last words to his elders before leaving.

They all smiled at him, waved, and turned back to discussing the issue of the day. Gracie left Lena and Colrolus house with a plan and a purpose. Thoughts were racing through her mind. Yes, she would prepare to move to Milwaukee and live by herself. Hell, maybe she might meet a beau. She wouldn't mind having running water, and all the luxuries of the big city. After all, she deserved to enjoy some of the comforts of life too. Besides, she also has a grandson there. She would be able to see little Codis again. Maybe she could make peace with Mae Ellen and still be the proud God Mother to baby Johnny as she had become. The more she thought about it the more excited she became about the relocation. She picked up her pace toward her house. Hell, those kids just don't know. Maybe they did me a favor. Now, that I think of it, I know they did. I have been trying to hold on to this old house for what seems like forever. For what? The kids don't care what happens down here. Her last thought, as she walked up the steps to her house, taking a seat in the swing on her porch, was how much she really loved her home.

A few tears rolled down her cheek as she looked out at the trees, and took in the silence amid the occasional sounds of nature. She walked through her unlocked door, which caused her to think of hearing that people in the city having to lock their doors to keep out potential burglars. Entering her house, it felt empty, even with all its furnishings. Her thought was she, after all these years, was alone. She glanced up toward the ceiling, and said out loud, "I didn't mean really alone, lord. I'll always have you by my side."

On Columbus Day, October 12, 1953, Gracie placed her suitcase in the car. She asked Lena to ship the rest of her cloths and a few belongings later. Colrolus and his sons, D.C. Frank, and Joe would keep an eye on the house. They had not found a renter yet. It was not her intention to sell the house either. It would somehow work itself out. Her daughter Lacirene and her husband, R.T., could still look out their back door and see the house too. She was moving to Milwaukee and riding back with Van D "Peach" Hampton to get there. He and Calvin had driven down to visit other relatives. She wrapped the shotgun in an old sheet, putting it in the trunk of the car. She packed the knife she always carried in her apron pocket in her bag. One thing was for sure, she thought, where ever she lived, she was not going to take any stuff from anybody and that would include her own children.

The End,
Continuation or maybe a New Beginning?

The Hampton family taken in the late fifties. The names are from left to right, Johnny Mae Miller (Rosalie's daughter), Codis Hampton Jr., Rosalie Hampton, Delores A Hampton as a baby, and Codis Hampton, senior.

Left from right top row,
Monroe Hampton, John Hampton, Willie Davis, Gus Hall, Elvin Davis,
Joel Johnson. Bottom row, Mansfield Davis and Frank Johnson.

Authors' Great Grand Parents, Sallie Davis-
Hampton and David "Sambo" Hampton.